Praise for *Lee*

"Too many other memoirs on this subject are fairly singular in their depictions. They often lack psychological insight, social understanding, or in-depth presentation of changing family relationships in favor of focusing upon either the narrator's impressions alone or the mentally ill character's perceptions. By contrast, Farmer's book is very nicely balanced."

—Diane Donovan, critic for Midwest Book Review

"Ken Farmer's book recounts a family history marked by secrets, schizophrenia, and abuse. This compelling true story is about the experiences we share and threads that hold us together as family, even as we work to find our own path...There is anger, loss, and regret but also crystallized memories we hold that become an enduring image...Generational scars are traced to both origins and effects, yet each person is shown as more than their scars, and deserving of understanding and forgiveness."

—Mary Bell, educator and activist

"Farmer's engaging and emotional account of his life tears open the wounds inflicted by his dysfunctional family and brother's schizophrenia. Unfortunately, families continue to be victimized by the unavoidable collision between the mental health and justice systems, and his story remains all too common."

—Todd Meurer, municipal court judge
and retired court commissioner

"Farmer is an expressive writer who deftly pinpoints emotions…
As the memoir develops, the author astutely captures how Lee's
mental illness revealed itself incrementally and also emphasizes how
potential signs of schizophrenia are often overlooked…"

LEE

The Tragic Story of a Family
Broken by Schizophrenia

by KENNETH FARMER

Ten|16
PRESS

www.ten16press.com - Waukesha, WI

To Mom and Dad:
You still never have to worry about Kenny

Author's Note

The events described in this memoir are based on police records, interviews of relatives, various documents and family photos, and my best recollection. Court and mental health records could not be accessed due to privacy laws. However, I was able to use some of such records that were sent to my family as a result of commitment proceedings.

The quoted dialogue reflects the spirit and intent of conversations, though not necessarily the precise words employed. I did not, after all, have a tape recorder or stenographer with me during these exchanges. When the book indicates a character always used a phrase in a certain context or when the words employed are unique or unusual, the quotes are exact. As to names, most people mentioned are dead. For those who are living or who have not given me permission, I have employed pseudonyms.

Foreword

I first met Kenneth Farmer, whom I know as Ken, when he applied for a job at the Louisville-Jefferson County Public Defender's Office in 1982. He was fresh out of law school, and I was the Executive Director of that office and thus in charge of hiring decisions. His interview revealed him to be a most interesting young man who possessed great potential as a lawyer. I offered him a trial attorney position, which he immediately accepted. During his tenure there, he handled thousands of cases, many involving clients with mental health problems. They included matters in which competency to stand trial or insanity was an issue, as well as court proceedings relating to involuntary hospitalization of individuals suffering from mental illness who were deemed a danger to themselves or others.

In 1987 Ken left our office and returned to Wisconsin, where he had grown up and attended college. At that time, he made a professional transition from public defender to prosecutor in Manitowoc and later in Madison. Other than an occasional phone call, our paths did not cross again until 2018, when he returned to Louisville to attend my retirement party. Afterward we agreed to have lunch the following February during a trip I was making to Milwaukee, where I was raised and had extended family. By then, Ken had left the active practice of law and begun a second career as a writer. Over lunch, we swapped stories about cases, judges, and attorneys we had dealt with over the years, as lawyers often do. Several notorious mentally ill defendants that I represented in my own forty-five-year career in the criminal justice system came up in the course of our conversation. It was at this point that Ken revealed to me for the first time that his only sibling, Lee, had struggled with paranoid schizophrenia throughout most of his life and had come close to becoming a notorious defendant himself.

The story about his brother struck me as extraordinarily unique and poignant, not only because Ken had a close relationship with him, but also because his mother raised Ken and Lee despite having a severe physical handicap that left her paralyzed. I knew immediately a book about the subject would offer tremendous insight into the challenges families of the mentally ill face in the court system and from the disease itself. I also knew that Ken had already written several novels dealing with criminal justice, including *Real Lawyers* and *Chez Betty*, which were informed by his experience as a defense lawyer and prosecutor. To me, this made him uniquely qualified to write about the subject from a personal and professional perspective. Earlier we had bandied about ideas for his next writing project, but after hearing his brother's story, I suggested that he consider writing a memoir about his relationship with him and the effects his illness had on him and his family.

At first Ken seemed very reluctant about my proposal. He told me that by going public about the subject he felt he would be betraying his family, particularly because his mother had specifically instructed him never to mention the problem to anyone. Even after the death of his parents and brother, the stigma of mental illness seemed to bridle Ken's ability to divulge fully what had happened. But as we discussed the matter further, it became apparent to both of us that neither his brother nor his parents would be viewed by readers in a negative light—the latter because they had suffered so much and tried so hard to rectify the problem, and his brother because Ken had so many positive things to say about him. By the end of the conversation, my former employee and colleague decided to write this book, and I offered him encouragement and whatever assistance I could provide. There was no doubt in my mind that, once committed, Ken would diligently explore every aspect of the subject matter, utilize his public defender training and legal experience to research thoroughly and investigate all facts and records involved, and then apply his considerable talent in telling this important story.

Now that the task has been completed, and I have read the work and its various drafts, I believe the finished product is every bit as inspirational as I thought it would be, if not more so. Lest I spoil the book for the reader, I will not go into more detail. However, I will say this: this memoir comes straight from the heart of a very thoughtful, passionate, and caring person, one who knew Lee the best and loved him the most.

Daniel T. Goyette
Attorney at Law/Defender Emeritus
Louisville-Jefferson County Public Defender's Office
Louisville, Kentucky

Introduction

I asked myself a thousand times if I should write this book, and a thousand times I said no. Reliving what happened would be too painful, I thought, however cathartic it might also be. I was worried I would make my family look bad by revealing its dysfunction, something I would necessarily have to get into since this contributed to the problem in the first place. In short, writing the story would make me feel guilty on top of all the other negative emotions I had experienced. I even speculated that my parents, who are now deceased, would somehow condemn me in the afterlife for having "exposed" their weaknesses, however much I also wrote of their strengths.

But somewhere in the process of sifting and winnowing the details, looking through family records and photographs, and interviewing those who knew my brother, I came to a different conclusion. If I did nothing, my experience would have no meaning and my family's suffering would be for naught. But if I did write the book, perhaps in some small way I would be able to contribute to the common good. If nothing else, I might even be able to encourage others to tell their story and thereby help reduce the stigma associated with this horrible disease. The fact that I professionally defended and prosecuted cases like my brother's might also provide a unique perspective on the problem.

If I were to summarize this book in one word, it would be struggle: struggle for my mother in having to overcome a devastating physical handicap, struggle for my father whose mother died when he was eight, struggle for my only sibling and mentor in not being able to achieve his true potential and essentially having his life destroyed, and struggle for me in having to be the only normal one in order to compensate for everyone else.

Now you might say something like a friend of mine once did when I tried to explain the situation to him, "Everyone has problems, Ken." I hate it when people dismissively say things like that. Yes, everyone has problems, but some have bigger ones than others, and ours was a huge one. This story is about what it was like to cope with it and to a certain degree overcome it.

PART I

My Big Brother

1

Erlanger, Kentucky, 1961

Running around in the rain with Lee is my most precious childhood memory. I don't know why this is the case. Perhaps it is because it concerns a time in my life in which I had the least responsibility and was the most spontaneous, when someone looked after me versus the other way around, when ego or shame did not guide my choices, and when worry or thought of consequence did not pervade my existence. Simply put, it was a period in which things were the least burdensome and thus the most enjoyable.

Our experience in the rain typically started when I noticed dark blue and purple clouds in the southwestern sky over my family's two-bedroom brick bungalow. Excited by an earthy, musty scent that wafted up to my face after the first few drops hit the ground, I would run inside and ask Mom for permission for us to put on our bathing suits and take advantage of the growing storm. Often she'd be sweeping the kitchen floor.

Her method of accomplishing this task was necessarily unique and laborious. She would grasp the middle of the broom handle with her left hand and slowly move the brush end across the floor in long, drawn-out strokes. During this tedious process, her right arm, benumbed and bloated from paralysis, would dangle at her side without purpose or direction. After accumulating a small pile of debris, she would lean the broom against the counter and place a dustpan atop her right foot. Though angled inward and deformed, the foot still had the wherewithal to prop up the dustpan at the appropriate angle. She would then retake the broom and in the same manner as before, sweep the pile into the dustpan, limp to the garbage can with it, and deposit it inside.

Mom's response to my request to go out in the rain always invoked the same admonition: "So long as you don't track!" Household tasks took longer for her, given her disability. So when we left mud, water or the slightest particle of food on her kitchen floor by accident, it required twice or even three times the effort of an able-bodied person for her to clean it up. So "tracking," whether it occurred in this context or another, was an unpardonable sin. To outsiders, this attitude may have seemed querulous or bitchy, but they didn't have to survive with half a body.

Against the advice of her doctor, Mom birthed us two boys and raised us like any other mother. She carried us around as infants, pushed us in a stroller, changed our diapers, washed us in a sink, cooked our supper, took us to Cincinnati on the bus shopping, and yes, disciplined us, all with one good arm and one good leg. So accustomed was I to her limitations, I was unconscious of them until I grew older. Curiously enough, we were not told why she had lateral paralysis, but this did not matter, for to me and everyone in our family including my father, she was just Mom. No one called her by any other name.

Mom could not work outside the home, even part time, and Dad earned little money as a professor since college teachers at small schools weren't paid well then. The resulting lower-middle-class income deprived us of many of life's comforts, and so just like her, Lee and I improvised and overcame. A case in point was going swimming. While we had a cheap, plastic children's pool in the backyard, our family did not have enough money to pay for a membership at the Triple E in Erlanger. No free pools existed in that area either, and public beaches were too far away. So running outside in the rain was a good alternative on a hot summer day—that and Kool-Aid popsicles that Mom would make us.

After getting her approval, I would march into the bedroom I shared with Lee. Usually he was lying on his stomach on his bed with the heel of his right hand propping up his head. Before him would be a book that he kept open with his other hand. Often it was a classic novel such as *Huckleberry Finn* or *Tom Sawyer,* but sometimes it was a work of pop fiction. In any event, he always had a book. It was as though he existed in two worlds: the one I experienced with him and the world portrayed in the latest story that he was reading.

Lee's bed was an old hospital one that somebody gave our family before I was born. It had a sagging mattress and metal springs that squeaked with the slightest movement. Until I was four, I slept in a crib. When my parents saved up enough money, they bought a new couch, a purple hideaway that followed us wherever we went. The old one became my bed.

"It's raining and Mom says we can go outside, if we don't track," I would tell Lee. Engrossed in his book, he ignored me, but when the rain began to pound on our house's metal awnings like a drummer rapping on a snare drum, he relented, though he did so reluctantly.

Once we exited the house, we ran up and down the backyard and around our rusted swing set, while the downpour drenched our bodies clean. When we tired of that, we lay on our backs in the grass, gazed at the clouds above us, and drank the rain as it hit the back of our throats. It tasted pure, fresh, and free.

By this point even Lee became excited, and he sprinted to the street in front of our house and plopped down into the gutter. Its gushing water flowed around his shoulders and cascaded over his stomach and legs. I then followed his example, and together we wallowed in the gutter without a care in the world.

Typically our next stop was the creek behind our house, where the storm's runoff rushed around fallen trees and rocks. We would slide down the creek's muddy banks on our butts and wade through the water, sometimes crouching to touch it and even sitting in it. As the storm intensified, a torrent of rain would drive into the creek, causing small splashes to jump from its surface. Here and there an oak leaf or a maple helicopter would fall upon it and float away without purpose, perhaps wishing it had control but resigning itself to the fact that it had none.

While watching this unfold, my mind turned to the possible dangers that lurked beneath the water's surface, and my brother would always exaggerate them, telling me wild stories of water snakes, cottonmouths, and black and blue racers. As a result of such harrowing tales, I clambered out of the creek as fast as I could, convinced a snake would bite me any moment. My brother would then chase me toward the house, and once he caught up with me, pinch my leg with one hand and my side with the other and tickle me until I begged him to stop. As we reached the clothesline by the patio, we finally slowed down and caught our breath.

Before Mom allowed us back inside the house, she always handed us a towel. After meticulously drying ourselves off, we retreated into the bedroom, changed out of our swimming suits, and hung them up in the bathroom. Despite the fact we were so careful, Mom inevitably scolded us for having left a few drops of water on her kitchen floor. We paid her reprimand little mind, however, for we did not want to spoil an otherwise glorious afternoon in our own special paradise.

Although running in the rain was a truly idyllic experience, I can only speak of it in general terms because we did it so often that discrete episodes of it are hard for me to distinguish. By contrast, I have a very specific memory of the ugliest event of my childhood since its particularly violent and traumatic character indelibly imprinted it on my brain. I am fairly certain it happened in the summer of 1961 since it was very hot out, and I know I was just five at the time. My brother was nine.

I was lying on my couch-turned-bed, and my parents and Lee were quietly having breakfast in the kitchen. Without any warning whatsoever, I heard my father bark my brother's name. Whenever he did this, the sharpness of his voice would cause me and everyone in the house to jump. Any thought in our head would evaporate, and any task we were performing would stop until such time as his anger mercifully subsided.

After my father yelled my brother's name, he chased him into our bedroom. As he did this, I slid back on my bed in a desperate attempt to stay out of the fray, for I knew from past experience such wrath could easily be turned on me. Mom, on the other hand, limped after my father and tried to stop him the best she could, but her valiant effort was weak and ineffectual, given her paralysis. All she could do was scream his name in protest: "Merl! Merl! Merl!"

"Don't you ever sass me!" my father hollered as Lee got up on his bed to avoid him.

"But I didn't sass you!" Lee responded, a little too sharply to draw a reprieve.

"What did you say?"

Lee did not respond as he cowered farther back on the bed.

"What did you say?" my father repeated, this time much louder.

"I said I didn't sass you!"

At this, my father yelled, "You goddamn devil, don't you ever sass me like that again, or I'll slap you to sleep."

"What's a matter with you?" Lee countered as he drew back even more. In response, my father climbed onto the bed and pinned my brother against the wall. With his other hand, he removed his belt, then without purpose, control, or reason whipped his legs and torso so many times I lost count. If Lee had not covered his face, he would have gotten him there too. This was not discipline. It was terror, pure and simple.

Finally, my father left the room. I could hear him bickering with Mom about how he had handled the situation, and I started to cry. But amazingly, Lee shed not a single tear. He was used to it, I guess, the same way a horse's mouth is accustomed to a bit.

"Don't worry, Kenny," he told me quietly. "Someday we'll get out of here."

"W-where will we go?" I asked.

"I don't know, but we'll find somewhere."

"What about Mom?"

"Maybe she'll come too. I don't know."

2

The Wise Guest House

My father, Merl Lee Farmer Sr., taught Economics in the late fifties and early sixties at the University of Kentucky-Northern Center just south of Cincinnati. We lived in Erlanger because it wasn't far from his job. My parents and Lee moved there from Chicago, where he was born in September of 1951. I came into this world in February of 1956 in Danville, Kentucky. The reason I was born in Danville was my grandparents lived there and would be available to assist Mom with my post-natal care.

Before our family moved to Kentucky, Dad had obtained his master's degree at the University of Chicago where he also did his course work for his doctorate. Because he wasn't Nobel Prize material, he never finished his PhD there. Instead he completed it at the University of Illinois. He wrote his doctoral dissertation on the Financial Administration of Kentucky from 1929-1960. My parents chose to live in Kentucky so we could be near where my mother grew up, and my father could have access to documents relating to his dissertation.

Our car during this phase of our life was a 1956 pink-over-black Plymouth Belvedere that we purchased after I was born. The four-door sedan had whitewall tires and sported two large fins on the back that housed the taillights. It had black and white patterned cloth seats and no safety belts. This particular model had an automatic transmission that was operated by push buttons on the left side of the dashboard. There was no power anything, but a giant steering wheel provided good leverage for parking.

Whenever we went anywhere as a family, we took the pink Plymouth. Lee occupied the left side of the backseat next to Mom's dresses that hung on a hook above the door. Since touching them was prohibited, he kept his butt slightly closer to the center. I sat to his immediate right, Mom rode shotgun, and Dad drove because she couldn't drive due to her disability.

Shortly after the belt-whipping episode, a milestone of time after which I remember events more clearly, we drove to Grandmother's in Danville, a trip of about 110 miles. I believe it was in August because we always went there when my father finished teaching summer school. Grandmother called her home the Wise Guest House since her married name was Wise. She periodically rented rooms to travelers and people who lived in town for an extended period. Such accommodations were common in Kentucky in that era, though guest houses were slowly dying off in favor of motels. Our trip started off like all the others—with a knock-down-drag-out argument. My parents settled everything that way whether it had to do with correct grammar in my father's dissertation, the timeliness of a bill payment, or the proper use of a deduction on their income tax return.

"Honey, we got to get to going!" Dad pleaded urgently as we were about to leave. "Grandmother is expecting us at two o'clock, and it's eleven now!" He used the phrase "got to get to going" whenever he was in a rush, which was most of the time.

"But I'm not ready yet!" Mom yelled from the bathroom. "If you had gotten out of the shower sooner, this wouldn't have happened!"

"Will you please hurry up?"

Ignoring Dad, Mom brushed her brown hair and adjusted her travel clothes in the bathroom mirror: a white blouse and a fifties-style bluish-grey skirt that went down to the middle of her calves. As to her shoes, she always wore a pair of women's slip-ons, and never pumps or high heels since they were easier to put on given her deformed right foot and provided better balance. She also did not need extra height, given that she was five-foot-nine.

While she finished getting ready, Dad stormed around the house, ran his fingers through his salt and pepper hair, and repeatedly looked at his watch. Normally he had on a suit and tie, even when traveling, but in the summer he wore a short-sleeved button-down shirt sloppily tucked in his pants. His overhanging gut suggested he might have a heart attack someday and even die. Perhaps there were times when we wished this would happen, so Mom would be able to raise us by herself. But when we had such dark thoughts, we erased them from our minds quickly; or at least I did.

When Dad couldn't wait any longer, he made his usual empty threat: "Kenny! Lee! Get in the goddamn car! We're leaving without her!"

"Fool!" Mom yelled back.

Lee and I had this part of the play memorized, for the lines were always the same. When Mom told Dad he was a fool, for example, Lee would mimic her and call me a fool using a similar tone of voice. We would then laugh together until our bellies ached. Some people might consider this insolent, but really it was nothing more than a way of coping with an absurd situation.

Eventually, we backed out of the driveway and began our trek to Grandmother's house. The trip took three hours with stops. The newly constructed Interstate 75 stopped about thirty miles north of Lexington. The rest of the way we drove two-lane roads that wavered like a shook blanket with constant hills and curves. That part of our journey was perilous, as oncoming cars would try to pass in sections of the road that offered little room. Then too, Dad wasn't exactly a competent driver.

As we made our way to Danville, we sang our song. Believe it or not, we actually had one, and the very idea of such a thing stood in sharp contrast to my parents' frequent disputes and my father's explosive anger. Mom started things off, presumably to encourage us, and everyone joined in, even Dad. "We have ninety-nine miles to go. Ninety-nine miles to go. We'll walk a while, we'll rest a while, but we have ninety-nine miles to go. We have ninety-eight miles to go. Ninety-eight miles to go…"

After ten miles and ten verses, the music trailed off. The entertainment did not, however, as we switched to our favorite game of naming states and capitals. Mom would read their initials off a paper placemat that she had saved from a truck-stop restaurant, and everyone except her would try to provide the city and state. I didn't know very many answers at the age of five, but I knew enough to participate.

Sometimes Lee and I would fight about the game. This would generally concern who got the answer first. When this occurred, Dad would say the word "Now" with ominous inflection. Occasionally, he would say it with our name attached to it. But it was always his first shot across the bow when it came to our transgressions. The second was, "I don't mean maybe." And the third was his fist. Most of the time, he would hit us when the car was stopped, but occasionally he would do so when it was moving. Since his eyes were fixed on the road when he swung, we had an advantage in being able to dodge his punches. Once in a while he connected though, but not necessarily with the right culprit. During a trip that took us through Iowa (or perhaps it was Illinois or Nebraska), he tried to hit Lee and got me instead. I loudly objected, of course, but Dad didn't give me "a get-out-of-fist-free card."

Mom wasn't immune from becoming physical, either. She could run us down, albeit slower than other mothers, and pin us back on a bed, car seat, or couch by the neck with great efficiency. She used her good hand to do this, which wasn't any old hand by the way, since it had necessarily been overdeveloped by double use.

On the way to Danville, we stopped for lunch. Mom normally fed us stale cheese crackers and crusty fig bars in the car so we could save money. But sometimes she would forget to bring them, and we would stop at Hayden's Restaurant. We called it the Halfway House since it was halfway to Danville.

Inside the restaurant, Mom, allocated each of us one dollar for lunch, and Dad was included to set an example. Lee and I each ordered a hamburger and a Coke. Dad got chili and coffee, and Mom a tuna sandwich. Naturally Lee and I marveled at the desserts, but Mom reminded us that extras would have to be paid for with our own money, earned while working around the house and usually spent immediately. Thus, we never got dessert.

When it came time to leave, Mom stuffed the unused sugar packets in her purse. She also saved the crackers that Dad did not add to his chili. As she did this, he asked: "Honey, are we going to leave a tip?"

"Oh, Merl."

"Well, we got to leave a tip!" Dad snapped, loud enough to silence the other patrons and cause their heads to turn in our direction. Lee and I sank down in our seats almost to the floor to avoid being seen. But Mom and Dad didn't take the hint, probably because they were so enmeshed in their argument that shame eluded them.

"I have no change," Mom announced after digging in her purse.

"Then leave a dollar!"

"Merl!"

"All right. Fifty cents then," Dad said, while slapping down a half-dollar piece, which was about ten percent of the bill and thus a miniscule tip.

"But we can't afford that!"

"It's just fifty cents, damn it! God all Christ!"

Mom turned her head away and pouted. Later, as we exited the restaurant, she lagged behind. At first I didn't think anything of it until I saw her grab the coin that Dad had left.

After Lexington and another argument, this time about directions in the bustling town, we had "thirty-six miles to go," and things became quiet as we took in the old stone fences and rolling hills of the Bluegrass Region countryside. Eventually, a tinge of exhaust leaked in the car, and I became nauseous.

"Mom, will we be there soon?" I asked weakly.

"Not much farther, sweetheart," she replied.

"Mom?"

"What?"

"I feel sick."

"Sometimes Daddy drives too fast. Merl, slow down."

"Stop!" I yelled suddenly. Having seen me vomit inside the car in the past, Dad slammed on the brakes and pulled over. I then opened the right side rear door, turned so I was on the edge of the seat, and threw up on the ground between my knees.

Mom handed me a Kleenex to wipe my mouth, and we resumed our journey. As we did, my brother cried out, "Don't come near me, Puke-Breath!"

"Mom! Lee's making fun of me again."

"Stop it! Both of you," Dad said. "And I don't mean maybe."

We knew better than to press our luck.

Soon we made our way to a light-green bridge that crossed a portion of Herrington Lake near Danville, and another educational session started as we wound our way down to it. It consisted of Dad's traditional lecture about different types of rocks. "Now those ones are sedimentary," he said with authority, while pointing to a cliff adjacent to the roadway. "They are caused by receding glaciers and rivers that leave sediment. Scientists sometimes find fossilized remains of fish and other water creatures in them." Dad could be a horrible tyrant and a bad example with respect to controlling his anger, but he was also a wonderful teacher. People are complicated, I guess, and he was no different.

About five miles after the sedimentary-rock lecture, we reached

Danville, a town of about 12,000 people. Its main attraction was a private liberal arts school called Centre College. The town had two separate social classes: a white, gentrified one and a poor black one. The first group lived in antebellum, Queen Anne, and bungalow-style homes, some with beautiful verandas and white columns. The second resided in falling-down frame and shotgun-style houses in separate parts of town. The Blacks also had their own business district, churches, schools, and swimming areas. Danville had two high schools until 1964: one for white students near the college and another for black students called the Bate School, several miles away.

While there was segregation, I can't recall anyone in our family ever speaking ill about people of color or using racial epithets. Mom always taught us not to "talk ugly," and this included such language. She sometimes referred to it as "gutta talk." Of course, the irony was she and Dad talked ugly to each other all the time, and they cussed us quite a bit. In effect there was justifiable ugly talk and unjustifiable. When my parents did it, it was justifiable, but when we did it, it was not.

Our trip to Danville finally ended when we saw a purple sign on the right side of Maple Avenue just past Centre College's campus. The sign read, "Wise Guest House, free parking." Dad turned into the driveway that flanked the residence on the left and parked the pink Plymouth in the back. We had made it to our destination and for the most part safe and sound.

Built in 1910, the Wise Guest House originally had four bedrooms. Later, Grandmother converted two other rooms in the home for her guests, so it now had six. The house had five fireplaces because central heat didn't exist at the time of its construction. Pocket doors, some out in the open and others hidden behind large pieces of antique furniture, connected many of the rooms. Nooks and crannies abounded, and one curiosity or another found on a shelf or in a drawer could occupy a child's attention for hours.

Despite its allure, the place did have one problem. It stood in stark contrast to the moderate home in which we lived in Erlanger, and this was a sore subject for Mom. She thought her parents should have done more for us. They were the haves, and we were the have nots, and she made this known every time we visited. Then too, there was the overlay of her paralysis, which caused her to feel slighted, relative to her siblings, Boyd and Mell.

After we entered the Guest House that trip, Grandmother greeted us with ebullience. She had gray hair, of course, brushed back into a tight curl. She wore horn-rimmed glasses and always a dress. "My, my, my, you never know what's going to happen next," she exclaimed, her refrain whenever anyone came over. Without hesitation she hugged and kissed us all.

While my parents and Grandmother caught up on things in the kitchen, Lee and I ran off to other parts of the house. In the front parlor, we saw Grandfather, slowly rocking in a chair by a fire. Behind him was a claw foot antique table that had a manual typewriter atop it on which he once wrote short works of literature. Sadly, it now stood idle. Though you wouldn't know it at this point since he was 87, he once taught Public Speaking, Rhetoric, and even Latin at Centre College. In fact, he formed the Journalism Department there in 1938. At various times he also taught at colleges in West Virginia, Tennessee, Arkansas, and Oklahoma. He obtained his PhD from Johns Hopkins in 1905 and wrote his dissertation on the arcane subject of the influence of Statius on Chaucer, something I find impressive since I have never read Chaucer much less Statius.

Besides the fireplace and claw-foot table, the front parlor had an antique bed with thin, hand-carved posts where Grandfather slept. He used to sleep on a cot in the attic until he could no longer go up and down the stairs to it. Below the bed rested a peach can in which he would urinate in the middle of the night instead of making his way to a toilet. In the morning, we would see him with the can in his hand, shuffling to the bathroom, where he would empty it.

We knew better than to bother Grandfather, for he did not have any tolerance for small children. To us, he was downright cranky and even scary. Sometimes he would get angry and yell at us for no apparent reason and make us cry. Most of the time, however, he would just mutter randomly at us. Perhaps in the past he had been approachable, but at this point, he needed to be avoided.

As we left the front room to explore other areas of the house that day, Lee and I heard a commotion in the kitchen, so we went there and discovered that Aunt Mell (Mom's older sister) had arrived. She taught Children's Literature at Illinois State University. Thus, she always gave us books. Since I couldn't read yet, she got me *The Cat in the Hat Comes Back.* Lee, being far more advanced, received a copy of *Robin Hood.*

In her forties and unmarried, Mell was five-foot-eleven and very self-conscious due to her height. Obsessed with her appearance, she wore upscale clothes, used expensive perfume, and sported a dark perm. Sometimes she would pay us a penny for every gray hair we plucked out of her scalp with tweezers. It was a nice source of income for us since she already had many gray hairs.

"Don't I get a kiss?" she asked, smiling. She towered over us and had to bend down considerably to expose her cheek. We each gave her a quick peck, though we did so with a boyish roll of our eyes.

After thanking her for the books, we excused ourselves from the conversation and retreated to a bench that was built into the woodwork in a hallway below the staircase. Our family called it the hall seat. Lee had already sat down on it before I got there, so I asked him if I could join him, and he grudgingly swung his legs around to make room. I watched as he read from *Robin Hood,* then requested something very important from him: "I'm going to start school next year, and I was wondering if you could teach me how to read."

My brother sighed.

"Come on, Lee, if you do, I promise I won't bug you about anything else."

He took the *Cat in the Hat* book from me and opened it up. "Now if you want to learn to read, you first have to look at a word and say it," he said. "Like this one here, 'work'. Now you try."

I pointed my finger at it and slowly pronounced "w-work." After doing so, I smiled in triumph.

"Okay, how about this one?"

I did my best to articulate it as well, and we repeated this process until I could say a sentence, then another and another.

"A book is just a bunch of sentences, Kenny. Pretty soon you'll know how to read the whole thing, but you got to practice first."

And so for several hours, I did just that. Each time I got stuck, Lee would come to my rescue. I developed the rest of my competence in this area on my own as I got older, but he was the one who got me started and monitored my progress at every juncture. He also set an example for me by his own effort in this department. For this I am greatly indebted to him, more so than anything else he taught me in childhood, and there were plenty of such things—everything from swimming to riding a bike without training wheels.

After I honed my fledgling reading skills some more, Grandmother announced supper was ready, so Lee and I rushed to the dining room table. Five chairs surrounded it. One of its sides abutted an upright heating register, and this was where the two of us took our places. A thick burgundy pad lay across it to prevent our butts from being burned. Around the rest of the table, the adults sat. In front of Grandfather was the main dish, a salt-cured country ham. My family called this Old Ham, a reference in the

South to an era in which such meat was preserved the old way, meaning without refrigeration and with salt.

Before we ate, Grandfather insisted on saying the blessing, something that Mom said he had worked on half the day. His delivery of it made it seem like we stood before God in fearful supplication. "Our father who art in heaven," he started off, his voice halting and even lurching. "We thank thee for the many blessings we have received..." Though he continued for what seemed like five minutes, we dared not clear our throats or show any sign of impatience. Instead we waited in silence, mesmerized by the prayer's eloquence until it finally ended with an appreciative round of amens.

The next ritual consisted of carving the meat. Armed with a knife with an ornate Sterling silver handle and a large fork of equal character, Grandfather began this process. Due to one affliction or another, he shook wildly as he cut, sometimes pushing the dish about the table. At one point Aunt Mell, apparently concerned he would slice his hand, insisted on taking over, but he adamantly refused to allow it. So the spectacle continued until he carved the entire ham, albeit into irregular pieces.

Once each of us had received our share of the meat, we passed the rest of the dishes around the table. They contained everything from turnips and sweet potatoes to red-eyed gravy and rolls. The fine china serving dishes perfectly matched our plates. Instead of using shakers, we pinched our salt from tiny metal cellars.

After dinner and before we had cleared the table, Mom asked without any lead up, "How come the tapestry is gone, Mother?"

"Well, I don't know, honey. What tapestry are you talking about?"

"The one that's supposed to be in the front room," Mom replied, turning toward Aunt Mell. "There's a large discolored space on the wall where it used to hang."

"If you're suggesting I took it, you are plainly mistaken," Mell said.

"Did Sam Cheek say you could have that?" Mom asked.

"Why, Sam Cheek is Daddy's lawya, and I have nothing to do with him. So the answer is no."

"Even though he's been doin' you and Boyd's biddin' for years, right?"

"I don't know what you're talking about."

"Grab, grab, grab, is what I'm talking about. Takin' Mother and Daddy's things before their graves are bought and paid for. Kenny dudn't even have a bed!"

"Honey, stop," Dad interjected.

"No, you stop! We scrimp and save, while she and Boyd help themselves."

"You're a bitter woman," Mell replied.

"Don't you care about Kenny or Lee?" Mom shouted back.

"Of course, I do. I've always done as much as I can for your boys."

"You have not, and neither has Mother or Daddy."

"Come on, honey," Dad said, while escorting her to a different part of the house.

"Grab, grab, grab. You and Boyd and that goddamn Sam Cheek!" Mom screamed from the hall.

An awkward silence enveloped the dining room. Grandmother broke the impasse with a smile as though nothing had happened. "Do you boys want some dessert?" she asked in her Georgia accent. "We have homemade pecan pie. Why, Miss Fant, who lives down yonder on St. Mildred Court, was kind enough to bring us some today."

Out back of the Wise Guest House, an intermingling of pear and walnut trees spread wide and deep. The pears painted hues of pink and yellow in the trees and across the ground, while walnut pods added lime green to this colorful palette. In the past, Grandmother would can the pears in mason jars, and Grandfather would pry the walnuts open using nutcracker picks that still could be found in the kitchen drawers. Now, due to their age and infirmity, my grandparents couldn't accomplish such tasks, and the pears and walnuts simply dropped to the ground and became food for the squirrels.

The morning after our arrival at Grandmother's that August, Lee and I searched for something to do. The old barn that stood behind the pear and walnut trees came to mind, so we hurried over to it. Its sliding door was jammed shut, but little by little we pulled and shoved it open. Inside the barn, a small amount of sunlight peeked through the vents near the roof as well as the cracks in the walls, and this allowed us to see tobacco hanging from the rafters, empty horse stalls, and a cast iron water spout. The tobacco was in the process of curing and offered a sweet scent. No doubt nearby farmers had rented the space from my grandparents for this purpose. We weren't supposed to be in the barn without express permission. Yet this made our experience all the more pleasurable, for we loved to explore prohibited areas, if for no other reason than to find out why they were prohibited.

We climbed an old wooden staircase that went up to a loft that overlooked the main floor. Here and there on the way up, we brushed aside dusty cobwebs mottled with egg sacs and the remains of spider prey. At the top of the stairs, we found a separate room but couldn't figure out how to breach the lock on its door. So we scouted out the rest of the loft, where we found rusted farm implements and tools: hoes, sickles, handsaws, block and tackle sets, pitchforks, and shovels. Some tools we did not recognize, either because we were unfamiliar with them, or they had become obsolete. But the biggest and most glorious object of our attention was an old two-seated kayak that rested on the floor.

"It's Grandfather's," Lee whispered urgently. "He and Uncle Boyd paddled it in Canada together. Come on, let's sit in it."

I took a place in the front and Lee in the rear, and he told me stories about the two men fishing and hunting together. I listened to his every word, spellbound by his description of their adventures. With equal enthusiasm, he tried to convince me that Uncle Boyd, who had a bedroom on the second floor of the Wise Guest House as a teenager, would get up in the morning and leap over the railing and down to a landing in the middle of the staircase. When I challenged Lee about the unlikelihood of such an accomplishment, he spun the yarn further and reminded me of the wear marks on the landing, where my uncle's feet must have hit when he jumped down.

It would be an understatement to say my brother and I idolized Uncle Boyd. Whenever he would come to Grandmother's or our house in Erlanger, we would become overwhelmed with joy. We would beg him for piggy-back and shoulder rides, and most of the time he would oblige. This gave us a great thrill, for he stood six-foot-five, much taller than our father who was five-nine and didn't engage us in such activities. Dad couldn't throw a football or baseball or shoot a basketball. He likely couldn't bait a hook either, though I can't be sure of this, since he never took us fishing or hunting. His interest was in supply-and-demand curves, price theory, fiscal and monetary policy, and things like sedimentary rocks. He lectured on and on about such subjects at the dinner table while not making eye contact with us, staring off into space, and gesturing as if he were speaking to a large class at school. While such information was important, it was hardly the domain of young lads.

My father was also older than other fathers. He was nearly fifty at my birth and fifty-five at this point in my life. He looked more like a grandfather than a dad. Sometimes people would even refer to him as such by mistake. If this deficit were his only problem, it wouldn't have bothered me, but it together with his anger and explosiveness, often displayed in public, made me feel far more short-changed than the stares I would receive due to Mom's paralysis.

After we left the barn that day, Lee urged me to follow him to the second floor of the Wise Guest House. Its cherry staircase turned to the right halfway up and creaked as we climbed it, serving notice to Mom that we were up to no good.

"Kenny! Lee! Don't be messing around up there," she cautioned.

"It's okay. We're just taking a look at Grandfather's books," Lee replied coyly.

At the top of the stairs stood a large walnut partner's desk, so called as it had the same drawers and ornate features on both sides. It is the desk on which I write this memoir today, for somewhere along the line, I inherited it. It sat in front of a pair of single-hung windows that led out onto the roof, where the attic stairway went up the side of the house.

"Boys, don't be going up to the attic," Mom shouted as Lee raised open one of the windows. Her hearing was highly developed when it came to our mischief, and we often mistook it for Extra Sensory Perception. Thus, she knew we were up to no good, though she was way down in the kitchen talking to Grandmother.

"We're just getting some fresh air in here," Lee hollered back. He put his index finger on his lips to signal that we should proceed quietly, grabbed a broom that had been resting against the wall, and exited onto the roof through the window. I followed him, and he led me underneath the attic stairs. There we observed a large wasp nest, perhaps seven to eight inches in diameter. I grimaced at the sight of its menacing-looking inhabitants and with a nervous whisper asked my brother what he had in mind.

"We're going to take that nest out," he replied, eyeing a can of Raid next to the bottom of the staircase that must have been left by someone who had previously dealt with the same problem.

"But we'll get stung really bad."

"Nah, it'll be easy. I'll knock the nest down, and you'll spray the wasps with that Raid can."

"But they'll come after us."

"Don't worry. We'll climb in through the window real fast, and they'll never know what hit 'em."

Under the stairs, Lee slowly moved toward the nest, armed with the broom. Then with a quick swipe, he hit it squarely, but it did not fall. Instead, the wasps chased us, and they were mad as hell. At first, we ran about the roof in panic, swatting them off us as best we could and spraying them with Raid, but they still managed to sting us. One even got me underneath my pinky fingernail, and man did that hurt. Eventually, we dove back inside the house through the open window, but our retreat was so uncontrolled and panicked that we knocked everything off the partner's desk before Lee could slam the window shut.

"You boys come down here right this minute," Mom yelled. "I told you not to mess around up there, and you promptly did it anyway!"

After we sheepishly made it down the stairs to the hallway where she waited with her good hand propped on her hip, Lee tried to justify our efforts. "We knocked a bad wasp nest down, Mom, or uh tried to at least."

"Well, let that be a lesson to you," she replied as she watched us nurse our wounds. "Now get some baking soda from the kitchen, wet it, and paste it on those stings. It'll help with the pain."

Once we accomplished this, Mom methodically climbed upstairs as best she could to assess the damage. Naturally, we raced ahead to fix things. Lee put the green blotter back on the desk that had been knocked off during our escape. I did the same with a few magazines. Unfortunately, we had broken something, which Mom immediately noticed once she got up there.

"That was Mother's good flower vase!" she said. "You'll have to pay for it out of your own money."

We immediately agreed to the terms of repayment and watched with amazement as Mom slowly descended the stairs. We had seen her do this hundreds of times, but the way she accomplished this task never got old. If she faced forward going down the steps, there would be a large amount of space in front of her which might cause her to lose her balance, tumble all the way to the first floor, and possibly sustain serious injury. But if she faced upward and limped backwards one step at a time while grasping the bannister firmly with her good hand, the space down the stairs would be less daunting, and she would be able to keep her balance more easily. If she did fall, she would only go down a short distance onto the steps in front of her and likely catch herself.

Now you would think that after all this excitement, financial set back, and pain and suffering, Lee and I would no longer be bored that day and retreat into more sedentary activities such as reading our new books. But we did not, since my brother suggested we play his favorite game. He called it "stalking".

I always thought it was odd he referred to it as such, as the name conjured images of criminals spying on innocent human prey. Really, it was nothing more than a sophisticated variation of hide-and-go-seek in which the players did not have to remain in place. The object of the game was for the stalker to observe the person who was "it" and move away before being spotted and tagged. If he tagged that person first, he won. But if he got tagged first, he lost. Lee liked to play this game since usually it took a long time, involved multiple hiding places, and constituted more of a challenge than hide-and-go-seek. I was always "it", of course.

Because the entire house was our playing field, I operated systematically in attempting to find Lee, starting first with the cellar. Eventually, I made it to the second floor, but I hadn't seen any signs of him. At the top of the stairs, I noted the window above the partner's desk was slightly ajar. I knew for sure that he had slammed it shut earlier when we dealt with the wasps. He had to have gone through it again and was now in the attic, I thought. If so, there would be no method of escape, for there was only one entrance to the attic, and I had that covered. So I slid the window up further and stepped out onto the roof. Slowly and quietly I crept up the stairs outside the house, being careful not to disturb the wasps. Soon, I reached the attic entrance, which consisted of a small bi-fold window that swung open outward.

After quietly slipping inside, I observed a cot on my right that Grandfather used, back when he could still climb the attic stairs. A floor lamp, draped with cobwebs, extended over the part of the bed closest to the entrance. Old books and boxes full of documents gathered dust seemingly everywhere. On a nearby table, I saw a pair of binoculars and some old-fashioned camera equipment. Leaning against the wall were several fly-fishing poles, and on the floor near them was a tackle box. Everywhere there were items of interest.

I continued past the cot and turned left down a passageway. A small alcove appeared on the right side of it, and I made the mistake of walking into it without covering my back. I then felt someone touch my shoulder and whisper, "You're still it!"

"Darn, I never get to win!"

"Maybe one day you will," my brother said, smiling. "Once you get a little older and smarter."

"Ha-ha-ha, real funny, Lee."

"Well, it's true."

"Maybe if I wasn't 'it' all the time, I'd win."

"How do you know that?"

"Because the guy who's 'it' has to chase, which is harder."

"Tell you what. Next time I'll be 'it.'"

"Okay."

"But if you lose, you'll always have to be 'it' after that."

"No fair, we should take turns."

"Fine, we'll do that, and I'll beat you every time anyway."

At this we took a seat side by side on the cot, where our conversation took on a more serious tone. "So how come Grandfather stayed up here so much?" I asked.

"Not sure. Maybe he could read and write better without people interrupting him all the time."

"But he was up here for days at a time. That's why there's this cot. Probably only came downstairs to empty his stupid peach can. And what about Grandmother?"

"What about her?"

"She was by herself all the time unless she had guests."

My brother shrugged indifference.

"Come on, Lee. Don't you think it was a little weird for Grandfather to be alone up here so much?"

"Not really. I kind of like being alone myself."

"But aren't you afraid?"

"Nah."

"Not even a little bit?"

"Nope."

We sat on the cot for a while and said nothing. Then Lee told me to go back downstairs so he could read. I did as told, making sure to close the attic window tightly behind me. As I made my way down, I thought about something that was quite significant: as much as my brother and I had in common, we were very different.

For the next several days, Lee followed Grandfather's example and spent most of his time alone. Generally this was in the attic. Occasionally, we would do things together, but he didn't show much enthusiasm or energy for our activities and would often disappear. Usually I found him up there reading, but instead of doing something with me, he would send me back downstairs and remind me I was not supposed to be in that part of the house. Of course, he wasn't either.

Because Lee had gone into hiding, I worked for Grandmother, sweeping the porch and sidewalk, mopping the floors, and gathering sticks for her to burn in the front room fireplace.

When I was doing this one day, I noticed Mom in the dining room standing next to one of Grandmother's cabinets, while meticulously counting her mother's silver place settings. Her lips mouthed numbers as she carefully handled each item and one by one put them back into a walnut treasure box in which they had been stored.

Mom then left the dining room, and I followed her to the front parlor. When Mom got there, she started searching a desk. Though she had shifted her attention to something else, she was just as determined as she had been with the silverware. Having not found what she was looking for, she slammed the desk's slanted top shut and stared at the floor in disappointment.

"What's wrong?" I asked her.

"Mell took Mother's sapphire ring and Daddy's Phi Beta Kappa key! She probably took some of the silver place settings, too."

By mid-afternoon, Mom was still searching for the missing valuables in the chests, cabinets, and other hiding spaces throughout the house. I didn't mention this paranoid episode to an adult, for it happened so often I wouldn't be reporting anything new. Besides, what good would it have done to complain? She was my mother, after all, and I wouldn't exchange her for anyone. Despite all her faults, I loved her more than anyone in the world.

On the final night of our week at Grandmother's, everyone gathered on the front porch. The porch was supported by multiple white pillars and stretched the entire width of the house. Each end of it had a dark green wooden swing that fit two people, and Lee and I swung wildly on them until Mom made us stop. Between the swings, several white grapevine benches and a couple of wicker rocking chairs provided the rest of the family a seat, as lightning bugs blinked on and off in the front yard. Grandmother brought us each a dish of lime sherbet, which we savored a half spoonful at a time. In the background, we could hear a symphony of cicadas that soothed us still further.

Lee and I retrieved from the cellar several of Grandmother's old mason jars. We ran around the front yard and captured about twenty of the lightning bugs, while the adults talked like adults for once. We put the bugs in the jars, being careful to poke holes in the top so that the little creatures could breathe. Once we did this, we watched the bugs glow on and off. When we finally became bored, we allowed them to fly away and relished a rare moment of peace in our family.

3

Left to Our Own Devices

From the fall of 1961 to the summer of 1963, Dad took a temporary teaching job at Kearney State University in Nebraska while we stayed in Erlanger. Lee and I were glad he wasn't around, since things were quieter at home, and we would be able to avoid his spare-the-rod, spoil-the-child approach to discipline. For the most part we didn't have a relationship with him. If we cared about any parent, it was Mom. Even though she was imbalanced, she at least loved us. Dad, on the other hand, never told us he cared about us, provided any physical affection, or did anything special with us. If he had feelings for us, it was only because he was trying to please Mom, whom he did love. At least that was our impression at the time. As a result, Lee took my father's place. He was my *de facto* dad.

In order to occupy ourselves one Saturday in this time frame, Lee and I asked Mom if we could take a hike to the Cincinnati Airport. Given the weather was still warm, she agreed and made us a lunch of peanut butter and banana sandwiches for our journey. She packed them in an empty bread bag and in turn put it in a Shillito's Department Store shopping sack. She never bought baggies or lunch sacks and instead used left-over packaging from the store. She also saved TV-dinner tinfoil instead of buying it in a box, converted cheese jars into juice glasses, reused containers that food came in versus Tupperware, and never threw away a rubber band, a piece of wrapping paper, or a grocery bag. She was the ultimate recycler before recycling came into vogue. This was not because she was environmentally conscious, mind you, but rather that she was obsessed with saving money having lived through The Great Depression. Her efforts, like so many other amazing things she did, evinced a highly capable woman despite her meltdowns.

Lee and I began our trek at the creek. Unlike the times we would run around in the rain, the water was shallow, and we could see it bubbling and winding its way around various rocks and boulders. After crossing a clearing, we came to a thickly wooded area that had a narrow footpath made by the kids in the neighborhood. "This is the Little Woods," my brother proclaimed, as though a map had designated it as such.

"Is there a Big Woods?" I asked.

"Yep."

"Where is it?"

"Just before we get to the Super Highway," Lee declared, while pushing aside overgrown tree branches that blocked the trail.

"The Super Highway must be pretty big, if they call it super," I called out.

"It's part of the new four-lane road system that goes state to state."

"What types of animals live in the Little Woods?"

"Squirrels, chipmunks, rabbits, and a few snapping turtles by the creek."

"Do the snapping turtles bite?"

"Yep. I saw one snap a stick clean in half last week."

"Really? How thick was the stick?"

"Maybe an inch."

"How big was the snapping turtle?"

"'Bout like this." Lee put his arms out as though he were hugging a tree.

"And the Big Woods? What animals live there?"

"Bobcats, fox, deer, sometimes bear."

"Bear?"

"Don't worry. They're more afraid of you than you are of them."

The path came to a point where the creek widened, and we stopped by the water's edge. At our feet were some small rocks, which Lee squatted to examine. "Sometimes you can find arrowheads around here," he said while staring across the water. "Gary Reinfelt found one once. Really it was just a chip, but you could tell it came from an arrowhead because it had marks on it that must have been chiseled by Indians."

Gary was a tall, strapping teenager whom my brother frequently spoke about. Even though I hardly saw him hang out with the guy, Lee sure talked about him a lot. "Gary built a treehouse by the creek," "Gary rode his bike no-handed down Fitzgerald Court," or "Gary got a job at Kroger bagging groceries," he would say.

After searching the ground, Lee bent down and grabbed a couple of flat stones. "Ya ever skip rocks?" he asked.

"Nope."

"Come on. I'll teach you."

Lee side-armed one of the stones he had picked up, and it skipped three times across the water. I tried doing it myself, but mine didn't work.

"You can't use round rocks," he said. "They have to be flat like this."

I found a stone that met his approval and tried again. This time it skipped, but just once. After multiple efforts, I skipped one twice. Satisfied with my progress, Lee had us return to the trail.

Another half hour passed, and we eventually made it to an area where the trees had been cleared and piles of branches dotted excavated ground. Several empty bulldozers drew our interest, but we dared not climb on them. Something about their massive nature made this too scary. On the edge of this destruction, some mature oaks towered above us, which Lee told me were the remains of the Big Woods.

He pointed to some houses in the distance that had dry shells, consisting only of roofs, outside walls, and framing. "Come on," he said, and we both ran to one. He hoisted me up by the armpits to a window opening so I could peer inside. I observed a series of unfinished rooms outlined by studwork. In the middle of the floor I noticed a large square hole. We crawled inside the house through the window opening, and from the hole, we could see the ground eight feet below where the basement floor would go. Concrete had not been poured yet, so its surface was sand. We also saw a space in the wall of the basement where the garage door would be.

"Betcha I can jump down there," Lee said as he sat on the edge of the hole and dangled his legs over it.

"You're going to get hurt. Don't!"

Suddenly, my brother slipped his butt off the edge and dropped down. He landed on his feet and stumbled, then straightened. He looked up at me and said, "See, it was easy. Now it's your turn."

"I don't know, Lee."

"What's a matter? You chicken?"

"No, but—"

"Come on, I'll catch you," he said, while reaching his hands toward me.

I reluctantly draped my legs over the hole while staring down at the sand.

"On the count of three. Ready?"

I nodded, mustering up as much courage as I could.

"One."

"Two."

My heart raced, and I grimaced hard.

"Three."

I jumped into Lee's arms, and we sprawled across the sand together. After I dusted myself off, I stood tall and exclaimed, "Let's do it again!"

"Maybe another time," my brother replied. "We need to get going."

We continued our journey and in time made it to the Super Highway, under which the creek disappeared into a concrete culvert. We climbed up the embankment and found unopened-finished roadway that stretched as far as we could see in either direction. "This way," Lee said, whereupon we hiked on the shoulder until we came to a dead bobcat. Its eyes had been eaten out by scavengers, but it still had its telltale pointy ears. The paws were the size of a dog's, and its fur was thick and mangy. With a stick, my brother revealed the animal's sharp teeth.

Farther up the new interstate, we came to Donaldson Road, which would take us to the airport. We trudged along the ditch beside this busy thoroughfare in an attempt to keep our distance from the traffic. We could feel the whoosh of cars and trucks as they sped by. We had to shout to be heard over the noise created by tires humming on the pavement.

Lee picked up a dirty pop bottle from the ground. "If we get enough of these, we'll be able to buy soft drinks for lunch and maybe candy for dessert," he said.

"How do you figure?"

"There's a liquor store on the way to the airport, and the man there will give us two cents a bottle," he replied. "We just need ten bottles. That's twenty cents, and a pop is a nickel. That leaves us five cents each for candy."

We found a discarded cardboard box by a garbage receptacle at one of the businesses along the way and used it to hold the bottles we recovered, as well as our sack lunches. We crisscrossed the ditches and scoured the ground until we got our quota. At the liquor store, I got a grape pop and Lee an orange one. I bought some jawbreakers, and he purchased several sticks of red licorice.

By noon, we made it to the airport fence. As we ate our lunch and swigged our soft drinks, we watched several DC 3s land. Then, a jet plane took off and made its way upward through the white puffy clouds. Once it disappeared in the distance, I said,

"Maybe someday we can fly across the country together, huh Lee?"

He shrugged without saying a thing.

"I heard they got pretty stewardesses and nice meals."

"That's true, I guess."

"Sure is nice to dream, isn't it?"

"If you say so."

"Why do you say that?"

"Because dreams like that never come true, Kenny. They're just dreams and nuthin' else."

Even though things were better for Lee and me when Dad was in Nebraska, this wasn't always the case, since Mom frequently got into it with the neighbors just like she did with her siblings. This time it was the Dusies. They lived to the right of us as you faced our house from the street, and the Mitchells to the left. The Dusies had a lower-middle-class income like our family, but less education. Mom didn't like them and prohibited us from associating with their children, because she said they were "poor-white trash."

Catholic, they attended St. Henry's Parish in Erlanger, and Mom, a devout protestant who had grown up in the South, didn't particularly like Catholics. In fact she voted for Nixon rather than Kennedy in 1960 for that very reason, according to Dad, at least. While this was part of her dislike for this clan, by no means was it all, for she quarreled with the Mitchells and all our neighbors no matter who they were. She was an equal-opportunity trouble-maker when it came to people who lived next door. Something about her personal space triggered such hate since the disputes always started as a result of the same pretext: trespass to land.

Having spotted a Dusie boy through the kitchen window running in our yard, Mom rushed outside and screamed a phrase from the depth of her lungs that we had heard a dozen times before,

"Get off our property!" Naturally this garnered our attention, and we followed her to investigate what the fuss was all about. By the time we got out there, the trespassing Dusie boy, a child of about eight wearing a mitt on one of his hands, had already made it back to his family's side of the line with a baseball that must have rolled onto our side. He gave it to his older brother, who tossed it up in the air and hit it to a third brother occupying a make-believe outfield, the boundary of which came precariously close to the edge of our yard.

"Get off our property!" Mom shouted as the ball rolled on our side again. Her jaw was clenched, and the cords of her neck throbbed. She had in her eyes what best could be described as a thousand-yard stare.

"What's wrong, Mom?" Lee asked, but she ignored him, as she did me when I posited the same question.

The Dusie boys eventually suspended the game and ran inside their house, presumably to seek reinforcements. After a few minutes, Mr. Dusie came out. He was a burly man with an abundance of tattoos and a reddish-brown complexion from having worked construction. Nevertheless his intimidating appearance did not deter Mom, not for a solitary second.

"You tell your goddamn boys to stay off our property!" she hollered at him.

"What in the hell's wrong with you?" Mr. Dusie responded, gesturing wildly as he approached her. "They just playin' ball!"

"Keep your white trash off our property!"

"We got no quarrel with you."

"Just stay off our property! Or you'll go to jail!"

The last remark was delivered with greater force than the others. But it must have had an impact, as Mr. Dusie returned to his home and slammed the door shut. Mom remained outside, however, keeping a vigilant watch for several minutes like a German shepherd aroused by a burglar. Finally, she reentered the kitchen, muttering bitterly, "Nothin' but poor-white trash."

Lee and I were embarrassed by Mom's tirades with the neighbors, but beyond that we were confused. We had no degrees in psychology or familiarity with what might have caused such belligerence. We were just kids being raised by a mother who periodically went berserk, and a father, who, when around, flew off the handle at the slightest back talk. As a result, we depended on ourselves for grounding and personal development. Sometimes we succeeded in that endeavor, and sometimes we did not, but we tried the best we could.

School on October 22, 1962 ended like most days at Erlanger Elementary. Children in my first-grade class slammed their desks shut after putting their workbooks and school supplies away. Some grabbed metal lunchboxes, colorfully decorated with cartoon characters. Others retrieved jackets from hooks on the wall. Eventually, everyone crowded by the classroom door, and once the teacher opened it, they rushed into the hallway, where older, more seasoned students swarmed about in a cacophony of voices shouting, lockers slamming, and feet running. The excitement continued outside, as kids yanked their bikes off racks, played on teeter-totters, merry-go-rounds, and swing sets, and ran back and forth in spirited games of tag.

Lee met me after school, and we walked home together as usual. The route consisted of several winding streets and two short cuts, one that went through a field and another on the edge of a hill. The oak, maple, and hickory trees along the way offered a kaleidoscope of brown, red, and yellow. Periodically the rushing wind sent leaves fluttering to the ground, where they mixed with banana-shaped locust pods and buckeyes.

For supper that night Mom fed us hotdogs and beans, something we had quite often. On our orange Formica-topped kitchen table, she plopped a red and white serving dish that had a batch of it inside. The ketchup bottle was almost empty, so she poured some pickle juice in it to scarf out the remaining dregs of ketchup. We used bread for the hotdogs, as Mom didn't want to pay extra for buns. After sitting down, she separated the bacon chunk from the beans for herself. She claimed that this was one of the few pleasures she had in life, so we dared not take it for ourselves.

Generally, we ate what Mom fed us, for there was no alternative menu or short-order cook at her restaurant. Only twice did I go to bed hungry. The first time was when she made liver and onions, and the second was when she cooked us brains and eggs. Besides hotdogs and beans, we had TV dinners, potpies, her version of chop suey (ground beef, onions, and bean sprouts), black-eyed peas and ham, fish sticks, cream-chipped beef, and boiled chicken. We did not have a grill and never ate out unless we were travelling, and fast food wasn't around much back then. If it had been, Mom wouldn't have paid for it anyway.

Having eaten our meal and cleared the table, we retired to the living room, where we watched a black-and-white television contained in a wooden console, for TVs in those days were an item of furniture. Our favorite show was *Leave It to Beaver*. I identified with Beaver, and Lee with Wally, but in every other respect our family did not resemble the Cleavers. I sat on the couch with Mom, and Lee sprawled across the room's worn-out grayish-blue rug with his face closest to the TV screen and chin propped up by his knuckles.

Normally the local news came on at 7 p.m., followed by the national. Instead, President Kennedy appeared, and for three minutes we watched as he explained what was taking place in Cuba. Specifically, he said that the Soviet Union had put missile sites there having "nuclear strike capability." He also announced that he had ordered a quarantine of all ships coming to Cuba in order to block further shipment of military equipment to that country and warned that any attempt by the Russians to fire missiles at the

United States or other countries in our hemisphere would result in "a full retaliatory response against the Soviet Union."

"Lee, where's Cuba?" I asked, after Kennedy finished.

"Ninety miles off the Florida Keys."

"What's a nuclear strike?"

My brother provided a detailed lecture about nuclear weapons, including a short course on atoms. "Atoms make up everything and are the fuel for nuclear bombs. So when one hits, there's a huge explosion and tens of thousands of people are dead. If enough bombs go off, everyone is dead. One moment you're here and another, poof, you're gone."

I closed my eyes and tried to imagine sudden vaporization, but I just couldn't grasp the concept. "Is there going to be a nuclear war?" I asked.

"Maybe," Lee replied. "Unless Kennedy stops the Russians in Cuba, and even if he does, they've still got hundreds of missiles that they can fire at us from clear across the ocean whenever they feel like. Most of them we'll shoot down, but some will get through, and the people who survive the first wave of bombs will die anyway from radiation poisoning and starvation."

I couldn't sleep that night. Through the windows in our room, open because of a fall heatwave, I gazed at the horizon and heard in the distance the lonely sounds of sirens screaming, cars racing, and trains rumbling on railroad tracks. While my brother slept on the old hospital bed, I wondered if the sky would soon glow and the world I knew would forever change.

Winter in northern Kentucky was relatively mild. Temperatures rarely got below the teens, and little snow accumulated. Cars did not have snow tires, and plows hardly ever cleared the roads before the snow melted on its own. When it did snow, Lee and I viewed it as a novelty rather than something to dread. We put on our boots, gloves, hats, and coats, and joyfully ran outside and played in it. We made snowmen, had snowball fights, and by golly, we ate the stuff.

In that spirit, we went sledding together in late December the year of the Cuban Missile Crisis. We had one sled between us, a wooden Royal Racer. With a rope attached to its steering bar, we towed it up Fitzgerald Court. By the time we arrived, a dozen kids had already gotten there. Whenever a vehicle approached, one of them would yell, "Car!" This in turn caused a ripple effect of other kids yelling the same thing. Then everyone scattered until the vehicle passed.

Lee gave me first dibs, so I lay stomach-down on our sled. He pushed me as hard as he could while running alongside, whereupon I experienced the thrill of being out of control as I barreled down the hill. After I made it back up, he got his turn. I tried my best to push him, but I wasn't much help. When we became bored doing this, we rode the sled together. Sometimes I sat in front of him, and sometimes I would lie down on top of him. After about an hour, we decided to head home. But another kid told us he was going over to a house on Forest Avenue that had a nice hill behind it and asked us if we wanted to try it out.

"Sure," Lee replied. Naturally I tagged along.

Though the new hill was not as long as the one on Fitzgerald Court, it was considerably steeper. Several trees dotted the slope, and we could see other kids weaving around them as they sped down it. Lee went first and managed to steer our sled to the left of a tree in the middle of the hill and narrowly missed another just beyond it. After running back up, he handed me the tow rope and said, "Your turn."

Nervously I got on our sled. As Lee shoved me off, I dragged the tips of my boots behind me to keep myself from careening out of control. Like him, I steered away from the big tree in the middle and the others beyond it.

For the next half hour we took advantage of this obstacle course. Soon we got used to the challenge, and the same kid who got us to come over to the house in the first place suggested we go down the hill in tandem and try to wrestle the person beside us off his sled. Lee agreed, and he was able to stay on each time. Later, a boy more my size challenged me. At first I was reluctant, but after a minute I worked up the courage. Heaven forbid, if I were called a chicken for backing down.

At first my opponent and I went down the hill slowly in order to grab ahold of each other by the coat before picking up speed. So focused was I on ripping the other kid off his sled, I didn't realize we were rapidly sliding into an area full of trees off the main route. Without warning, I felt my face plant into one of them. I put my hand on my nose and mouth and looked at it. I was bleeding badly. I started to cry, but only when I saw the blood.

Lee ran down the hill and assessed the situation. "Your nose and mouth are really messed up, and your forehead is cut too," he said. "We need to get you home right away."

"But it hurts!"

I bawled the whole way back. Lee put his arm around me and repeatedly reassured me as we went along. He even dug out a crumpled Kleenex from his jacket pocket and wiped my nose and mouth with it.

At the house, Mom cleaned the rest of my face and dabbed my wounds with a washcloth, but she did not call a doctor to see if I needed stitches or was concussed. She rarely sought medical attention for anyone in our family. When I got the flu, she took my temperature, and no matter how high it was, never consulted a nurse. In the summer, I would get severe rashes from seasonal allergies that left large, open sores on the inside of my thighs. Often they would become infected, but she never took me to see anyone. Aunt Mell noticed the infected sores one year and brought me to a doctor in Danville, but not Mom. Sometimes these allergies caused my eyes to swell shut. Even so she would simply have me cover them with a cold washcloth rather than obtain a prescription. I even used my own money to buy over-the-counter drugs for this condition, as she refused to do that for me. She responded similarly when I got poison oak on my ankles and could barely walk. I still have scars from it. It was the same with Lee. An older kid once knocked him out when demonstrating a judo move on him. Mom gave my brother some aspirin and told him to go to bed early.

My point isn't to complain about my mother not getting us medical help. The last thing I want to do is look like a whiner. Indeed, our minor medical issues paled in comparison to her paralysis. Like many families, we didn't have decent health insurance or extra cash to pay extraordinary bills. In looking back on it, however, I wonder if her reluctance to seek medical attention had more to do with her extreme mistrust of outsiders. The words she used during her many battles with the neighbors come to mind—"Get off our property!"

4

The Picture Darkens

With a poor excuse for a pop singer's voice, Lee quietly sang, *Goodbye Cruel World, I'm Off to Join the Circus.* James Darren's hit song had come out recently and was often played on the radio. It was about a young man who ran away after being jilted by his girlfriend.

"How come you're singing that?" I asked.

"Because I like it. What's it to you?"

"Just wanna know is all."

"Well, maybe I'll join the circus someday," my brother said with a half-smile. He was probably trolling me, but given his threat to run away earlier, I had to take him seriously.

"That's not funny, Lee. Cut it out!"

Instead of obliging me, he sang the first line of the song again, this time right in my face.

"Stop it! Will ya? You're scaring me!"

Lee laughed.

I stormed into the living room, while he continued singing the tune to himself. There, I noticed a glossy-covered magazine called *Grade Teacher* on the coffee table. It was the February, 1963 issue, and I still have a copy of it today. I opened it to a page marked by a scrap of paper where I saw a dozen or so poems penned by kids from all around the country. One was entitled "Abraham Lincoln," and its attribution said, "Lee Farmer, Grade Five, Erlanger Elementary School, Erlanger, Kentucky."

While I didn't understand all the words, I read the poem out loud the best I could:

Lincoln was born in a humble place
And was very homely of face.
Lincoln was very poor
And yet always a book he bore.
Lincoln, wise and good,
For his country strongly stood.
Melancholy, gentle, strong of will,
We remember Lincoln still.

Since my brother had written the poem in the fifth grade or the 1961-62 schoolyear, he would have been ten. When I saw the magazine just after it came out in early 1963, he was going on twelve. Regardless of the age mechanics, I was very proud of him for having accomplished this feat at such a young age, so I went back to our room to congratulate him.

"It was just something my teacher liked," he replied, very much unenthused.

"Yeah, but it's published in a magazine!"

Lee shrugged and went back to humming *Goodbye Cruel World, I'm Off to Join the Circus.*

I returned to the living room and started re-reading the poem, but before I could get very far, Mom rushed in, snatched the magazine from me, and put it away. "I'm saving this, and I don't want you drawing on it," she said sharply. "You're such 'a little tearer-upper,' you know." Being a "tearer-upper" was a reputation I had earned around the house because I would often take things apart and not put them together right. Sometimes I would remove something from a box or drawer of hers without asking and not return it to the precise location where I had found it, which unfailingly caused her to lose it.

Instead of becoming upset with Mom for being so harsh, I changed the subject and asked her what "melancholy" meant. I'm sure I mispronounced the word, as it was well beyond my vocabulary.

"Why do you want to know?"

"Because Lee used that word in his poem."

"Melancholy means sad," Mom replied, sighing with irritation.

"Hmmm. I wonder why he decided to call Abraham Lincoln that."

"Just don't worry about it!"

When Dad was in Nebraska, the only time we would see him was when we went to Grandmother's in August or for holidays. Otherwise he made only one cameo appearance at home the entire two years he was gone. I didn't actually see him, but I knew he had been there since he had left a book for me on a table next to our living-room picture window. It was called *Barney Beagle*, a story about a kid who got a dog from a pet store. It was the only present Dad ever bought me, so I wanted to thank him for it. Unfortunately, by the time he came back from Nebraska for good, we both had forgotten about it. Other than this, my father made no effort to communicate with Lee or me when he was gone—not one phone call, letter, or postcard. It could have been he just didn't care or it could have been that was what fathers did back then. I don't remember any fanfare or affection when he came home permanently, either; there was no jumping up and down, hugging, or shaking of hands among us. It was as though he had returned from the office. The pink Plymouth simply appeared in the driveway.

Though there was not much excitement over Dad's return, I do recall Mom and him discussing his next job while they were in the kitchen. Either he didn't like Kearney State or it didn't like him. Dad mentioned he had an opportunity for a position at a university in Stevens Point, Wisconsin. The mandatory retirement age in Wisconsin was seventy, which made taking a job there attractive to him since in Kentucky that age was sixty-five. Mom did not approve of this proposal for two reasons involving cold weather: first, she had been raised in the South and wasn't used to it; and second, it might aggravate her paralysis and already poor circulation.

As this conversation continued, my brother and I became interested in the portable TV Dad had brought home and used in Nebraska. It sat on a cheap metal stand with white-plastic wheels in the hallway between the kitchen and the bedrooms. Always the instigator, Lee thought it would be cool to move the TV into our bedroom so we could watch it privately. Up to that point we had been a one-TV family, and Lee and I having our own one, even for a short time, seemed like a good idea.

The plan my brother concocted involved quietly rolling the TV on the hallway rug while my parents were consumed in conversation in the kitchen. After talking about this proposition briefly, we each went to separate sides of the stand and started pushing it. But the rug bunched up in the process, the wheels got caught in it, and the TV crashed to the floor.

Dad rushed toward the hallway, screaming, "Lee! Kenneth! Goddamn your blackhearts, what have you done now?" He only called me Kenneth when he was hopping mad since that name could be yelled more sharply than the innocent sounding, Kenny. He frequently used the term blackheart or damn little devil when referring to us. I assumed at the time he actually thought we were evil, even though it would have been more accurate to conclude we were just devious and/or rebellious. Unfortunately, the subtle nuances of words escaped my father when he was angry as did just about any other notion of rational thought.

Luckily, Lee did not respond with any sass during this verbal explosion, and Dad's belt remained fastened, though his fists were tightly clinched. Instead, my brother admitted what we did was a stupid mistake. I apologized as well.

But this was not good enough, and our father vomited another series of profanities, punctuated in such a way as to make us jump: "Honey, can't you watch these goddamn kids? God all Christ!"

"I was in the kitchen with you, Merl! Why is it my fault?" she asked. She had a point, of course.

While my parents argued, the TV sat on the floor with its beige-plastic casing smashed. When Lee plugged it in, it wouldn't turn on.

"Now it doesn't work!" Dad yelled. "Do you know how much I paid for that? Well, do you? Huh? Huh?"

Lee hung his head and didn't answer.

"Merl, calm down," Mom said. "You're gonna have a heart attack."

"What do you mean calm down? These goddamn little devils broke my TV!"

Dad stormed into living room and sat on his easy chair. For a few minutes he was able to collect himself, but then out-of-the-blue he slammed his fist on the chair's arm and roared, "Goddamn it!"

Such was my father's inglorious return from Nebraska after being gone for two years.

During the summer of 1963, Lee became even more socially isolated and spent most of his time alone. For a while he had a couple of friends, though none of them ever came over to our house. In time, even they drifted away, and he only had in his life satellite figures such as Gary Reinfelt, whom he talked about, but we never saw. There were also shadowy troublemakers, like a kid named Bobbie Emhoff. Rumor had it Bobbie had been sent to reform school at one point, something Lee was quick to point out, as if it were a badge of honor.

The only time I remember seeing my brother with anyone outside our family in this period was at a backyard gathering up the street from our house. I am not sure of the occasion, but when I arrived, he was in the middle of a fight. And this wasn't any old tussle in which the participants grabbed each other and wrestled for a while until someone gave up. It was an outright fist-fight in which the combatants danced around like boxers in a prize-fight ring, the ring being formed by about twenty kids. At one point, Lee charged at his opponent, and as the other boy retreated, Lee skillfully landed a flurry of punches on his face. When he did this, I saw in his eyes the look Dad had when he used his fists on us. After the fight was over, I could hear several other kids say that they hated my brother's guts, and if given a half a chance, they would take him on themselves and beat the shit out of him. Not one person took his side.

I caught up with Lee after he had stormed away from the house where the fight was and asked him what it had been all about, and he told me that the other kid had smarted off to him. "When someone gives you trouble, just knock his teeth out!" he said angrily. "Don't even give him a chance to hit you first!"

On September 15, 1963, Lee turned twelve and had just started the seventh grade in Erlanger. Dad had taken the job in Stevens Point and had already begun teaching there that fall. The rest of our family stayed behind until our house got sold. Mom busied herself during this period eliminating unnecessary junk and packing things in boxes for the move. Even though she had a lot to do, she made time for Lee's birthday. The party was pretty much like the others, except no friends were there, since he had none.

Mom decorated the kitchen table with a white-plastic covering that had orange and light blue animals printed on it. Before a birthday party, she would retrieve it from a kitchen drawer, and when the party ended, she would carefully scrub it off, fold it up, and put it back. In the middle of the table, she positioned a cake, adorned with twelve pink-plastic candle-holders and candles. She had made the cake using store-bought angel food and chocolate icing. She always did this for birthdays instead of baking a cake, for she preferred simplicity when it came to food preparation. When you have only one arm at your disposal, you do things like that.

Mom carefully held a closed matchbook down on the table with her little finger. Then with the thumb and index finger of that same hand, she struck a match on the flint and lit the candles. Strangely, Lee and I didn't copy such mechanics. We swept a floor using two arms, cracked an egg and struck a match with two hands, and descended steps going forward. And that was the way Mom wanted it. She absolutely demanded that we be as normal as possible and enjoy every advantage she lacked. I remember one time I tried to strike a match the way she did, and she angrily scolded me, not because I didn't have permission to light one, but because I had done it with one hand.

"Okay, make a wish and blow out the candles," Mom said.

Lee reluctantly complied, while rolling his eyes. I did not dare ask him to identify his wish, for I doubted he believed in wishes in the first place. Then too, I feared what it might entail: running away or perhaps wanting Dad to drop dead. Whatever it was, it likely wouldn't be positive. So I kept my mouth shut.

At the kitchen table we gobbled down our cake and some vanilla ice cream on the side. Between swallows I asked, "Mom, does Lee get any presents?"

"Yes, I have three: one from Uncle Boyd, one from Aunt Mell, and one from me, or rather Daddy and me."

We retired to the living room after taking our dishes to the sink. Mom dragged out the presents from a closet and put them before Lee, who now sat in Dad's easy chair. For obvious reasons, they were not wrapped. She kept them in the packaging in which our aunt and uncle had sent them and in the bag in which she had taken her own gifts home from the store. From Uncle Boyd my brother got a backpack, from my aunt a sleeping bag, and from my parents, a new Scout shirt, short pants, and knee socks. If my father had been there, he would have learned of the gifts for the first time once they were opened. That was how it worked: Mom bought the presents, and Dad went along for the ride.

"How about putting your new Scout clothes on for a picture with Kenny?" Mom asked. Lee complied, and we went outside and to the back of the house. I had on some oversized jeans and an undersized shirt, and Mom dangled her Kodak camera from her neck by the cord. It was the boxy kind you look in from the top before snapping the shutter. She took pictures of us with it when we went to church on Easter Sunday or otherwise did something unusual. Sometimes we did not cooperate in her efforts to record family history and made faces, poked each other, or gestured in some way before the photo was taken.

"Come on. Say cheese," Mom said as she looked downward and readied her left index finger on the shutter button. We smiled and did nothing to ruin the photo, thus giving the false impression that all was well in our messed up lives.

5

Touches of Death

All Americans old enough to remember John F. Kennedy's assassination know where they were when it happened. I was in my second-grade classroom. Toward the end of that day, my teacher, Mrs. Jeffries, used reverse psychology to encourage students to perform work for her. Whoever had behaved the best got to clean the blackboard erasers with a machine in a nearby closet and wipe the board down with a wet sponge, and I had won the contest. After I completed these tasks, I sat quietly while waiting for the bell to ring to go home, as did the other students.

Normally school was over at 2:30. At 2:15, or 1:15 Dallas time, the principal announced over the loudspeaker that the president had been shot by a sniper while riding in a motorcade. He revealed no details about Kennedy's condition and let us out early. I assumed the president would survive, as I couldn't imagine him being dead. Perhaps the lack of urgency or panic in the principal's voice convinced me as well. Still, his making an announcement using the PA system and allowing us to leave before the official end of the day was quite unusual. As a result I was very curious about what had happened. So I hurried home and watched the television coverage of the event.

I arrived in time for Walter Cronkite's somber announcement that Kennedy had died. Mom's reaction to the news was, "They"—meaning those who supported him—"will make a martyr out of him." I didn't know what the word "martyr" meant, so I did not respond. Instead I stayed glued to the TV as events slowly unfolded. I vividly remember seeing Lyndon Johnson being sworn in on Air Force One in front of Mrs. Kennedy, while she still wore her now-famous blood-stained pink dress.

Sometime during the television coverage, a reporter mentioned that a man name Lee Harvey Oswald had been arrested for the murder of a police officer and was being questioned concerning the assassination. Another announcer referred to him as "a lone nut." My mind shifted to another Lee, the one with whom I lived. I didn't view him as an assassin or "a nut", but I did worry about his sadness and isolation, even though I was just seven years old.

In the year Kennedy died, our black rotary-dial phone sat on a small table between the living room and the kitchen. Since we had only one phone, it had to be centrally located. So when Mom answered it on Monday, December 16, 1963, I could hear her side of the conversation from the living room, where I was playing army after school with miniature plastic soldiers and wooden blocks.

"He lived a long life, but suffered greatly at the end," Mom said. "It was a blessing in disguise for this to have happened."

I stopped playing and focused on the call. Now I could hear the muffled words of the person on other end of the line. I could tell it was Aunt Mell, who sobbed as she spoke. "Honey, I know it's hard, but we knew this day would come," Mom kept saying.

"Yes, I do understand how close you were to him."

"It's going to be just fine."

"I love you too."

"Yes, we'll be coming down to Danville directly."

"Oh, sweetie, stop crying. Everything is going to be okay."

"I understand. You'll be there tomorrow too."

"We'll talk more later. Bye now."

"Yes, that's true. But I have to go now."

"Okay then. Goodbye."

After hanging up the phone, Mom turned to me and in a peaceful and mature voice said, "Grandfather died." The event was not surprising to me, so I did not react with shock. The last time we had been in Danville during Thanksgiving, we had seen him at a nursing home called the Friendship House. He'd had a stroke, and we were told his days were numbered then.

"Will Aunt Mell be okay?" I asked.

"She's very sad, but she'll make it."

"When did Grandfather die?"

"Earlier today."

"How come you're not crying?"

"Well, Kenny, we all die," Mom said matter-of-factly. "When someone is as sick as Grandfather was, it's better that he or she not linger on and go to heaven as soon as possible."

"Is that where Grandfather is? Heaven?"

"Yes, of course, sweetheart."

Mom's calm and reassuring demeanor on the phone after her father's demise melted away once we got to the Wise Guest House. Something about the physical surroundings angered her. Maybe they brought back bad memories. More likely it was the same-old-same-old in which she thought her siblings had somehow achieved an advantage over her.

The most heated argument started at an early supper before the visitation that Thursday night. As usual it had to do with material things. Mom wanted to know how much money had been spent on Grandfather's coffin. When she learned it had cost nearly $2,000, she threw a fit, presumably because the funeral expenses would be paid by Grandmother. Since my uncle had already received his bequest in advance, which was a rental house down the street, any extraordinary money spent by Grandmother would disproportionately be incurred by Mom and Aunt Mell, once they received their share of the estate through their mother. Hence Mom demanded Uncle Boyd pay some of the costs. This in turn led to a discussion of the purchase of the gravesite. Mom wanted to know if other gravesites were being bought at the same time that would accommodate our immediate family. She objected to the high cost of this and sarcastically scoffed at the cemetery's promise of "perpetual care" of the grave.

"Honey, we need to be there by six o'clock, and it's ten minutes to," Dad said, in an effort to end the acrimony. "We got to get to going."

We drove to the Stith Funeral Home, where Grandfather had been laid out, or "fixed" as my aunt had put it. Lee and I laughed at the name, referring to it as the Stiff Funeral Home. Mom didn't appreciate our dark humor and sharply corrected us. Dad said nothing, until Lee brought the name up again, at which point Dad said, "Now."

Inside, the undertaker, whom my mother knew by first name, greeted us. He had the look of a corporate executive, with his white hair and dark and expensive suit. He told my mother in a subdued, whispered tone, how much he respected "Dr. Wise." Near the front door, people stood in line at a registry perched atop a pedestal. Their reverent conversation, muted by soft, soothing elevator music, made me think I was in a dream, or possibly a nightmare. One by one they signed in and shuffled to the viewing room, where they were drawn to Grandfather's body in a hypnotic march. Lee and I followed them, acting just as mesmerized, controlled, and expressionless.

Although I knew I'd be seeing a dead body, I was startled by the sight of Grandfather lying motionless in his light-green metal casket. He appeared perfectly coiffed and dressed in a freshly ironed brown suit. Frilly-white satin lined the coffin's edges and made him appear like he was floating on a bed of clouds. Flower arrangements that emitted a sweet scent flanked him on both sides.

The lighting cast a brilliant hue upon his face, the kind one might expect to encounter in heaven. Stonelike, he had a permanence that I had not seen before. I dared not touch him, for I did not want to be haunted by the feeling later. Many thoughts invaded my mind, everything from what it would be like to be dead to whether Grandfather wore shoes inside the casket.

Mom must have noticed Lee and me, transfixed at Grandfather's side. She moved in between us and said, "See, he looks like he's asleep." Her words provided little comfort, and Lee and I walked away, wanting to leave the premises at the first opportunity. Yet the ghoulish spectacle continued. Various people whom my mother knew growing up came forward to greet us. Some of the guests were old and ready for death themselves, and I wondered what they would look like in the casket.

That night Lee and I slept in an upstairs bedroom at Grandmother's that had two twin beds. As I lay awake in the dark on mine, I imagined myself buried in a coffin. I even pretended I was Grandfather, closing my eyes and putting my hands together across my stomach. Feeling anxious over this, I turned toward Lee and asked if he was asleep.

"Not yet," he replied. "Why? What do you want?"

"I have a question, but I'm not sure if you have the answer."

"What is it?"

"What happens to us when we die?"

"What do you mean?"

"Well, do we go to heaven like Mom says?"

"No."

"Where do we go then?"

"Nowhere. When you're dead, you're dead. You experience nothing."

"Not even being in the dark inside a coffin?"

"Not even that."

"What about God?"

"He doesn't exist. That's what they tell stupid people who are afraid to die."

"How do you know there is no God?"

"How do you know there is?"

"I guess I don't."

"Go to sleep, Kenny."

"But I can't, because I'm scared to die."

My brother did not respond further. I assumed he had fallen asleep, so I went back to closing my eyes, crossing my hands over my stomach like Grandfather in the coffin, and practicing for the day the Grim Reaper would take me. Maybe if I knew the drill well enough, death would be easier, I thought.

The funeral activities the next day commenced with a limousine picking up our family at the Wise Guest House. Fascinated by its electric windows, Lee and I opened and closed them repeatedly despite Mom's protest. From the right front passenger seat, she turned around and grabbed my hand hard. "I said, stop it!" she snapped.

"But we've never seen electric windows before," I whined.

"Kenneth," said Dad, who was sitting between Lee and me. "Don't give your mother any sass!"

"How long does a funeral take, anyway?" I asked.

"About an hour," Mom replied.

"Why does it take so long?"

"All the boring speeches," Lee said.

At the Stith Funeral Home, a queue of cars lined up behind a hearse for the procession to the cemetery that would take place later. A cold-winter rain fell. All around us, old people milled about in Sunday clothes, protected by umbrellas. We had our best clothes on also, such as they were. Mom touched us up with her left index finger that she had moistened with her own spit. She wiped away some "sleep" from the corner of my eye and some breakfast from around my mouth. She handed me a Kleenex she retrieved from her purse and told me to blow my nose. She did the same for Lee.

Once we got inside, the funeral home director escorted us to a room off the main area, where the open casket was again drawing people's attention. The room was occupied only by family members—Mom, Dad, Lee, Uncle Boyd, his wife, Lura Jane, their kids, Aunt Mell, and Grandmother. The non-verbal communication told a lot. Grandmother looked glum. She had not cried at all about her husband's death from the moment we arrived in Danville, at least not that I had noticed. I wondered if she even liked him. Aunt Mell demonstrated more emotion than anyone, bawling at the slightest instance of sympathy. She must have been the closest to him. Uncle Boyd buried his face in his hands as he sat on a couch next to his wife, perhaps to shield his emotions from public view. Mom had a bitter, angry look. Dad managed a pleasant one, probably in an effort to keep Mom from making a scene. Lee's face was passive and uncaring.

Before the service began, the funeral home director carefully folded the coffin's satin accoutrements inside it. After closing the lid, he screwed a hole in the side of the coffin with a crank of some sort. I later learned this was how it was locked. Once the director did this, a Methodist minister started the funeral with a prayer. I don't remember much about it, but I do know it was long. The eulogy rambled as well. It described Grandfather's efforts as an educator and his many virtues. While this was going on, I shifted in my seat impatiently until Mom pinched my knee.

"How much longer?" I asked in a desperate whisper.

"Shhh," she mouthed.

I tried to catch Lee's eye and make a face at him so he would smile at me. Instead of accomplishing this, I drew another sharp pinch from Mom.

Finally, the minister wrapped things up, and we filed out. The trip to the Bellevue Cemetery didn't take long, it being just four blocks away from the funeral home. By the time we got there, the coffin was already resting on a lowering device and under a large tent. In front of it were folding chairs surrounded by fake grass. As we sat on them, I wondered how deep the coffin would be buried and if the idea of six-feet-under was true. Soon I became bored again and asked Mom, "Is this another funeral service? I thought we already had one."

"Stop being so impatient!" she said. She had the ability to yell at me with a whisper.

Once everyone gathered, the minister commenced yet another prayer, this one having the traditional graveside words of "ashes to ashes and dust to dust." With a few more "our fathers" and "amens," he cast Grandfather to the ages, and my first personal experience with death came to a close.

6

A Memorable Christmas

We spent Christmas of 1963 at Grandmother's. Since the holiday occurred a few days after the funeral, we stayed in Danville rather than Erlanger. Mom's siblings and their kids hung around as well. Though this holiday followed a somber event, I have a fond memory of it.

It started off with the adults purchasing a real tree a couple days after the funeral. Once they dragged it inside and put it in the stand, Lee and I searched the storage spaces of the Wise Guest House for decorations: the hall seat, the pantry, the closet beneath the gable in the upstairs bedroom, the sewing room, and even an overhead cupboard that connected the dining room and a hallway between two of Grandmother's guest rooms. We found in these hiding places vintage tree lights that had large bulbs and did not blink. On the floor, we unraveled the cord that connected the lights and tested them to make sure they functioned. With the aid of the kitchen step stool, we wrapped them around the tree that stood next to the fireplace in the main hallway. We then festooned the tree with garlands and beads and hung ornaments that had been acquired by Grandmother over the past five decades.

On Christmas Eve, Mom told Lee and me to stay away from a bedroom adjacent to the dining room. Its door was shut tightly, but once in a while an adult would open it and go inside or outside the room quickly. When this occurred, I could briefly observe Dad and Uncle Boyd putting together something made of metal. I concluded it was a present for us since we were specifically told to avoid the room.

In addition to being curious about this, I was heartened by the fact that Dad was actually trying to construct something for us. This effort involved mechanical skill, which under normal circumstances he did not have. Thus, it must have been extremely difficult for him. Likely Uncle Boyd had to do most of the work, but Dad definitely got an A for effort, and I was proud of him for having at least tried.

That night Lee and I slept in a bedroom off the opposite side of the dining room. The bed was a three-quarter one, meaning it was smaller than a double bed but larger than a twin. Long after everyone at the Wise Guest House had fallen asleep and the commotion of Christmas Eve had ended, we were still awake, and we stared at the ceiling together.

"Did you hear that?" I whispered. "Must be Santa on the roof."

"Yeah, I heard it too," Lee said. "Maybe it was one of his reindeer."

"How is he going to get down the chimney? He is so fat he'll get caught in it."

"Because he can do things humans can't."

We continued this fanciful conversation for some time, listening for any noise that might have been caused by Santa. Oddly enough, Lee didn't try to dispel my ingenuous thoughts on this topic. In fact, he participated in them, though in the past he had always been so frank about the ethereal and never tried to protect my tender ears. He had bluntly denied the existence of God, for example, after Grandfather's wake. Then there was our discussion about nuclear war during the Cuban Missile Crisis that made me worry about whether the world would come to an end. But with Santa Claus, Lee was different. Perhaps he didn't want to spoil my Christmas and the myths that went along with it. Maybe he also believed that since so much was already missing in our family, it was best not to remove anything else.

The order of events Christmas Day was as follows: stockings, breakfast, and presents.

The stockings that hung over the fireplace were knee-high boot socks. They were red, of course, and had a lumpy, irregular shape due to their contents. Larger items that could not fit inside them rested on the mantle. Mom made every effort to assure that the stockings had exact equality so that no claim of discrimination could be made by the kids. Grandmother contributed walnuts, pears, apples, and oranges, and also gave each child a washcloth doll, something she made us every year. Mom and Dad sprung for small toys (jacks, marbles, and games involving tiny metal balls), toiletries such as nail clippers and toothbrushes, and most importantly, candy. In regard to the latter, we each got Pez dispensers and tabs, a lifesaver book, and numerous candy canes.

After breakfast, we finally opened the real presents. Lee and I received a board game called Stratego, Cub and Boy Scout wallets, and assorted clothes. Dad got two gifts: a giant box of Whitman chocolates, and the present that he got every year, the latest World Almanac. Dad gave Mom an electric card shuffler, as shuffling was an impossible task for her at bridge club functions. I had bought her a couple of small kitchen gadgets, and Lee some shampoo and special soap.

But the best gifts were saved for last: two Schwinn bikes, a red 24-inch Typhoon with coaster brakes for me and a black 26-inch three-speed Racer with hand brakes for Lee. I doubted my parents could afford such purchases, so I assumed Aunt Mell or Uncle Boyd must have contributed. Mom told me the bikes were what Dad and my uncle were working on the night before in the bedroom. I remember sitting on my bike for the first time next to the Christmas tree with Lee holding me up. Needless to say I was excited. I had just gotten off training wheels, and my old bike was ready for the dump. Now I had a gleaming new one that I could show off to my friends. I could ride it to school, the store for Mom, and most anywhere else I wanted. Thus, it would give me greater independence as I became older. One day I might even be like Lee, I thought.

After marveling at my new bike for a while, I asked my brother about his: how the brakes worked, what advantage the gears had, and how he would use it once we moved to Wisconsin. Since I was so enamored with mine, I figured he would be about his own. But he wasn't. He just answered my questions as if he were bored, then retreated to the attic with one of his books.

7

Tropical Fish

In the first half of January, 1964, while Mom and Dad dealt with the sale of the house in Erlanger, Aunt Mell cared for us at her apartment in Normal, Illinois. During this time, Lee and I attended Illinois State's Lab School. That way we would not "be underfoot," Mom said. The plan was for Mell to drop us off with our parents in Erlanger once the house was sold, and they were ready to travel north with us to Wisconsin.

The weekend before this rendezvous, Aunt Mell brought us to the Wise Guest House from Normal because she wanted to visit Grandmother, given that she was alone after Grandfather's death. Things didn't exactly go well between Lee and our aunt, either in Normal or at Grandmother's. The morning of the meetup in Erlanger, for example, Mell asked him to pack his suitcase, but he refused, offering no explanation whatsoever. When she repeated this request, he ignored her and said something nasty to her, the words of which I don't remember. In response to this, she chased him into the bedroom where he and I were staying. He easily eluded her by hopping to the other side of the bed. From there, he taunted her and laughed at her inability to catch him. When she climbed over the bed to get him, he escaped to another part of the house, as though he were playing a game of Stalking. Frustrated, she gave up, stating to me: "Your parents are going to be very unhappy when I tell them how terrible your brother has been."

After speaking with my aunt, I eventually caught up with Lee upstairs, who was sitting behind the partner's desk. I wanted to warn him about what she had said, so he would be ready to tell his side to Mom and Dad that afternoon when we drove up to Erlanger. He was reading a copy of *Argosy Magazine* that had on its cover a diver chasing a large fish on the ocean floor. The picture was striking and colorful and diverted my attention away from what I wanted to talk to him about.

"What's this?" I asked, grabbing the magazine from him and flipping through its pages.

"Something I found around the house."

"What's it got in it anyway?"

"Adventure stories," Lee replied as he snatched the publication back.

"Adventure stories about what?'

"Tropical fish for one thing."

"Tropical fish?"

"Yeah, I want to learn how to hunt them just like that diver on the cover."

"Well, you're not going to do that in Wisconsin, that's for sure. You'll have to wait until you're an adult and live by the ocean."

"That won't be a problem."

"Why do you say that?"

"Because I'll be living in Florida soon."

"Florida?"

"Yeah, I'm going there so I can make a million dollars hunting and selling tropical fish."

"You're running away?"

"Yep."

"Come on. Stop scaring me again and tell the truth."

"I'm not trying to scare you, Kenny, and it is the truth. I'm running away to Florida so I make a million dollars hunting tropical fish."

For the first time in the conversation I realized my brother was dead serious. So I nervously posited a litany of practical questions in hopes of dissuading him from this bizarre proposition.

"How are you going to get to Florida?"

"Take the bus. I've already saved the money for the ticket."

"Where will you stay?"

"I'll make friends and live with them."

"But you don't know anybody there."

"I'll find someone."

"Do you know anything about skin diving?"

"No, but I'll learn."

"Where are you going to keep the fish once you catch them?"

"In an aquarium."

"Where will you get the money for that?"

"Working odd jobs."

"But you're just twelve years old!" I yelled and ran downstairs crying.

On the way to Erlanger from Danville, I considered telling Aunt Mell what Lee had said about hunting tropical fish, but I decided against it. I took the same approach with Mom and Dad when we got there. I just didn't want to violate my brother's confidence and hoped the problem would go away on its own once he came to his senses or fixated on something else.

At seven years old, I was also very confused about it. Kids I knew sometimes threatened to run away from home, but their plan didn't include making a million dollars. That was the part that bothered me. It was like Lee wanted to be a big shot or thought he had some special talent that had gone undiscovered. Obviously, I didn't know anything about schizophrenia and how it could include grandiosity. I didn't even know what the word grandiosity meant. Had I known and been much older, I probably still would have been confused since the onset of this disease usually doesn't occur until late adolescence or early adulthood, and Lee was twelve. I say usually, because there was the possibility he suffered from childhood schizophrenia. Interestingly enough a risk factor for that disease is having a much older father, which we did have. But again at seven, I had no clue about that, nor would any adult other than a trained psychiatrist or psychologist. The bottom line was I didn't know what to do, so I did nothing.

That evening, we stayed at Mom's pastor's house in Covington since our home in Erlanger had now been sold. While Mom and Dad spent time with the pastor and his wife, Lee and I shot pool with their teenage son downstairs. My brother acted friendly and polite during this encounter, as if nothing were wrong. In fact, his usual morose and withdrawn demeanor disappeared, and he was quite social. As much as I liked seeing him act this way, it seemed very much out of character for him, and I wondered if something was up.

The next morning my suspicions were confirmed: Lee's bed was empty. I frantically searched for him throughout the pastor's home, but couldn't find him. I went outside and looked around the yard and down the street. Again I had no success. So I told Mom and Dad that he had gone missing. The pastor and his wife summoned their son and asked him if my brother had indicated any plans to him. He responded that he had not. Finally, I worked up the courage to mention to my parents what Lee had told me about tropical fish.

Not surprisingly, Dad exploded. He stormed around the pastor's house, blaming me for not having said something earlier and cursing Mom for not watching Lee more carefully. He did not call the police and instead waited for his return. It turned out to be the right decision, for Lee slipped in the back door about an hour or so later and acted as though he had never been gone.

"Goddamn you! Don't you ever run off like that again," Dad hollered. More colorful expletives followed, despite the fact we were staying at the house of a man of the cloth. Lee did not respond to Dad's tirade. But eventually, my father asked him a logical question: "Where the hell were you?"

"I took the bus to Bobbie Emhoff's house in Erlanger," Lee replied. His tone was flat and matter-of-fact, as if he were explaining why he was late for school.

"Bobbie Emhoff's?"

"He was supposed to go to Florida with me to hunt tropical fish."

"Why that's ridiculous!"

"He wasn't home, so I came back."

"Don't you realize you have an orthodontic appointment the day after tomorrow in Wisconsin? We may not have time for that since now we'll be getting such a late start!"

"But Dad, Lee was running away from home," I said, wondering why my father's priorities were so obviously messed up.

8

The Trip North

Given the tropical-fish debacle and some other delays, we didn't leave the Cincinnati area until mid-afternoon. Since the distance to Stevens Point was 554 miles, we likely wouldn't complete our trip in one day, but we gave it a shot. As we drove through Ohio, the elephant in the room, or in this case the car, was Lee's attempt to run away. But the topic never came up. We just pretended it didn't happen, and given the explosive nature of Dad's temper and his complete misunderstanding of the subtleties of the problem, that was probably better anyway.

By Indianapolis, darkness had set in due to our late start and the time of year. Hundreds of cars on its bypass, together with wet snow, caused serious glare. Our windshield wipers didn't help, either, as Dad never got the blades changed. He also needed glasses, but Mom wouldn't let him go to an eye doctor. Effectively, he was partially blind.

In Lafayette, Indiana, the situation got worse on Highway 52, a two-lane road under construction. This caused many lane deviations, and the approaching headlights created the illusion that cars were coming right at us.

"I can't see!" Dad yelled, as he steered our car to the right side of the road to avoid a possible head-on.

"We just need to get to Kentland, and we'll stop there," Mom said.

"But I can't see!" By now Dad's voice had a desperate, childlike whine to it.

I started to say something to Mom, but she turned around and snapped, "Button your lip!"

Lee and I did exactly that, perhaps because we didn't believe our father could control the pink Plymouth under such conditions while swinging his fist at us. Instead we glued our eyes on the road and braced ourselves against the back of the front seat in the event of a collision.

"I can't see!" Dad wailed again.

"Calm down, Merl. It's going to be all right!"

"Honey, we're gonna have to stop at a motel in Lafayette!"

"Well, all right then, damn it!"

Dad slowed down and turned into the parking lot of a business. "Is that a motel?" he asked, while squinting at the place.

"Fool! It's a car dealership!"

The same drill occurred when Dad drove into parking lot of a real estate office. In time, we found a motel north of Lafayette, and he went inside to see if a room for four would be available. After five minutes he returned.

"They have one room left," he said, his voice now hoarse from yelling.

"How much is it?" Mom asked.

"Sixteen dollars."

"Well, that's way too high. The one in Kentland will be ten."

"That's forty more miles from here, and I'm not going to endanger our lives any longer over six goddamn dollars!"

"Go on then, you old fool," Mom replied. She turned her face away, stared out the window, and commenced the dreaded silent treatment, something she only used when all else failed.

"All right, we'll go to Kentland! God all Christ!"

After almost an hour we made it there. Mom was right about the price, though, and we saved six whole dollars.

We started out early the next day in order to make up time, but not before getting breakfast at a truck stop. The usual frugality rules applied—extras came at our own expense. I wanted a glass of chocolate milk with my breakfast, which raised Mom's eyebrows nearly to the ceiling. Technically, milk was a drink, and we always had the right to have one with our food, but the chocolate in this one made it similar to a dessert. Most significantly, it cost a nickel more.

When Mom started to complain, Dad interrupted and said, "Honey, just give him the goddamn chocolate milk!" Patrons dropped their forks, stopped their conversation, and looked in our direction.

Mom yielded to Dad with an irritated sigh. So rare was my victory that I savored that chocolate milk, right down to the last drop in the truck stop glass it came in. Then too, I had paid dearly for it with the currency of embarrassment.

After breakfast, and in anticipation of the customary tip argument, Lee and I asked to be excused and went outside. For about five minutes we watched semi-truck after semi-truck whoosh by. The flat farmland spread out around us as far as we could see. It had no corn on it due to winter, which made it look all the flatter. Soon my parents left the restaurant, and we got in the car and continued north.

When we made it to Hammond, Indiana, Mom, who had been chief navigator, told Dad to exit the road in order to get on I-94 West and go around Chicago. We must have gotten off on the wrong ramp because we ended up going straight north instead, and this made Dad blow up. "Now we're in Gary, Indiana!" he yelled, returning to the desperate voice he had used the night before in Lafayette.

"We'll just have to turn around and go back," Mom replied, looking around at the traffic.

"There's a sign that says 94 West...but we just passed it," Lee said with chagrin.

Soon the smell of steel-mill fumes invaded our car, and Dad went into crisis mode even deeper. "Chicago Skyway?" he blurted as a sign to that effect flashed by.

"Just get off at the next exit," Mom said.

"But there is no exit. Honey, I don't want to end up in downtown Chicago!" Of course, no one else in the car did, either—especially with Dad.

Soon we got off the road, but there was no corresponding entrance back onto the highway going the other way. So for ten minutes we drove the streets of Gary with Dad swearing and Mom telling him he was experiencing a second childhood, which was in fact an apt description. By sheer luck, we stumbled across an entrance ramp and got on the highway in the right direction.

But our troubles did not end. At a toll booth on the I-294 bypass, Dad asked Mom for the 35 cents for the toll. She gave it to him, and when he tried to toss it in the basket, part of it went on the ground and the gate wouldn't lift. So Dad asked Mom for another 35 cents. She vigorously protested and stated she did not have change. He exploded and demanded a dollar, which she finally gave him after searching her wallet for several seconds. Dad then got out of the car, went to a manned toll booth, got change, and tossed it in the basket. By now the cars behind us were honking, and Lee and I had slumped down in our seats, despite the fact we didn't know anyone in Chicago.

"Why does everything have to be so difficult?" I asked myself as we finally drove off.

9

A Struggle to Adjust

Stevens Point, a small town in central Wisconsin, was named after George Stevens. In the 1830's, Stevens had established a trading post for loggers at a point on the Wisconsin River, hence the name Stevens Point. When we arrived in January of 1964, the population was about 17,000. The chief feature was the university, which at that time was called Wisconsin State University-Stevens Point. The school had about 4,000 students, and by the end of the Vietnam War this doubled to 8,000. Besides the university, the main employers were Sentry Insurance, the Soo Line Railroad, and several paper mills.

As we drove around town late on the afternoon of our arrival, Mom noted with muted acrimony, "There's a bar on every corner." To her, we had crossed into Siberia, and in a social sense, she was right. We knew absolutely no one, and none of Mom's relatives lived within three hundred miles. If they had been ten miles away, however, she would have prohibited contact with them because she had decided to disown her side of the family. I am not sure why she did this, but based on the arguments she had had with Aunt Mell and Uncle Boyd in the past, it had something to do with her potential inheritance. As for Dad, he had only told us he was from Utah. For all we knew he had emerged from a dark abyss somewhere in the mountains of that state and had no family.

The neighborhood of our new home reinforced Mom's Siberian trope. Few houses had been built there, and intermittent jack pines and open fields, covered with drifting snow, abounded. Our street and the other roads in this section of town had not been paved yet and their surface consisted of pink-granite gravel. The streets did not have curbs or gutters, and there were no sidewalks, meaning that if you travelled anywhere on foot you had to walk on the road amongst the cars, trudge the fields, or make your way through the woods. Rather than mailboxes being beside the front door, they stood next to the street and looked like the kind you would find in a rural area.

Our single-story ranch-style home on Lorraine Street had orange brick and white siding. It had 1,300 square feet of living space and no finished basement. On the left side of the house was a single-car garage and driveway. The front door had a four-by-four-foot concrete stoop instead of a real porch. Beneath the snow, the yard consisted of sand. According to Dad, by the time the builder had slapped the house together, winter had set in and no grass could be grown. Thus, it would have to be planted in the spring, which didn't come in Wisconsin until May. The yard also had no trees or shrubbery. Mom didn't want such extras, probably because it would make the home more inviting and discourage a return to Kentucky.

The chief upgrade to the house was the fact it had three bedrooms instead of two, a master and two smaller ones. This meant Lee and I got our own digs. My room was to the right as you walked down the hall from the living room. Across from it, the house's only full bathroom offered me a small measure of convenience. Farther down the hall on the left was the master bedroom, which had a quarter-bath on the other side of it that also connected to the kitchen dinette. Finally, a second small bedroom, given to Lee, could be found at the very end of the hallway.

Within a few days of our arrival in Stevens Point, the movers put our meager furniture into our new home. Until then we stayed at "the Castle" near downtown Stevens Point, a three-story, red-brick house built in the 1880's that had the smell of oldness and reminded me of Grandmother's. Today, it is considered a historic landmark. The place had two turrets, which Lee and I climbed up into until Mom made us come down.

The first night that we actually slept in the house on Lorraine Street, Lee and I had to shovel the driveway. We'd had some experience with this in Kentucky, but it was not the same as in Wisconsin. For one thing, the snow was much deeper. For another, the wind would blow it in our faces when we tried to toss it aside. We didn't have face masks or thick gloves yet, making the problem all the worse, and a snow blower was not part of our garage repertoire. We only had a heavy coal shovel that Grandmother had given Mom. A lighter, flatter aluminum one had not been purchased.

With the coal shovel, Lee established a single path from the garage to the street. He then widened the path a little at a time until he grew tired and leaned on the handle, apparently disappointed there was so much left to do. Dad then took his turn, but due to his age and weight, he quickly lost his breath. So I finished what was left. As soon as I did, the city plow came along and dumped several feet of hard-packed snow in front of the driveway. So we had to start our rotation over, wondering if the task would ever end.

Because the driveway had not been cleared when we arrived, Dad parked the pink Plymouth on the side of the road in front of the house, which was a mistake since the plow later inundated it with snow. Unfortunately, the car did not have front wheel drive, which made our attempt to extricate it nearly impossible. At first we shoveled around it, but the snow underneath it prevented Dad from driving a single foot forward, despite the fact that Lee and I pushed it from behind as hard as we could. With each attempt we heard the rear wheels whine and whistle as they spun without traction. In addition, the tires flung ice and gravel backwards, stinging our legs. After ten minutes of this futile process, Lee came up with a different approach: clear as much snow as possible from underneath the car, put it in reverse, burn a path backwards, then switch to drive and go forward on the path created. Dad did this several times and eventually was able to move the vehicle into its proper place in the driveway.

Back inside, we removed our coats and gloves and stood by the radiator. After warming up and blowing our noses, we went to the living room to marvel at what we had accomplished through the picture window. Instead we saw Mom, bending over the sidewalk, grasping the heavy coal shovel toward the bottom of its wooden handle with her one good hand, sticking it in the snow, and pitching that snow aside, a quarter-shovel-full at a time. Lee and I rushed out and tried to do the walk ourselves, but she refused to let us until she had made a small path to the house from the driveway.

After Mom finished shoveling and came in the house, she removed a mitten from her bad hand. Because the fingers of that hand involuntarily curled together in a swollen knot, they could not be separated into the fingers of a glove. So she wore a mitten, but it did not match the style, fabric, or color of the glove on her good hand. This did not matter to her, however, for years of coping with paralysis had made her oblivious to appearances.

The mitten was made of cheap, thin fabric, and it did little to protect her paralyzed hand. So when she took the mitten off, I noticed her hand was mottled with gray. No doubt she had suffered frostbite and didn't notice it due to the numbness that existed there already. When I asked her if her hand was okay or if she needed medical attention, she responded in the same manner as she did when anyone showed her concern: "Oh, don't bother."

Next, Mom limped into the kitchen, where she started boiling some hot water on the stove. Dad followed her and tried to comfort her by telling her that everything would be all right. But instead of responding in kind, she narrowed her eyes at him and bitterly declared a phrase I shall never forget: "This is a godforsaken place!"

I attended Jefferson Elementary School in Stevens Point for the last half of second grade because the newly constructed Washington School, which was three blocks from my parents' house on Lorraine Street, had yet to open. My teacher, Mrs. Leary, announced to the class one day that my dad had guessed the correct number of bricks used to build the new Campbell's Department Store downtown. This entitled our family to a $100 gift certificate, she told everyone, which was not a small amount in those days. "Your dad must be pretty smart to have figured something like that out because there are a lot of bricks in that building," she said.

"Mrs. Leary?"

"What, Kenny?"

"That wasn't my dad. It was my brother, Lee."

"But the radio said it was Merl Farmer. Isn't that your dad's name?"

"Yes, but it's also my brother's. He goes by his middle name, Lee, even though his real first name is Merl."

"How old is he, anyway?" Mrs. Leary asked.

"Twelve."

"And where does he go to school?"

"Down the street at Emerson Junior High. He's in the seventh grade."

"Well, you're very lucky to have such a smart older brother."

At lunch that day I walked over to Emerson with a friend from my second-grade class, a girl who taught me how to make flowers with folded Kleenex. We went there because Jefferson didn't have hot food, and we had the choice of a cold lunch there or a hot one at Emerson.

Emerson was built in the 1920's and had close to a thousand seventh and eighth graders jammed into its aging three floors. In addition to Stevens Point, it serviced several surrounding small towns and various rural areas. Within the school, there was a cultural divide between kids coming from blue-collar families, whose breadwinner worked at a paper mill or on a farm, and white-collar ones associated with the University or Sentry Insurance. Such differences, together with the overcrowded conditions, made fights at the school common.

After we entered, my friend and I felt intimidated by the sheer volume of students in and around the lunch room, which was the size of a large classroom. A long waiting line extended down a hallway and around a corner from it. Here and there teachers dressed down one rowdy group of students or another in a futile attempt to establish order. As we made it to the front of the line, I saw my brother pushing someone in the lunch room. The principal, Mr. Oelke, then yelled, "Farmer, get your ass to class, right now!"

I considered saying hello to Lee as he left the cafeteria, but decided against it, given the chaos and obvious animosity of Mr. Oelke. Instead, my friend and I ate and exited as quickly as we could. I don't think we ever came back and always brought a cold lunch after that.

To say that my brother was a discipline problem in junior high school would be an understatement. He idolized the troublemakers and would frequently tell me about their exploits in disrupting class or bullying weaker kids in the hallway. Several times Mom told me that Mr. Oelke had sent Lee home because she had refused to allow him to paddle my brother for one serious transgression or another. As to his grades, he barely passed his classes, despite his academic talent. It was hard for teachers to see that ability since it got buried in his back talk, association with school hoods, and general negativity.

I remember well when Lee came home from school and announced that he had won the school chess championship. He had beaten some of the top students, the ones who got A's while he got D's. I congratulated him on his success, then almost by accident, I asked him a question that perfectly illustrated his contradictory nature: "How come you can figure out the exact number of bricks at Campbell's Department Store and win the school chess championship, but get bad grades?"

Lee's answer was telling: "Because I hate my school, I hate my teachers, and I hate this town."

Mom purchased some ice skates for me at the Sport Shop in downtown Stevens Point for my eighth birthday on February 15, 1964. A children's size 2, they were black figure skates with white laces. I knew nothing about skating, having never done so in my life. Lee didn't either, but that didn't keep him from trying to teach me how to do it at Iverson Park.

Iverson had more structured winter attractions than the sled-riding hill on Fitzgerald Court in Erlanger or the steep slope where I had face planted. For one thing, it had a saucer slide, which consisted of a semi-circular chute formed by hard-packed snow and sheer ice. Bigger kids would spin smaller ones around and around in their saucers before they sent them down the chute backwards, forwards, sideways, and sometimes over the edge of the slide entirely. Nearby there was a toboggan tower, where people dragged toboggans up a wooden ramp next to a staircase. Once they got to the front of the line, they put the toboggans on a platform restrained by a brake. When everyone was seated securely, the operator released the brake, which caused the platform to tilt forward, and a perilous ride down a narrow ice-covered runway to begin. We didn't even know what a toboggan was at this point, much less had gone down a hill on one. But the most hair-raising activity by far at Iverson was ski jumping. The area for this purpose had two scaffolds: the yellow junior tower and the lime-green senior tower. The latter was about forty feet tall, though it sure looked like it was a hundred. Ski jumpers would whoosh down it until they reached a small drop off at the end of the tower itself. Then they flew through the air and bent forward over their skis in silence until they landed with a thud on the hillside below.

After Lee and I got to Iverson that day, we went to the edge of the skating rink, which appeared to be about fifty by a hundred feet. On the half to our right, a pick up hockey game was taking place in which kids skillfully passed a puck about. They started, stopped, and turned effortlessly, and sometimes even skated backwards as they shot the puck toward a goal marked by a couple of gloves. On the left side, figure skaters practiced pirouettes and glided backwards gracefully in a circle with their arms out. Needless to say, I was impressed, but at the same time, I felt intimidated.

"There's no way I can do that," I exclaimed.

"You gotta at least try," Lee replied. "Now change into your skates at the warming house."

The warming house consisted of a small cinder block building with a ramp that led up to a doorway. Inside, people hobbled to and from a series of wooden benches where they changed in and out of their skates. Most were much older than I was, and their voices loudly echoed off the concrete walls and wet cement floor. After putting my skates on, I could barely stand up, much less walk. My ankles had already started to hurt by the time I reached the door to go back out. On the ramp, I clung to the railing at every step while other kids whipped around me without hesitation. Finally, I made it to the snow-packed lip of the skating area.

"Try getting on the ice," Lee said immediately. "Just to get a feel for it."

"But I'll fall," I replied.

"I'll stay behind you and catch you. Now try it."

Trembling, I slid forward slowly on my skates while Lee walked behind me in his rubber snow boots and gently pushed me. I started to fall, but he picked me up by the armpits and kept me from doing so, whereupon I tried again. Eventually, I learned to use my skates to move forward by myself. Several times I lost my balance completely and hit the ice hard. Some kids, who had been watching the spectacle, laughed at me when this happened. But Lee glared at them and got me back up, and I earnestly resumed my nascent effort, often wandering about the ice as other skaters raced around me and nearly hit me. Finally, my ankles grew tired, and I asked if we could go home.

Lee agreed. As we passed the monument marking the entrance to Iverson Park, I asked him if he was going to get some skates someday and try this himself.

"No way," he replied, "I'd probably fall and break my neck."

I thought it odd he would say this. He wouldn't do something at twelve that he expected me to do at eight. Years later I realized why he said this: Lee lived through me rather than himself. Why did he feel the need to do this? Perhaps because he had such a dim view of himself that he needed a surrogate, and that surrogate was me.

Winter dragged on through March and even into April. When Lee and I weren't shoveling snow, we played board games like Risk, Stratego, and Monopoly. He even taught me to play chess. In all such games, I never beat him. He was just too smart.

During this time, we would go swimming at the indoor pool at PJ Jacobs High School as a diversion from the board games. Every Saturday morning it was open for this, and we took advantage of it. The twenty-five-yard-long pool probably had over a hundred kids in it at any given point. There was hardly enough room to swim, and people sometimes kicked or hit each other by accident. The ratio between swimmers and lifeguards was hardly sufficient. Simply put, the activity was an overcrowded free-for-all.

Lee and I met up after one such swim day and walked to the bike racks at the back of the high school. Despite the fact it was still fairly cold, we had ridden our bikes, the ones we had received as Christmas presents in 1963. We really didn't have much choice because Mom couldn't drive and Dad never drove us anywhere. As we approached the racks, a kid who was a good six inches taller and thirty pounds heavier than Lee came up to him and asked, "You the one who kicked me in the pool, hey?"

"I don't know what you're talking about," my brother responded.

"Come on, Lee. Let's get out of here," I said.

"I've got five reasons why he's stayin'," the big kid replied, closing his hand one finger at a time to form a fist.

"You leave my brother alone!" I yelled.

"You want some too, hey?"

I thought about what Lee had said about punching someone before he had a chance to react. But the young man we were dealing with was much too large and strong for that.

"So what's it gonna be?" he asked my brother. "You gettin' down on your knees and beggin' for forgiveness or me kickin' your ass?"

"I already told you I didn't do anything."

The big kid reached toward Lee and grabbed him by the collar with one hand and readied his fist with the other. When I saw this, I dove into the guy's stomach. No one was going to hurt my brother, and I didn't care how big he was. But the thug threw me on the asphalt like a sack of potatoes, and he hit my brother in the face and stomach with his fist several times.

As we rode our bikes out of the parking lot, Lee angrily asked me a rhetorical question, "Now do you see why I hate it here so much?"

10

Boys Will Be Boys

In the fall of 1965, Lee and I were super interested in football, and our favorite team was the Green Bay Packers. Uncle Boyd had told us about them before we moved, but at that point, we knew little about the subject since basketball was king in Kentucky. After some time in Wisconsin, however, we became converted—quite literally, in fact. On Sundays, the Packers were our church, the NFL was our religion, and the players, who we believed were paragons of virtue and moral righteousness, were our idols. If we ever prayed, it was only when a game was close, and our team needed a boost. We actually memorized the players' numbers and rattled them off faster than we could say our ABCs. While going to a home game was out of the question since we had no access to tickets, we watched the road and Milwaukee contests on TV. The ones in Green Bay we listened to on the radio because the TV broadcast for those games was blacked out. If the Packers lost, which wasn't often, our mood was sour until the next game, when the mere possibility of redemption rejuvenated our spirit. I remember one time I actually cried after a loss. I think it was to the Vikings. I know it wasn't to the Bears, because we never lost to them.

Anyway, our enthusiasm for the Packers inspired Lee to teach me how to throw a spiral in our back yard. He showed me the basic patterns receivers would run and expected me to hit him in stride as he performed them. I would be Bart Starr, and he would be Boyd Dowler or Carroll Dale. Later, we would change it up, and he would be Starr. "Cut-out, cut-in, corner, post, fly, and button hook," he would yell, and I would perform the patterns like a marionette.

After our first season rooting for the Packers came to an end, it was January of 1966. We could no longer play football in the back yard, as it was winter. Board games had gotten old, and I didn't ice skate as much as I did after I first got my skates. While we watched nearly every heavyweight-championship bout that year (Muhammad Ali versus George Chuvalo, Henry Cooper, Brian London, Karl Mildenberger, and Cleveland Williams), there weren't any fights in January or February. So we longed for something to do, and Lee, being the instigator, came up with an idea.

"There's a gym inside Washington School, you know," he said, grinning mischievously.

"I know that. In case you've forgotten, I'm in fourth grade there."

Lee continued to smile despite my insolence.

"Look, the doors are locked, and besides we're not supposed to be in there."

"There are other ways to get in, that is if you really want to."

"Such as?"

"A certain window in the cafeteria the dumb-ass janitor forgot to lock."

"And how do you know this?"

"That's for me to know, and you to find out."

"Okay, which window is it then?"

"One that is too small for me."

"But big enough for a kid like me, right?"

"You got it."

I sighed with disgust and turned away.

"Come on, let's get our coats on, and go over there."

"But we'll get in trouble, Lee. Jeez."

"They'll never even know, and if they do, we'll be long gone by the time they find out."

I reluctantly agreed to my brother's proposal, despite the fact I knew better. Sometimes he was a bad influence on me. Older brothers tend to do that at times.

In addition to our coats, we put on some face masks that Mom had bought us. We must have looked like burglars. Effectively, we were.

At the school we cased the unlocked cafeteria window by walking back and forth along the sidewalk in front of it. Our effort at stealth was pathetic, quite obviously, as we did this in broad daylight. When the moment was right, Lee and I dashed toward the window. He raised it open while surveying the area for observers, and I slid through it with his help. Once inside, I ran around and opened a side door for him.

"See, piece of cake," Lee told me confidently.

"I'm still nervous though."

"Don't worry, we'll look around first, and see if anyone is here. That way we can get the hell out before they have a chance to catch us."

"Okay, sounds good."

We quietly roamed the dark hallways of the school, listening for any noise or conversation, but heard nothing. The classroom doors and offices were all locked, and the custodial room was empty. Finally, we yelled "Hey" several times in order to draw out any person we had missed, but got no response.

"Looks like the coast is clear," my brother said, whereupon we went to the gym.

It was different than in school. No adults supervised our every movement, and other kids didn't monopolize things, so the space seemed larger than it really was. We could hear our footsteps and voices echo off the walls.

We found some basketballs in a large closet, practiced free throws, and played one-on-one. When we tired of that, we retrieved a football and ran the patterns my brother had taught me in the back yard. As soon as we became sick of that, we threw dodgeballs at each other, only to start over with basketball.

After an hour of such activity, we decided to exit the building and not press our luck. As we left, Lee put a rock in the jamb of an outside door to keep it ajar.

"You're not gonna come back here, are you?"

My brother shrugged. "Maybe I will. Maybe I won't."

Later that day, I noticed he wasn't around the house.

"Do you know where Lee might be?" Mom inquired, with a worried look.

"No," I answered without making any eye contact with her whatsoever.

A knock at the front door interrupted our conversation, and Mom opened it. Before her stood a police officer and Lee.

"Someone saw your boy trespassing at Washington School," said the cop. "I caught him inside."

"Lee!"

"Because nothing was missing or damaged, I'm not referring him to juvenile. But the next time, I can't guarantee it."

"There won't be a next time, officer," Mom assured.

Once she was done yelling at Lee and grounding him to his room, I joined him there. "It was that Little Prick Weaver who squealed. He must have seen us go in," he whispered coarsely. "Little Prick Weaver" was known around the neighborhood for ratting kids out. So he was a prime suspect.

"Did you tell the cops I was with you at the school earlier?" I asked.

"Nah. They never even brought it up."

"And if they had, would you have told them?"

"Of course not," Lee replied, smiling and showing me his braces.

In the middle of March of 1966, Lee and I went back to Iverson Park to "mess around." Boys our age employed that phrase euphemistically. It really meant socializing with friends or siblings with no particular agenda, and sometimes getting in trouble when the opportunity arose. Breaking into Washington School was a prime example.

I remember we could see our breath, so it must have still been fairly cold out. Because Iverson no longer offered winter sports, it was virtually devoid of people. Not even the animals ventured out of their hiding places yet, and the birds knew better than to return to an early spring that might never come. The result was a peaceful and reflective stillness, interrupted only by an occasional plop of snow from one of the tall majestic white pines that overshadowed us.

Iverson had a stream running through it called the Plover River. This had several tributaries that meandered about the park and under its stone bridges. In late winter and early spring, large flat ice chunks floated down it that had broken off from shore. They were sometimes as big as a room, but more often the size of a dining room table.

This process captured Lee's boundless imagination. "I bet we can get on one of those ice chunks and float down the river like Huckleberry Finn," he said. Near the edge of the woods, he grabbed a tree branch and fashioned it into a pole. After spotting a large piece of ice near the edge of a channel, he hopped aboard it and used the pole to guide himself. It seemed safe enough, so I stepped onto an ice raft myself, and together we moved down-stream.

This lasted all of five seconds. The weight of our bodies caused the vessels to break in half, and we tumbled into the icy water, which was over our heads, unfortunately. Immediately, I lost my wind due to shock. Though I knew how to swim by then, it didn't do me much good, since I couldn't breathe. I gasped for air over and over as I treaded water, but it did not get past the top of my throat. Neither of us could scream or yell, either, and the only noise we heard was a staccato-like sucking sound that came from our mouths. After what seemed like an eternity, I adjusted to the cold and began to breathe. Finally, I swam to shore, where Lee, who had already gotten out, helped me to safety.

"Are you okay?" he asked, desperately.

"I-I think so."

"We need to call Mom so she can get someone here to drive us home. Otherwise we might become hypothermic," Lee warned.

"What's that?"

"It's where your body gets so cold that you freeze to death!"

I started to panic. "What are we going to do, Lee? No one's around. Winter sports are over, and there's no phone booth!"

"We'll just have to walk back."

By now darkness had begun to set in, and I felt my clothes begin to freeze. "We might not make it, Lee," I shouted. "We could die!"

"Shut up and calm down. Otherwise that's exactly what will happen."

"But I'm freezing!" I replied, chattering my teeth.

"Stop whining and keep moving!"

We hurried through the woods to a parking lot, just in case someone was there. Finding no one, we made it up the hill that led to the highway. We tried to flag down some motorists, but the drivers looked at us indifferently and drove off.

"The hell with them," Lee said. "We'll walk home."

We trudged for ten to fifteen minutes through the subdivision streets that led to our house on Lorraine Street. With our clothes frozen, we entered the door that went from the garage to the kitchen. I am sure we looked like cryonic specimens to Mom, but she didn't exactly greet us with open arms or offer any sympathy.

"Get those goddamn wet clothes off and don't even think about tracking in my house!"

"But Mom, we almost drowned and froze to death," Lee protested.

"I don't care what your excuse is. Just take those clothes off and get in the bathtub!"

We peeled off our stiff, ice-covered clothes and even our underwear, but we did it too slowly for Mom's liking. "Right this minute!" she screamed, whereupon we finished undressing and ran naked to the bathroom with her chasing us with a broom. She moved pretty quickly when she was pissed off, despite her limitations. The trouble was we didn't know what made her so angry: our stupidity for trying to float down the river on an ice raft, or our negligence in tracking water on her kitchen floor. Most likely it was the latter.

11

Grandiosity or Healthy Ambition

During third and fourth grade, I attended Washington Elementary. After our arrival in Stevens Point, Mom put me on the waiting list at the University Lab School, or Campus School as it was known around town. By fifth grade, I had risen to the top of it, so she enrolled me there.

She felt this would give me an advantage academically. To a certain extent this was true, as its classes had a maximum of twenty-five kids as opposed to thirty-five or forty in the public school system. Also, the curriculum offered a more advanced and innovative learning experience. For example, the school abandoned numerical levels altogether in sixth grade and kids learned according to their level of achievement.

Despite the fact that going to Campus would have been in my best interest, I protested changing schools because I thought the kids there came from upper-crust families and wouldn't accept me. Lee, who was in tenth grade by then at the local high school, called me into his bedroom one evening in order to advocate for the change. When I first came in, I noticed he was shelving a novel on a make-shift bookcase he had constructed out of wood planks. The bookcase was out of kilter since he hadn't put any support braces on it.

"Mom says you have a problem with going to Campus," he said while propping a chair against the bookcase to keep it from sagging. "I don't understand why you are so opposed to it."

"Because it's a snob school."

"But it has more to offer than where you go now."

"Like what?"

"For one thing, you learn to speak French while you're in grade school. You also learn to type. Those things don't happen in the public school system until junior high."

"Yeah right, sounds like real fun."

"School is not supposed to be fun, Kenny, but if you are worried about something like that, Friday is 'Freeday' at Campus. Starting in seventh grade, you get to do whatever you want that day—swim at the University pool, run on the indoor track, or read a book at the college library."

I took a seat at Lee's card-table desk. "You mean I get the whole day off?"

"Well, you're supposed to be learning something."

"What about my friends at Washington School?"

"You'll make new ones at Campus," Lee said, smiling.

"But we're gonna play basketball on a real team in fifth grade, and I'll miss out on that."

"They have basketball at Campus."

Lee went over to his book-shelf and retrieved a manual of some sort. "See this?" he asked.

"Yeah."

"It's a college entrance-exam prep book."

"Uh-huh."

"I'm studying it to improve my test scores. That way I can get into a better college." Lee threw the manual on the card table and looked me in the eye. "You need to be concerned about things like that because Mom and Dad aren't always going to be around to take care of you."

"But I'm just ten. I can wait until later for things like that."

"No you can't, Kenny. The time for you to start is *now!*"

I stared at the card table and the test manual without saying anything. I didn't know what to make of my brother's sudden and adamant interest in my future, so I was taken aback, if not stunned. Finally, he broke the uncomfortable silence with a challenge: "Do you want to live in a tract house like this the rest of your life?"

"No."

"Then tell me what you're going to do for a living when you grow up?"

"I don't know," I replied, frowning confusion and perhaps even fear. "I'm not smart enough to be a doctor or anything important."

"How do you know that?"

"Because I'm just an average student."

"You're more intelligent than you think. So don't sell yourself short."

"But I didn't even make the Blue Birds in first grade, and I barely got assigned to the smart class at school after that."

"Well, you do have good verbal skills. So how about being—"

"A lawyer?"

"Now you're talking," Lee said with intensity in his eyes.

"Yeah, I have seen lawyers on TV. I love how they solve murder cases, question witnesses on the stand, and make a fool out of them."

"All right then," Lee replied, smiling. "It's settled. You're gonna be a lawyer!"

"Just like that, huh?"

"Nope, you'll have to go to law school first, and getting in will be difficult, but if you work hard at it, you might just make it."

I pressed my lips together, emphasizing my determination. I didn't want to let my big brother down.

"Okay, so what's your plan?" Lee asked.

"Plan?"

"Yeah, how are you going to get from where you are now to law school?"

"I-I have no idea."

"Well, for one thing you need to read more," Lee said flatly. He went to his make-shift bookcase and retrieved a copy of *Little Men* by Louisa May Alcott. "Start with this, and when you're done, I'll give you *Little Women*."

"This seems kind of hard," I said as I flipped through the pages. "I don't know if I can do it—"

"You can, and you will."

"All right, all right, I'll do my best."

My eyes shifted to Lee's card table. Toward the back of it, I noticed a slick and colorful brochure. "What's this?" I asked.

"It's about a prep school in Missouri."

"What does that have to do with you?"

"I want to go there," Lee said confidently.

"But we live here."

"It's a boarding school, moron!"

"Okay, okay, but why do you want to go there?"

"To better myself, just like what we've been talking about. They make you learn Latin, Greek, and a third language of your choice, and all the subjects are taught at an advanced level by good teachers."

"Sounds like tropical fish to me."

"I'm serious, Kenny."

"You were serious about tropical fish."

"That's not funny. And besides quit changing the subject."

"All right then, who's going to pay for it? It's gotta cost a lot."

"Dad."

"But he doesn't make much money, and Mom can't work."

"Then he'll have to borrow it."

"Well, that's not going to happen. Besides, what makes you so special?"

Mom called us to supper before Lee could answer that burning question. A bowl of Mom's chopped suey, four slices of white bread on a small plate, and several place settings she had gotten for free by opening up a small savings account at a local bank rested on the Formica table. In the corner of the room and behind the table, the portable TV that Lee and I had broken served as a reminder of Dad's potential for over-the-top wrath. Its plastic screen border was still severely cracked despite the efforts of a repair shop to glue it together.

Halfway through the meal, I allowed the smart ass in me to come out and brought up the conversation that Lee and I had had in the bedroom. It was a mistake, of course, but discretion is not a ten-year-old boy's strength. "Dad, Lee says he's going to prep school in Missouri."

My father responded with a sardonic chuckle.

"He's right," my brother boldly countered.

Everyone stopped eating, and an unusual calm took over the room, the kind that precedes a tornado. Dad turned to Lee and flat out said, "I'm not sending you to prep school, and that's all there is to it!"

"But I need a better education than I can get here," Lee insisted.

"The schools in this town are just fine!"

"No, they're not! The teachers are worthless and stuck here just like you, at some podunk college!"

"What did you say?"

"Merl, stop," Mom cautioned.

"When I was your age, I was on my own," Dad stated, jamming his index finger into the kitchen table to emphasize his point. "My mother died when I was eight. By the time I was sixteen, I worked for a dollar a day on farms and ranches out west, not because I wanted to, but because I had to. Sometimes I sold water cress. Sometimes I did other things, but I didn't worry about goddamn prep school!"

"What does this have to do with me?" Lee asked.

"Just that you have plenty of advantages," Dad replied sharply. "And it's time for you to get off your high horse!"

"I don't care what you say," my brother continued. "I want something more than is offered here."

"Well, we can't afford it. Now finish your food!"

Lee abruptly stood up from the table and headed down the hall to his room. On the way, he said something I thought for sure would cause Dad to explode: "You don't give a damn about me or Kenny. If you did, we wouldn't be living in this shithole!"

Dad started to give chase, but Mom somehow managed to get in his way. "Let it go, Merl. Tomorrow it'll be something else."

I complied with Mom's and Lee's wishes and went to Campus School that fall, and obviously Lee didn't go to prep school. The kids at Campus weren't as snotty as I thought they'd be, though they certainly wore nicer clothes than the ones Mom bought me at Tempo Department Store.

Despite things going well in school, I worried about what Lee had said about prep school. It was hard for me to distinguish between his legitimately being concerned about his future and there being something wrong with his mind. Maybe it was good for him to focus on lofty goals, but expecting my parents to pay for something that cost more than my dad's annual salary wasn't exactly realistic. I mean, it was hard for Mom to buy us a football to toss around in the back yard.

Several weeks after the prep-school gambit, Lee floated another expensive proposal. Again it was at supper. "Kip Johnson's dad bought him an organ and an amp," he opened, while passing the main dish.

"His family has more money than we do," Mom replied. "They own a successful clothing business downtown."

"Actually, his dad hocked his car for the $900 the organ cost," Lee continued. "Now there's a parent who cares."

"Well, I don't believe it," Dad replied, now getting irritated. "I don't know why you're even bringing this up."

"Because I want an electric guitar."

"But you've never had an interest in music," said Mom.

"I do now."

Dad laid the hammer down. "We're not gonna buy you an electric guitar!"

"And why not?"

"Because you're not a rock star!"

In his anger my father had hit on something. Maybe Lee thought he was just that. Sure, kids in town would often make outrageous demands of their parents, and being in a band was cool. On the other hand, this was not an isolated incident of his having unreasonable goals: trying to make a million dollars off tropical fish; going to prep school four-hundred miles from home though my parents couldn't afford it; and now wanting Dad to hock something essential to our family in order to pay for an electric guitar that would likely be a passing fancy. *What's next*, I asked myself. *A campaign for political office?*

On my birthday in 1967, Lee invited me into his room, indicating that he had something he wanted to talk to me about. When I came in, I noticed that the Boy Scout Handbook was positioned exactly in the center of his card table. There were no other books or items surrounding it, so it actually looked quite lonely. My brother got a second chair for me so the two of us could sit together at the table and talk.

"You're eleven now, and it's time for you to start Boy Scouts," he said. "Your first troop meeting will be at the Methodist Church tomorrow night at six-thirty."

"What are you talking about?"

"Well, you're going to be joining, right?"

"I hadn't planned on it until later."

"If you're going to be an Eagle Scout, there is no later."

"Eagle Scout?"

"Yes, and at twelve years old, Kenny."

"What?"

"Eagle Scout at twelve. Nothing else is acceptable."

Lee grabbed the handbook from the card table and showed me the length of service requirements for each rank. "If you add up all the waiting periods, you should have just enough time," he said.

"But I don't understand why being an Eagle Scout is so important."

"Because many great men in our country were Eagle Scouts that's why, and doing it at such a young age would be a remarkable accomplishment."

"Well you only got to second class."

"That doesn't matter. What matters is you."

I didn't say a word, but I'm sure confusion was written all over my face.

"Do you know who General William Westmoreland is?"

"No."

"He is a four-star general and commander of our armed forces in Vietnam."

"Okay."

"He was an Eagle Scout. Don't you want to be like him?"

"I don't know. I-I guess."

Lee took the handbook back from me and opened it to another part he had marked. The page listed the Tenderfoot requirements, including knowing the Scout Oath, Law, Motto, Handshake, Sign, and Salute, and six knots. "If you memorize this and do a few other things, you'll be a Tenderfoot and well on your way to Eagle," he said, smiling. "Now go to your room and come back before the end of the evening so I can test you."

I should have just ignored him, but this was my older brother talking. So I went along with the plan and wandered to my room with my fingers stuck in the handbook at the place he had marked.

"On my honor, I will do my best, to do my duty to God and my country," I recited as I sat on my bed.

By the time I went to sleep that night, I memorized everything Lee had told me and passed his test. I was well on my way to the goal he had assigned me despite the fact I was hopelessly confused.

I got my tenderfoot right away just as Lee told me. As a matter of fact, I whipped through Second and First Class at lightning speed with him chasing me at every requirement. My first experience at scout camp took place in late July of 1967, and I was excited because I would now be able to earn merit badges that would qualify me for my next rank: Star Scout.

Our troop car pooled that year to Camp Castle Rock in Mauston, Wisconsin, and Mom and Dad volunteered to help, something I dreaded. I did not want my friends to witness their petty bickering, which usually got worse on road trips. But I couldn't get out of going, since I needed to earn some merit badges in order to carry out Lee's plan.

In front of us on the highway, a neighbor kid's parents also drove, and we were supposed to follow their car. Since Mom hated them, as she did all our neighbors, she complained the entire drive about them. They didn't know where they were going. They drove too slowly. They disobeyed traffic laws. At one point she even suggested that the dad in the family, who also worked at the university as a professor, had something up his sleeve to obtain tenure over my father. After my parents dropped us off, one of the other scouts in the car asked, "Why is your mom such a bitch?" I did not respond, though I probably should have.

During camp, things didn't get much better. My goal that week was to earn two merit badges. Yet this particular camp required scouts to cook their own meals over an open fire and clean up afterward. In addition, we had to hike down to the commissary to get our food and bring it back to the campsite. This meant that breakfast, lunch, and dinner took five to six hours a day all told. Granted, we divided the responsibility among seven or eight scouts in a patrol. Nonetheless this process left little time to work on merit badges and achieve my goal.

I quickly determined that I would only be able to earn one merit badge and decided to pursue Swimming over Cooking. I figured I could get Cooking done at a weekend campout with my troop and that Swimming would best be pursued at camp. Yet both merit badges were required for Eagle, and I felt disappointed that I had to drop one.

The problem became even more painful when I passed every requirement for Swimming Merit Badge except one: performing a racing dive. For some reason I could not skirt over the water properly for the merit-badge counselor's satisfaction. Sometimes I belly flopped, and at others, I dove under the surface too far. The counselor spent a lot of time with me, but refused to give me anything other than a partial, meaning I would have to finish the merit badge later. Thus, I earned no merit badges that week, and this meant I had failed my brother. He would likely lecture me about how I had fallen behind.

The Friday before camp ended, I must have appeared depressed, as Scott Hall, a friend and fellow scouter, asked me what was wrong. I shook my head, so he suggested we go into his tent to discuss things. "I didn't get one stinking merit badge this week," I told him in tears.

Scott, who wasn't as driven as I was about advancement, couldn't understand my problem. "The only merit badge I got was basket weaving," he said, jokingly.

I stared at the tent's dirt floor. I felt like telling Scott about my brother's insistence that I become an Eagle Scout at twelve and all the problems I had at home. But I didn't want my family to be an object of ridicule any more than it had been already as a result of the trip down. Mom had done enough for that cause.

"Why not get the merit badges later?" Scott asked. "I don't understand what the big deal is."

"Because without them I won't get Star at the next court of honor, and that means I won't be on my way to Life and Eagle."

"Man, you're just eleven years old. You got until you're eighteen for that."

"But that's not good enough! I have to get my Eagle as soon as possible."

"Says who?"

I knew the answer, but didn't reply. The conversation with Scott ended without resolution, and the next day I returned home from camp. I found Lee sitting in Dad's easy chair in the living room, looking defeated. He had scrapes, sores, and bruises all over his knees, arms, and elbows.

"What happened to you?" I asked. "Did you fall off your bike?"

"Tried out for football," he replied.

"You never said anything about that. What position?"

"Quarterback."

"But that's the most important position on the team."

"That's right."

"Kind of a reach, don't you think?"

Lee bore a look of shame. "Yeah, I quit after the first practice."

"You? Quit?"

"Yep."

"So how did you get those marks?" I asked, pointing to the injuries on his knees and elbows.

"Let's talk about something else, okay? How was camp? Did you get those two merit badges?"

"No, I didn't, but I'll make up for it somehow. I promise."

"That's okay, Kenny."

"But you said I needed to be an Eagle Scout at twelve."

"It's all right. Whenever you get it done is fine with me.

Now I was even more confused. Lee had been pushing me to become an Eagle to the point of ridiculousness, and now he suddenly stopped. Mom must have told him to back off, I thought. On the other hand, I missed his encouragement. Such was the irony of my brother: his pathological ambitiousness was a good thing and a bad thing for me at the same time.

12

The End of Early Childhood

On a cold day in November, 1967, Lee and I tossed a football around in the back yard. By then the trees had completely shed their leaves and the ground had hardened. Though snow had yet to fall, increasingly overcast skies produced a gloomy, subdued feeling. With temperatures in the thirties, our hands stung when we caught the ball.

As I ran a post pattern toward the edge of our yard, I noticed a thin, yellow-coated wire several inches above the ground that stretched along the entire left side of our property. It wasn't there the last time we played, so someone must have put it there recently. Lee heaved the ball long, but the wind took it, and in order to catch it, I had to jump over the wire and into the neighbor's yard. As I did, he mimicked the Packer announcer Ray Scott and yelled, "Starr, Dowler, touchdown!"

I hustled back to our make-believe huddle with a smile on my face, only to hear Mom yell, "Kenny, Lee, stay out of the Kostuch's yard!"

"Why?" I asked. "They don't care."

"We stay on our side, and they stay on theirs. Understood?"

"Come on, Mom," Lee said. "Not this again."

"I put that wire up for a reason. Now stay off their property!"

Lee, now older and more rebellious, confronted Mom. "You did that crap down in Erlanger, and now you're doing it here."

"Don't talk ugly to me."

"The Dusies. The Mitchells. And now the Kostuches. What's a matter with you?"

"You stop your ugly talk, or you'll go downstairs to the basement for the rest of the afternoon."

"You need a psychologist. You know that?"

"A what?"

"A psychologist!"

"You come inside right this minute!"

"Have you lost your mind completely?" Lee hollered as he entered the house through the back door.

I quickly followed him and tried to get in between the two. As I did, Mom ordered Lee into the basement.

"Anything to get away from you," he replied, while slamming the door at the top of the basement stairs behind him.

"You'll stay down there all day until you apologize," Mom yelled. "And when Daddy comes home, we'll see what he has to say about your ugly talk."

At this, Lee pushed at the basement door to get back to the main level, but Mom put her shoulder on the door to block him. After the two struggled for a few seconds, she let him through and told him to go his room. I retreated into my own, where I reflected on what my brother had said about Mom needing a psychologist. One phrase came to my mind: "It takes one to know one."

Later that year, Mom got into another serious fight, this time with my father. Lee and I were in the living room, watching TV, when we heard her scream, "Let Boyd and Mell pay for it!" We rushed into the dinette to see what was going on.

"You need to stop this!" Dad yelled back at Mom.

"Boyd and Lura Jane have two incomes, and Mell doesn't even have kids. But according to them, we're supposed to pay the same amount for Mother's care!"

Mom then read aloud from a letter written by Uncle Boyd. "When you get old, I hope your children treat you the same way you have treated your mother," it said.

"Just ignore him," Dad replied.

"Grab, grab, grab, that's all he and Mell ever do!"

"We'll just have to pay our share. Now get off it."

"Our share? They never do their share. Instead, they just take and take and take!"

"What would you prefer? We move down to Danville and care for your mother ourselves?"

"That would be better than staying in this goddamn place!"

"Well, we're not going to do it!" Dad said, while leaning forward and sticking his pursed lips right in Mom's face.

"And why not?" she snapped back.

"Because I have a job here! We can't just pull up stakes and leave!"

Mom limped to the kitchen sink, then started crying.

"Honey, we can't live in Danville without any money! Now stop it!"

"Then get a job there!"

"But I can't! Besides, I won't be able to work until I'm seventy like in Wisconsin. The retirement age there is sixty-five. We've been over this a dozen times."

"But I can't take it here any longer!"

"We're not going to Danville, and that's all there is to it!" Dad yelled.

"And I'm not staying here!"

"Stop it, or I'll be the first to leave myself."

"Fine, then I'll move down to Danville and take Kenny and Lee with me."

"You will not!" Dad snapped, now charging toward her.

But Mom stood her ground and stuck the index finger of her good hand in his face. He in turn batted her finger away, which caused her to lose her already poor balance and fall back against the wall and onto the floor. Her bad arm was now scraped and bleeding as a result. "Get out of this house!" she screamed as she rolled on the floor.

"All right then, I'll get a motel," Dad shouted back, while grabbing his overcoat and storming toward the front door. As Lee and I helped Mom up, he slammed it shut behind him, sending several pictures in the living room clattering to the floor.

After a few minutes he tried to open the door again, but by then Mom had already locked it. We could hear Dad pounding on it and yelling over and over, "Open the goddamn door!"

But Mom refused and summoned Lee and me to help her keep the door shut just in case Dad had an extra set of keys. We didn't know whose side to be on, but we believed that if he came back in, it wouldn't be pretty. So we all three put our shoulders against the door.

Eventually, Dad calmed down, and Mom let him inside. But for the rest of the evening they didn't speak.

As I tried to sleep that night, I worried about whether Mom and Dad would get a divorce. Mom was the angriest I had ever seen her, and her talk about breaking up with Dad and taking us down to Danville underscored this concern. She was not stable. Dad was not stable. Lee was not stable. And I was beginning not to feel so stable myself.

Grandmother Wise died on January 22, 1968. During the previous year she had suffered a stroke and lost her ability to talk. A small rest home in Danville cared for her until she took her last breath. I'm not sure how the place was paid for, but it must have gotten worked out somehow. Regardless, she had always been an example of graciousness and kindness, so her death took me aback far more than Grandfather's.

Now you might think that the shock associated with such an event would have brought the best out of Mom. Instead, it embroiled her in another hot sea of paranoia.

"Sam Cheek says we need permission from Citizen's Bank to stay at Mother's," she said as we drove through Danville after a two-day trek down from Stevens Point for the funeral-related activities.

"Why's that?" Dad asked.

"Something about the bank being the executor of the estate."

"Maybe he's right. They have control at this point."

"Well, I'll be goddamn if I'm going to get permission from some bank to stay in my own home."

"It may have been your home growing up, but it's not now."

"The hell it isn't, and I'll not put up with Sam Cheek sayin' otherwise."

In the backseat, Lee and I both shook our heads, disappointed Mom had slipped into another one of her paranoid rants. But we managed to keep our mouths shut and not enter the fray.

By now we were on Maple Avenue, near the Wise Guest House. Due to the indecision about where we would be staying, Dad calmly drove past it. As he did, Mom stared bitterly at the house and asked, "Where will we go if the bank says we can't stay at Mother's?"

"A motel," Dad said with aplomb.

"Oh, hell's bells, Merl, we can't afford that."

"Maybe Boyd or Mell will be staying at your mother's, and we won't have any choice."

Mom turned her face away from Dad and said, "They got more money than we do. Let them pay for a motel."

"But they have a right to stay at your mother's as much as you."

"Well, I won't put up with that. Not for a goddamn second."

"Let's just call the bank and see what they say first, okay?"

By now we were near Jerry's Restaurant on the edge of town. Dad stopped the car at a phone booth there and attempted to call the bank. He came back and said, "No one knows anything about the estate or Sam Cheek."

"Let's just go to the house then."

"All right, but if Mell or Boyd want to stay too, you'll just have to get along."

Fat chance of that, I thought.

The evening of Grandmother's wake, our cousin B.A., the son of Uncle Boyd, attempted to visit the Wise Guest House. Up to then, things had been okay, for Boyd and Mell stayed at a different location. B.A. rang the doorbell, and Lee and I gleefully ran to the front of the house to let him in. We had not spoken to him at the wake, due to Mom's no contact rule. In fact, we hadn't communicated with him in years for this very reason, so we were very excited to see him. Just as he rang the doorbell, however, Mom locked the door. Then she hollered through the decorative glass on the side of it for him to leave. Yet he persisted, stating he just wanted to come inside and show his new wife the place for old time's sake. Mom refused to allow him in, screaming at him, "No! No!" and "No!" B.A. looked befuddled as did Lee and I, whereupon our cousin turned and shuffled back to his car.

At the Stith Funeral Home prior to the service the next day, Mom did not speak with her siblings or their children and kept a watchful eye on us to make sure we did the same. Occasionally, Lee and I snuck in a conversation with our cousins anyway, only to be strongly reprimanded for having done so. We then awkwardly walked away and conversed with people Mom knew growing up in Danville.

Prior to the commencement of the ceremony, I noticed the funeral home director consulting with Uncle Boyd and Aunt Mell in a hushed tone. Thereafter, he spoke with Mom in an animated conversation in which her face became red and contorted with fury. He then ushered our immediate family into the same private room from which we had viewed Grandfather's funeral several years before. As he did, I noticed Uncle Boyd, his family, and Aunt Mell were seated in a completely different family room. Something definitely was up. I wasn't sure if the separation was caused by Mom's insistence, her siblings', or the funeral home director's.

After the ceremony, no member of the respective family factions said a word to each other, though non-family attendees mingled as they went out the door. I did not see Mom's relatives after this occasion until I became an adult, as she continued to stand in the way of any contact with them. I remember this event as a sad and ugly end to my formative years in which I lived in a family full of dysfunction, anger, and madness. Unfortunately, the worst was yet to come.

PART II

Losing Lee

13

Approaching the Precipice

Around the time of Grandmother's death, a series of articles about a local double-murder case appeared in the *Stevens Point Journal*. This was uncommon in a town as small as ours, so naturally it hit the headlines.

The defendant was an eighteen-year-old named Mark Leroux, who was accused of killing his mother and father. Mark and his fifteen-year-old sister, Jeannette, called the authorities and reported their parents' rural home was ablaze. Mark, who lived in Stevens Point, had been visiting his parents and sister that night. He claimed that his parents had been sleeping in an upstairs bedroom when he and Jeannette were awakened in the middle of the night by the fire. He said the house was full of smoke, so he was unable to rescue his parents from their bedroom. Jeannette gave the identical story, so identical, in fact, that the police called it "pat."

There were substantial problems with the teenagers' account. First, they reported the fire from a farmhouse two miles away, though nine closer residences existed that would have provided a better opportunity to do so. One was almost visible from their parents' home. Second, the police did not smell smoke on them during their initial interviews. In fact, they were neatly dressed. Finally, Mark told the cops that while he and his sister took the time to retrieve personal papers and guns from the house, they did not try to rescue their parents.

In the days that followed the initial police interview, Jeannette told a friend that her brother had suggested prior to the night of the fire that they shoot or poison their parents. Jeannette also said that after going to bed the evening of the fire, she was awakened by gunshots, whereupon Mark admitted he had just shot her parents. She then watched as he set the house on fire using kerosene lamps. Before and after the parents' funerals, Mark bragged to Jeannette that he had committed "the perfect crime."

But it wasn't so perfect after all, as the friend told her parents what Jeannette had said, and this eventually got back to the investigating sheriff's officer. An autopsy was performed on the parents' bodies, and it determined that they had died from gunshot wounds and not the fire. Jeannette ended up cooperating with the authorities and testifying against her brother, and the police found several handguns at his residence in Stevens Point, one of which proved to be the murder weapon.

Mark had been involved in several crimes as a juvenile. On one occasion, he attempted to force a man at gunpoint to drive him to Chicago. He also committed a string of burglaries and stored the stolen property from them in his mother's garage. When the property was found, she told the police, "Look what he does—he puts it in a place I'll find it so he can hurt me." She provided the sheriff an essay written and signed by Mark. It was entitled: *Epitaph of an Unwanted*. A psychiatric nurse who dealt with the family when Mark was a juvenile said she believed he had severe emotional problems involving his mother, and the investigating officer in that case indicated he believed Mark was very much a threat to her and would hurt her if given the opportunity. Thus, the authorities had their motive: Leroux hated his mother.

At trial, Mark Leroux cleverly testified that his sister did the shooting and gave him the gun for safekeeping. His lawyer claimed Jeannette was mixed up in the case as deep as Mark—that every fact pointing to his guilt made her guilty too, and she could be lying to save her own skin as easily as he could his own. The jury chose to believe Jeannette because Mark was more familiar with guns and the police had found the murder weapon at his residence, together with more bullets that matched its caliber. He also could not provide in his testimony a motive for his sister to kill his parents, though he had plenty of motive himself, given the missive he had written about being unwanted. At sentencing, the judge found, based on his observations of the defendant, that Mark Leroux was "a brilliant young man." He then gave him two consecutive life sentences.

The day after the sentencing concluded, I remember talking to Lee about the case in the living room of our home on Lorraine Street. The front-page newspaper article reporting the results of the trial and displaying a photo of Leroux, lay on top of a drop-leaf table next to Dad's easy chair. Lee slouched in the chair with his arms draped listlessly over its sides.

"I see they found this guy guilty," I said after picking up the article and reading it.

"Whatever," Lee replied indifferently.

"That's all you have to say, 'whatever'? Look, he killed his parents and burned down their house with them in it."

"So?"

"So don't you think that's pretty bad?"

"He may have had his reasons."

"What do you mean?"

"Just that it wouldn't be the first time a kid hated his parents," Lee said matter-of-factly. He then mentioned another case in town in which an insane teenager had attacked his mother, severely injuring her. His father, who witnessed the incident, died of a stroke immediately after it. My brother seemed overly knowledgeable about the details and was downright callous about that case, too.

Over the past several years, Lee had become more and more withdrawn, depressive, grandiose, and even anti-social. More importantly, he intensely disliked my parents, particularly my mother. As a result, I became hyper aware of the parallels between him and Mark Leroux. Both my brother and Mark had emotional problems and were highly intelligent. Both were of similar age and had trouble with their parents. Most significantly, Leroux had a younger sibling. Maybe I was imagining things, but I wondered if one day I would be awakened in the middle of the night like Leroux's sister had been.

During the spring and summer of 1968, Mom became interested in a split-level house located just east of the Stevens Point city limits. It was owned by the Contents, a university family who would soon be leaving town. She wanted to buy the property, and the receipt of a small inheritance after Grandmother's death, together with the money she and Dad had scrimped and saved over the years, would enable its purchase. Dad believed this would keep her in Wisconsin, so he had a stake in the venture as well.

In an effort to facilitate the sale, Mom and Dad became good friends with the Contents and learned all about them and their home. She mentioned the Content family was going on vacation for two weeks and needed somebody to water their lawn. She asked if Lee and I might be interested. The pay would be $5 a day for a total of $70 or $35 apiece, so we agreed.

By now Mom had learned to drive and said she would drop us off there each night. She had obtained this skill at the local technical school when Dad replaced the pink Plymouth with a light-green 1965 F-85 Oldsmobile. The new car had power steering and brakes, but it had to be further customized to account for her disability. A piece of metal widened the gas pedal enough so that her bad right foot could depress it, and a spinner knob, the kind farmers use on tractors, was added to the steering wheel. Once she got her license, she took us everywhere, including fishing. She even got up at 5 a.m. and drove me around on my paper route when it got too cold outside to ride my bike.

Something Lee and I failed to anticipate our first day of watering was the ubiquitous presence of mosquitoes. The Plover River was not far from the Contents' house, and it provided a perfect breeding area for them. The fact that we watered in the evening didn't help the situation. We thought we were prepared for the mosquitoes since we had plenty of repellant, but the ones in Wisconsin were particularly resilient to it, so this remedy didn't work well. Further, we had no key to the house and thus no avenue of escape.

"These bugs are bad, man," Lee said, as he bent down to change the location of one of the sprinklers. I could see that a large mosquito had taken advantage of the temporary occupation of his hands and landed on his forehead, so I swatted it away.

"You're not kidding," I replied, slapping one on my own arm, a second on my neck, and a third on my leg. I ran around the yard in an effort to get rid of them, but they caught up with me and buzzed annoyingly in my ears.

"When's Mom coming back for us?" Lee asked.

"Not for another hour," I replied, looking at the one-acre lawn.

"We may go crazy first."

"Maybe we should just finish watering and walk back," I suggested.

"I have a better idea," Lee said.

I frowned. "Okay, what is it this time?"

"You remember when I hoisted you through a window at Washington School?"

"No way, we're not doing that again!"

"Just tell me when you're ready."

A mosquito whined in my ear. I itched where one had already stung me on the back of my knee. When I finished scratching, a different one buzzed my other ear. "All right. All right. You win!" I yelled.

"See that basement window?"

"Yeah."

"I'll pry it open. Then I'll drop you through it and into the basement, and you'll go to the front door and let me in."

"I don't know, Lee. We could get in trouble."

"No one will be the wiser. Besides, this is an emergency."

Lee bent the window just enough to pop it off. The only problem was he accidentally dropped it on the concrete basement floor below. The crashing and splintering of glass caused me to jump and my butt to tingle with anxiety. Now we had a bent and broken window to deal with besides the mosquitoes!

"We're in serious trouble," I said. "Mom's going to kill us."

"We'll replace the window using our own money," Lee said confidently. "In the meantime, let's get in the house. Come on, these bugs are eating us alive."

Lee lowered me into the basement, I let him in, and we cleaned up the glass. We put a piece of cardboard that we found in the garage in the window space. God help us if the mosquitoes and other bugs got inside the house through the hole, we thought. After temporarily plugging the opening with the cardboard, we sat in the living room and tried to figure out what to do next.

"So where are we going to buy a window, and how are we going to get it back here?" I asked.

"Mom can't take us. Otherwise, she'll find out what we did," Lee replied.

"Well, you better come up with another plan, Mr. Smart Guy, since breaking in was your idea in the first place."

"Okay, I got it," Lee said, snapping his fingers. "We'll ride our bikes to Duralum Lumber on the south side of Stevens Point and take the window frame with us so they can match it and sell us a replacement."

"But it'll cost a fortune."

"Would you rather face the wrath of Dad?"

"No, but—"

"Look, we got to stick together on this."

Mom eventually picked us up that night. We did not say a thing about the window as we rode home, but we did note that the mosquitoes had been horrible. "Well, that $70 will go a long ways in making you feel better," she said.

Yeah, right, I thought.

The next day Lee and I struck out on our bikes for Duralum Lumber & Supply. We first rode to the Contents', where we retrieved the window frame. The three-mile trek from their house to Duralum was not easy. Lee slowly rode his three speed, while holding the window frame with his left hand. I pedaled feverishly behind him on my red Schwinn Typhoon. I thought Lee would surely drop the frame when he bumped over some railroad tracks three-quarters of the way there.

At Duralum the store clerk told us that he didn't have the window in stock and it would take several weeks to order it. This wouldn't work, as the Contents would be back by then. So we left the business disappointed. We tried several other ones, but got the same response.

"We'll just have to put the window back in the best we can and hope that they don't notice it. Maybe enough time will pass before they do, and they won't be able connect us to it," Lee said.

After Mom dropped us off at the Contents' that night for watering, Lee and I sat around their living room while periodically dashing outside and moving the sprinklers. We dreaded the day the family would return and find the broken window. "If they ask about it, we'll deny it," Lee said. "Besides, I have another idea."

"What's that?"

"A friend of mine knows this girl who's really loose."

"So?"

"So I thought maybe I would have her over here."

"You have got to be kidding me, Lee. For what possible reason?"

"To mess around with her."

"Come on, man. We broke in this place to get away from the mosquitoes, and now you want to turn it into a bachelor pad."

"Look, all you have to do is keep your little yap shut."

"Okay, okay, but don't expect me to help you with your hare-brained scheme any more than that."

At twelve, I knew enough about sex to understand exactly what Lee had planned. I also believed that at almost seventeen, he would feel like a conquering hero if he could pull it off. At the same time, the plan seemed to be the product of more than just hormones gone wild. I thought of my brother, sitting in the living room of this beautiful home, pretending to be a bigshot with this unknown girl. Grandiosity had once again emerged!

In the days that followed, an acquaintance of my brother who knew the girl tried to arrange the liaison and toured the Contents' home to make sure it was appropriate for my brother's purpose. He even gave him some birth control devices that he had stolen from a medical clinic where he worked. Despite all of this preparation, Lee's plan never came to fruition. I don't know if he thought better of it, or the girl simply refused to come over. More likely it was the latter.

After the Contents returned to town, Mom asked us about the window. She said that Mrs. Content had told her that someone had broken into the house through the basement and that the sheriff wanted to know if we had seen anything suspicious. "He felt it strange that nothing was missing," Mom said with accusing eyes. "He also pointed out that the person or persons who did this cleaned up the broken glass and covered the window hole with a piece of cardboard. Usually real burglars aren't so conscientious."

We denied knowing anything about it, of course, but we never asked for the money from the Contents for watering their lawn. They didn't offer to pay us any, either. We were lucky, I guess. We hadn't been arrested, and more importantly, Lee never got caught inside the house with that girl. That would have been just too embarrassing for us to explain.

My parents purchased the Contents' house in late August of 1968, and we moved in when I started seventh grade at Benjamin Franklin Junior High School and Lee became a senior at PJ Jacobs in Stevens Point. By now Mom had aged quite a bit. The vicissitudes of life had greyed her hair some and given her a wizened look. I had braces and curly locks that went over my ears and spoke with a child-like voice because I hadn't reached puberty.

As to Lee's appearance, it had taken a turn for the worse. He didn't use a comb or brush and had patches of unshaven whiskers mixed with infected acne on his face. His clothes did not match, and he did not tuck in his shirts or keep them clean. I could not tell if this had come about as a result of his lack of concern for social convention or something more pernicious. But the precipitous decline in his appearance was quite noticeable.

So too was his complete absence of a social life. He had had a problem with this already in Erlanger, but in high school it became worse. He did not participate in any school functions or attend a single dance. He dated no one. In the past he had played Avalon-Hill games with a few intellectual classmates once in a while, but now he hardly mentioned their names. He also didn't watch the news or TV, and we hadn't viewed a movie together in some time. Something was definitely wrong, but I didn't know what it was.

Because I had a close relationship with Lee, Mom would constantly urge me in a desperate, pitiable voice to talk with him about his despondency and be the friend he lacked. I reluctantly agreed to this and effectively became resident psychologist, a role I was obviously unqualified to perform. But I did it anyway since Mom would have made me feel guilty if I refused.

My "counseling" sessions with Lee would usually take place in the den. He would sit on the purple couch that ran along a paneled wall on the left when entering the room, and I would plant myself on Grandfather's rocking chair directly across from him. Between us, there was a coffee table that had a tiled top. To my left and Lee's right, an old floor lamp dimly lit his face. Next to the lamp was Dad's hi-fi, on which Lee would repeatedly play sad songs from the Beatles' *Sergeant Pepper's* album and Don McClean's *American Pie.*

The rest of the den had an eclectic feel. A pink-brick fireplace faced the interior of the room. Orange-flower-patterned drapes covered a window on the wall opposite the fireplace, and a sliding door with the same kind of drapes was across from the purple couch. The den had an abundance of Grandmother's antiques: the partner's desk, the claw-foot table that had once held Grandfather's typewriter, and various knickknacks. In short, this part of the house was a disconnected enclave of past and present, old and new, and given the nature of my conversations with Lee, clarity and confusion.

"So I see you got a letter of commendation from the National Merit Scholar people," I said in one of our sessions. In my brother's junior year of high school, he had taken the PSAT, like all other college-bound kids. He had received his test results recently and learned how he ranked for scholarship consideration.

"I wasn't a quarter-finalist, Kenny. It doesn't mean dick," he replied.

"So your mopey attitude these days has to do with this test?"

"It determines where I go to college, so it's not just any test.'"

"Well, most kids don't even get a commendation. So lighten up."

Lee frowned instead.

"You got A's in two courses you took at the university while still in high school."

"At some crap-state school," he replied in a far-away voice.

"Well, how are you doing in your classes at PJ Jacobs?"

"I got kicked out of French."

"Why? What happened?"

"Ms. Schultz, the teacher, asked me, '*Où est Madame Thibaut?*' and I told her, 'Up your ass.'"

"Well that wasn't a very good idea."

"No, Kenny, it wasn't."

"So why did you do it then?"

Lee turned his head away and did not answer.

Years later I learned what may have motivated my brother's crude rebellion in French class after I discussed it with a classmate of his in preparation for this memoir. The classmate had been allowed to attend foreign language classes at the university, and my brother may have been jealous of this, for he was stuck in Ms. Schultz's high school class. This jealousy was exacerbated by the fact that the fellow student was a National Merit Scholar finalist, when Lee only received commendation status.

The same kid, as it turns out, was my brother's debate partner. He told me in the interview that they made it to the state debate competition together that fall, but that at the tournament Lee walked off without explanation. No one could find him, and the partner had to debate by himself. Afterward my brother returned to the school bus that took the team home and acted as though nothing had happened. His life was obviously spiraling out of control, according to the classmate. Given what I had seen as Lee's "therapist," this was unquestionably true.

In the beginning of the second semester of Lee's senior year, I remember another session we had in the den. This time the topic was his future. It was ironic that I was the one doing this with him, given that in the past he had done this for me.

"I'm starting up something called the Film Appreciation Series," he said while reposed on the purple couch.

"What's that?"

"I plan on ordering films for free through the Public Library and renting them out to people. This will yield one-hundred percent profit, as I will have no cost or overhead."

"Why wouldn't they go to the library and do that for themselves?"

"They may not know they can."

"But don't the filmmakers have copyrights on the movies?" I asked, now completely confused.

"Not on the ones that have become part of the public domain. That's why I'm calling it the Film Appreciation Series. Old films are to be appreciated," Lee said, smiling. He handed me a card that had the name of his company on it.

"W-where did you get this?"

"Mail order. I bought five-hundred." He pointed to a small box on the coffee table that contained the rest of the cards.

"What if no one rents films from you?"

"Oh they will. By this time next year, I'll have numerous customers."

"And if you don't?"

"I have a few backup plans."

"Like what?" I asked, squinting at him and furrowing my brows in confusion.

"A snow-shoveling business."

"Seems like a lot of work."

"I don't plan on doing any shoveling, Kenny. I'll hire kids like you and pay them a couple of dollars an hour. My customers will give me five, meaning my margin will be three."

"Hmm. So what's the other back-up plan?"

"Buying houses and moving them to better areas of town where they'll be worth more."

"What?"

"Yep, location, location, location."

"Do you have any idea how much it costs to move a house?"

"Twenty grand or so," Lee replied calmly.

"And how much does the house itself cost?"

"Quite a bit."

"But you don't have any money!"

"Well, capital is a slight problem."

"Haven't we been through this before, Lee?"

"What do you mean?"

As I had done before with Lee, I listed his prior grandiose plans, everything from tropical fish to trying to have a girl over after we broke into the Contents' house.

"Now, Kenny," Lee replied, smiling sheepishly. But I didn't smile back.

After our counselling session, I tried to convince myself that my brother's recent business plans were just a joke designed to troll me. Then I realized he was dead serious about them since he had taken action steps on each one. He did buy the business cards for the movie rental business. He did demand Dad pay for prep school and an electric guitar. He did push me to be an Eagle Scout at twelve and monitor my progress. He did have a friend tour the Contents' home and attempt to arrange the date with the girl. And he did take the bus to Bobbie Emhoff's.

Later that winter I heard an announcement over the PA system at Ben Franklin. It offered a job to students interested in shoveling snow. I knew the identity of the sponsor immediately and sank down in my classroom chair.

14

A Glimmer of Hope

In the spring of 1969, another PA system announcement piqued my interest, but this one had more merit. It said a meeting would take place regarding participation in forensics in the auditorium at 3:45 p.m. I knew Lee had been involved in this activity in high school, so I decided to check it out.

About fifteen kids showed up. Everyone except me did extremely well in school, and I felt uncomfortable even being there. One of the students, whom I knew from Campus School and my neighborhood, was present. He had gotten all A's throughout grade school, even in handwriting. While we waited for the teacher in charge to arrive, the kid spoke to me privately in the aisle of the auditorium. He whispered so as not to embarrass me and asked, "Are you sure you want to do this, Ken?"

"Not really, but I thought I would at least see what it was all about."

"Well, I don't think you're going to be very good at something like this."

"What do you mean?"

"Just that you should try something less challenging and more within your ability. I don't want to see you get hurt."

I looked down at the floor and said nothing. I wondered if the kid was right and whether I truly belonged. I even considered walking out of the meeting entirely, but something kept me there, and I listened to the presentation anyway.

That night I talked to Lee in the den about the meeting and what Mr. Know-It-All had said.

"Don't worry about what some punk at school thinks," he said. "It's what you think that matters."

"But all the other kids in this are way smarter than me."

"Look, you want to be a lawyer, right?"

"Yeah, I guess."

"Well, this would be perfect preparation."

"Come on, Lee."

"What are you, afraid?"

"No, but..."

"Then do this activity and prove that little prick wrong!"

"Okay, okay, but the teacher says I have to pick a category, and I have no idea which one."

"Try Four-Minute Speech," Lee replied. "It's a good introductory one, and later you can do Original Oration, which is eight minutes."

"What should the speech be about?"

"Something persuasive."

"But I have no idea."

"You like current events, right?"

"Yeah, I read the paper every day."

"Remember how we used to talk about nuclear war?"

"How could I forget?"

"Well, there's one brewing in the Middle East right now. Go up to the living room and take a look at the latest *Time Magazine* on the coffee table. It has an in-depth article about it."

I did as told and reported back to Lee. "Wow, that's quite a situation."

"So how are you going to start your speech?"

"I don't know. Maybe talk about nuclear explosions like you did with me in Erlanger?"

"Not bad, but the first line has to draw people's attention. So how are you going to do that with the word explosion?"

"There might be a nuclear explosion in the Middle East if we aren't careful?"

"All right, but you need to say it stronger."

I hesitated, then it came to me. "Explosion in the Middle East."

"Yes, excellent. Now the next line has to explain that."

"The article talks about how World War III might start between Russia and the United States."

"So your second line is what?"

"World War III is about to begin between Russia and the United States?"

"Now say the whole thing louder and project your voice to the back of the room."

"Explosion in the Middle East. World War III is about to begin between Russia and the United States."

"See, you're a natural!"

I walked out of my meeting with Lee feeling encouraged, not only for myself but also for him. As the years went by, I did forensics and later debate at the high school and college levels. In fact, I won many public-speaking contests at various local, regional, and statewide competitions, even one in which I beat Mr. Know-It-All. As a result, my grades improved and college and law school became a reality for me. My life could have gone in a completely different direction given my family background, but it didn't, because my big brother took the time to mentor me at a critical point in my personal development.

15

A Long, Hot Summer

Sadly, in May of 1969, Lee barely finished high school despite his intellectual promise and high test scores. In order to make sure he went to school his last semester, Mom had to drive him there every day. He did not even attend his graduation and refused to pick up his diploma from the office. She got it for him instead.

My parents initially rationalized my brother's problems as being part of a rebellious phase. "Most kids these days don't like the establishment," Dad would say. "Just look at what's on TV." In a superficial sense he was right. Each night Walter Cronkite pronounced the toll of those killed or wounded in Vietnam earlier that day. Frequently anti-war protests occurred in one part of the country or another. But there was something else wrong with Lee besides youthful rebellion, something he would not just grow out of, something far more malevolent and destructive.

One event in that time frame illustrated this proposition well, though there were plenty of others. A kid, who had graduated from PJ Jacobs High School the year before, had just been killed in an automobile accident. I brought up the subject since Lee knew him. He was sitting in a worn-out easy chair in Dad's office, looking morose. A reaction of grief would have been perfectly normal for someone who had lost a friend or fellow classmate so tragically, but my brother said something that went well beyond this. "Why couldn't it have been me who was killed rather than a person who had so much going for him?" he asked. "My life has been such a complete failure. I should have been the one who died."

I gaped at Lee's reaction. Thus far he had been isolated, withdrawn, and even grandiose. But he had not said anything that would suggest a desire to harm himself. Moreover, he had never deprecated himself to this extent.

"Are you okay?" I asked him.

He shrugged without giving me a definite answer.

"Because if you're thinking of hurting yourself—"

"Just leave me alone, will ya?"

"Your life is not a complete failure, Lee."

"I said, 'Leave me alone!'"

At first Mom thought my brother's problem was depression, and rightly so given his substitute death wish. So she took him to a psychologist, which under normal circumstances she never would have done, since she was averse to outside intervention. I think she agreed to this because the shrink offered his services for free. He was also a professor at the university and may have been extending a courtesy to my father. His name was Dr. Lloyd Beck. Lee saw him a couple of times, but Dr. Beck mentioned nothing about schizophrenia. The problem was Dr. Beck was an academic and expert on psychological testing rather than a trained psychotherapist. So maybe he just missed it. Alternatively, he didn't spend enough time with Lee to recognize what was really going on. It was possible as well that Lee's schizophrenia hadn't manifested itself to the point where it was obvious enough to diagnose. It could also have been the case that Lee suffered depression as well as schizophrenia.

As to other counseling, we didn't have insurance for that, and there was no guarantee it would work. Then too, we hoped against all odds that my brother's problems would resolve spontaneously. We were optimists in a completely pessimistic situation. Sometimes people do that when things go wrong. It's called denial.

A short time after his last appointment with Dr. Beck, Mom called my brother into the kitchen and said she wanted to talk to him about something. I followed him up there, as her voice sounded ominous. Dad was at work at the time. She had in her hand an application for admission to the University of Wisconsin. My brother hadn't sent it in yet, and it was long overdue. "I found this while cleaning up in the basement," she said. "I told you that you needed to take care of this."

"Let me see that," Lee replied, snatching it out of her hand.

"Don't talk ugly to me," Mom said.

"You're the one who's talking ugly, constantly riding my ass about one thing or another."

"I was just trying to help."

"You can help by staying out of my business!" Lee yelled.

"Maybe you need to go back to Dr. Beck."

"If anyone needs to see a shrink, it's you. You're the one who's crazy!"

"I'm so sick and tired of unappreciative children. When they are young they are such a joy but when they get older—"

"You should have never had children!" Lee shouted at her.

"You stop talking to me like that, right this minute."

"The doctors should have fixed you a long time ago!"

Given all the effort Mom had made to birth us and raise us despite her disability, such words had to be particularly painful for her. Yet she remained steadfast and continued to try to persuade Lee to fill his college application out and send it in. But he did not listen and charged across the kitchen toward her instead. I thought he would hit her or knock her down, given how angry he had become. So I moved in between them. He then went to the other side of the kitchen, where he opened a drawer, retrieved some matches, and lit one of them. With his other hand he waved his college application in the air.

"What are you doing?" Mom asked. "Burning the house down?"

"Maybe I should," Lee shot back. Then, as though he were destroying his draft card, he lit the application with the match and held it steady for several seconds next to the wall and underneath a kitchen cabinet. The flame shot up the wall and scorched it. Mom gave out a terrifying scream.

I didn't know if I could prevent my brother from hurting her or damaging the house, so I got on the kitchen phone and called the police. Meanwhile, Lee took a bottle of booze from another kitchen cabinet and ran out the front door with it. The dispatcher asked me what was wrong. Unsure of my brother's intent or whether he'd come back and harm Mom, I told the dispatcher he had attacked her and I was worried he would set the house on fire.

After about five minutes, a sheriff's officer arrived. His lights and siren were on, and I watched as his squad car roared up the street to our house. *What an embarrassment,* I thought. *Now the entire neighborhood will know about our family's problems.*

Mom showed the cop the scorched drywall and cabinet and told him what my brother had done and said. A few minutes later, Lee returned while the officer was still there. "Have you been drinking?" the cop asked him.

"A little bit," he replied quietly. Perhaps his sheepish attitude had something to do with the officer being six-foot-three and having shoulders as wide as a pro-football lineman's.

"How old are you?"

"Seventeen."

"You understand it is illegal for you to drink?"

"Yes."

"Your mother says that you became threatening with her and lit some paperwork on fire. Is that true?"

"Yes, my college application."

"And you held it under a kitchen cabinet, right?"

"Well, I didn't mean to start a fire."

"I saw the burn marks, young man," the cop replied. "Those

cabinets are coated with flammable material. Now, do you think you can put a lid on this?"

"Yeah, I guess."

"Okay, I'm letting you go this time, but if I have to come back here, I'm going to take you down to juvenile. Got it?"

"Yes, sir."

The cop left, and Lee went downstairs to the den. Mom stared at the kitchen floor and said something quite prophetic: "It's going be a long, hot summer."

Lee never held down a job for more than a couple of days since turning sixteen and being eligible to have one. He worked at Richard's Drive-In for one night and got fired because he couldn't get the orders out quickly enough. He only lasted two days at Green Giant, picking blighted leaves off bean plants. He got a job as a forklift driver at Del Monte, but didn't know how to drive a forklift. Then there was his experience delivering pizza. His first night on the job, he hit another vehicle with the manager's car, causing minor damage and no injuries. That got him fired again. As for working around the house, he did very little. He never mowed the lawn or watered it or helped Mom with anything.

When Lee indicated he did not want to go to college and tried to burn his application, I became even more concerned, if not obsessed, about him and his future. So I decided to become his career counselor in addition to his therapist. Since I was already above my pay grade, it didn't seem to matter.

My first effort in this regard started at the Portage County Public Library, where I noticed a brochure on a table for a diesel-truck-driving school in Sun Prairie. The brochure touted how much money truck drivers made and how little time it would take to learn to drive a semitruck at the school. Given my distress about Lee's future, I took one of the brochures home to him.

"What the fuck is this?" he asked, when I dropped it on the coffee table in the den.

"It's about a school where you can learn to be a truck driver," I answered pleasantly.

Lee threw the brochure in the waste basket next to the couch.

"Come on, you gotta do something," I said.

"Well, it's not going to be driving truck."

"Then what about technical school?"

"I'm not going there, either."

"But you can't just hang around here and do nothing."

"Will you stop worrying? You're neurotic. You know that?"

"Maybe you could start college here and transfer to Madison later."

"Just stop it!"

"How are you going to support yourself if you don't get some type of education? With one of your stupid business schemes?"

"That's for me to decide."

"Look, you need something to fall back on."

"Now you're sounding like Mom and Dad."

Lee was absolutely right, for that was what I had become.

One evening later that June, I decided to watch TV with Mom and Dad, while Lee was downstairs. Because we didn't have a functioning aerial, we only could get two stations. The first had on the Billy Graham Crusade from Madison Square Garden, and the second displayed Dairyland Jubilee, a show involving live Polka dancing. We chose Billy Graham.

Because I had an interest in public speaking, I enjoyed watching the preacher. I even mimicked his voice during commercial breaks and practiced his gestures and facial expressions in my room. Toward the end of his presentation, he promised that Jesus Christ would resolve all our country's difficulties—"social problems,

problems of race, poverty, and war." As the show ended, I listened carefully when he invited people in the stadium to come down to the podium and accept Christ. I could hear the hymn *Just as I Am* being played as people gathered.

I didn't necessarily believe in Billy Graham's promise, but I did think about my brother's plight as the show ended. I knew that people had turned their lives around through religion. So in an act of desperation, I jotted down the mailing address for a brochure and a Good News Bible that flashed on the TV screen. Within a short time I received them in the mail and presented them to Lee.

"You have got to be kidding me, Kenny," he replied.

"I know, I know, you don't like stuff like this."

"That's right, I don't."

"Look, maybe religion will help you."

"Yeah, sure."

"It's worth a try at least."

"That shit is for Jesus freaks. Now leave me alone!"

"Maybe this book will help." I left the Good News Bible on the couch for him just in case he would change his mind.

"I'm not going to read that crap!"

"If you accept Jesus, Billy Graham says all your problems will go away."

"That's not true. Now get out of here!"

I went upstairs feeling embarrassed. I was so determined to get my brother to change and establish direction in his life that I had made a fool of myself about a religious thing that I didn't necessarily believe in myself. That's how much I cared about him.

A week or so after the Billy Graham fiasco, Lee told me about another business proposal. He wanted to obtain an ice cream truck and sell ice cream. He knew nothing about this subject, but this had never stopped him before. As usual he took action steps that demonstrated he was not bullshitting. Fortunately, one of those steps included consulting with the city about the cost of a vendor license, and that ended the idea. He would have to sell one hell of a lot of ice cream to break even.

However, the ice-cream-truck plan did lead to a more sensible way for my brother to make money. We lived near the airport, where the fireworks display occurred every year on the Fourth of July. Several hundred people gathered at the end of the runway for the event, which was only a couple of blocks from our house. "Why not sell hotdogs to people there?" Lee asked.

At first I was skeptical. My brother certainly couldn't make a living doing that, as the opportunity occurred only once a year. Besides, he might still have to pay for an expensive vendor's license. I joked about the idea with Mom. "Just another one of his schemes," I said.

But she didn't view it that way. She thought it would be a good experience for him. It might even give him some confidence. As to the vendor's license, the requirement likely wouldn't be enforced if the hot dogs were sold only one night. So I agreed to help my brother on the project.

We divided the labor up as follows: Mom would buy and cook the hotdogs; I would sell them; and Lee would be CEO and accountant since it was his idea. In preparation for the event, we got an empty box from the grocery store and lined it with tinfoil. The box would enable me to keep the hotdogs warm and carry them to the customers.

I didn't have to work hard to sell the hotdogs the night of the fireworks. I must have sold seventy or eighty of them. In addition, I hawked cans of soft drinks. I even had packets of ketchup and mustard and napkins ready for the customers. The main advantage I had was I looked much younger than my actual age. People viewed me like a pathetic, enterprising little kid at a lemonade stand. Lee took advantage of this by making me wear a white shirt, an apron, and a paper restaurant hat. I was irresistible.

At the end of the evening, Lee added up the proceeds. It came to almost a hundred dollars. Mom didn't charge him for her work or the wholesale cost of the hotdogs, buns, and pop. I decided not to ding him for any sales commissions. We just wanted my brother to have a feeling of accomplishment. And for once in his life, he did.

After the Fourth of July, the summer did indeed become long and hot as Mom had predicted. The grass turned brown despite our efforts to water it and died altogether in some parts. Water mirages shimmered on the asphalt road that led up to our house, making us wonder if we really lived in the South or out west in the desert. Our home had most modern conveniences, but air conditioning was not one of them.

On one evening the heat came in a different form, and it blew in at supper. We had taken our usual places at the orange Formica table in the dinette. I sat at one end and Dad the other. Lee was to my left and Mom directly across from him. As was customary, we began the meal with a perfunctory prayer, whereupon Dad joked about Mom's attempts to be frugal, perhaps in an effort to enliven an otherwise sour mood.

"She drives to the store everyday looking for sales," he said, smiling thinly. "She never buys anything unless it's on sale. The trouble is it costs money to put gas in the car for all those trips, and that more than outweighs what she saves. It's called opportunity cost, boys, and you always have to factor that into your financial decisions. But I suspect there are other rewards for her in doing this. For one thing, going to the store gets her out of the house."

"Oh, Merl, stop," said Mom. The passage of time and a brain condition we suspected was associated with her paralysis made her sentences shorter. She refused to go to the doctor about this, of course, just like with everything else. When we discussed current events, she spoke haltingly and could no longer offer much insight.

Dad reached out and patted Mom's bad hand. Though it had no feeling in it, she blushed at his effort at affection. "I'm kidding, of course. Mom does a wonderful job around here," he said.

While my parents engaged in this quasi-loving exchange, Lee did not pay attention. His lips were compressed and jaw was tense. He slapped a piece of bread on his plate, as though he wished to draw attention to his anger and unhappiness. He slopped some beef stew onto it from the serving bowl, hitting the plate hard with the serving spoon and causing us to pause and take note. A pall had now spread across the dinner table, and all I wanted was for it to go away.

"Would you like some milk?" Mom asked Lee pleasantly.

He ignored her, and the mood became even more subdued. He angrily chomped his food without making any effort to close his mouth. Several times he coughed without covering it with his hand. It seemed like he was trying to provoke Dad since in the past my father had screamed at him and physically jumped on him for this transgression. I thought the same thing would happen that night, but Dad managed to keep his cool—at least for a while.

"Lee, honey, what's wrong?" Mom finally asked.

"When are you going to stop feeding us crap like this?" he replied. He glared at her, despite the fact she had done nothing. His sharp retort even made me angry, but I knew better than to confront him and possibly aggravate the growing tension.

"Now Lee," Dad cautioned sharply.

"I thought you liked beef stew," Mom said sadly.

"It comes out of a fucking can," my brother replied. "Can't you cook anything better than that?"

Dad's face tightened, and my palms went clammy. I nervously tapped my foot in anticipation of a Mount Vesuvius-like eruption. "She works hard all day, and you have no right to criticize her," he told Lee firmly. Under the circumstances and given my father's explosiveness, the response was quite measured.

"Look at that mess over there," my brother continued, pointing to some unclean dishes next to the sink. The truth was Mom couldn't keep up with everything given her limitations, especially since our home had increased in size. On top of this, Dad didn't exactly have the skills necessary to fix things. Still, Lee saw our home's failings as an opportunity to provoke trouble for reasons completely unknown to us.

"You'll not disrespect your mother, do you hear?" Dad responded.

"She's not my mother; she's nothing but a goddamn bitch!"

At this, Dad could no longer contain himself and dove toward Lee. He wrapped his hands around his neck, and my brother did the same to him. As soon as I saw this, I ran around the table and tried to pry them apart, but the three of us became entangled. Picture a thirteen-year-old who appears to be ten playing referee with two grown men in a roller derby fight because that's what it must have looked like.

"She's the one!" Lee screamed with sudden rage.

"What are you talking about?" I asked, while struggling with the two combatants. I didn't mean this as a challenge to Lee. I genuinely didn't understand what he was trying to say, much less his justification.

"She's the one!" Lee screamed again, this time pointing his finger over my shoulder at Mom. "Put her in the mental hospital!"

"No one's talking about putting anyone in the mental hospital," I said.

"She's the one!"

Now it was Dad's turn to escalate. "If you harm her or me, you'll go to the penitentiary!" he yelled.

"She's the one!"

"Come on, Lee, stop," I pleaded, but he would not. He just shouted the same mantra as the three of us grappled in the kitchen.

After several more seconds, Lee changed his refrain, making

my father the object of his hate. "You're a worm! You don't stand up to her, so that makes you a worm!"

"Get out of my house!" Dad yelled back.

"You're a worm!"

"I said get out of my house!"

"You're a worm!"

By now we were at the top of the stairs that led down to the laundry room. Dad thrust his hands around me and was able to get a grip on Lee's shirt. This caused Lee to produce an animal-like shriek from deep inside him. At the same time as he screamed, he grabbed onto my father and yanked him down the stairs. Lee fell too, for Dad had a hold of him. Because I was in between them both, we all three sprawled onto the laundry-room floor at the bottom of the stairs. In the meantime, Mom was making her way down the steps backwards and yelling for them to stop. Dad tried to hit Lee, Lee tried to hit him back, and I did my best to block both their punches.

"Stop it!" I begged each time a blow was thrown. My world had crumbled into a seething pile of fists swinging, arms flailing, and legs scrambling. All I wanted to do was run away and get a new family, but I didn't have that choice. With all the adrenalin I could muster, I stayed in between them until somehow they lost the energy or will to continue.

And then it ended. Lee got up from the floor and left the house. As he did so, I could see he had scratches all around his neck and blood on his shirt from being choked. Dad had similar injuries. But the wounds went much deeper than the superficial ones I could observe, and I knew damn well it would take a long time for them to heal.

16

Hide the Knives

Despite Lee's lack of direction and general decline, he was admitted into the University of Wisconsin and started school in the fall of 1969. We felt very much relieved, not only because he was admitted, but also because he wouldn't be living at home. Perhaps our attitude was selfish, but the dinner table row had changed things. As a result, we did what people commonly do when faced with irrationality and potential violence: keep the source of it away as long as possible, and get rid of that source whenever it comes around. Sending Lee off to college was a great way to accomplish these objectives. Most of the time he was at school, and when he came home, we had the perfect excuse to encourage him to leave. Usually he travelled to Madison by Greyhound Bus, and my parents were more than happy to drive him to the bus station and pay for his ticket.

Compounding this conspiracy of exclusion was the fact that Madison in 1969 didn't exactly present a level-headed and tranquil environment. On the contrary, it was a cauldron in which student protests regularly turned ugly over the Vietnam War and a variety of other social issues. Lee was lucky to get to class at all, and when he did, he likely couldn't concentrate with the burn of tear gas in his eyes. Consequently, malfunction occurred around him as well as inside him. Some of the latter occurred as a result of mental illness and some resulted from alienation we had imposed upon him. By October, this complex dynamic manifested itself in the form of another violent episode, but this time it went outside our family. Mom announced what had happened at breakfast.

"Lee got arrested," she said, while I was eating my Wheaties and Dad was preparing his Shredded Wheat. The local news, followed by a Point Beer jingle, blared from my parents' Zenith radio that sat beneath the scorch mark on the kitchen wall where my brother had burned his college application.

"Was this the result of a protest?" I asked after swallowing.

"Worse," Mom replied wearily.

I breathed in deeply and braced myself for the story, which I knew would take a while given the hesitation she had developed in her speech.

"He hit a girl," she said bluntly.

"What?"

"He had been at a party. When he got there…she answered the door. She told him he was not invited…and she asked him to leave."

"And did he?"

"Well yes…but he came back."

"And then what happened?"

"She answered the door again…and he said…"

"Said what, Mom?"

"'You hurt me emotionally…so now I'm going to hurt you physically.'"

At this point, Dad took over, as Mom was crying and could no longer continue. "He hit her in the mouth, Kenny, and with his fist."

"So is he in jail?"

"They let him out this morning."

"What's going to happen to him?"

"He wants us to pay for an attorney who does civil rights work and sometimes criminal cases."

"That'll cost way too much, Merl," Mom interjected.

"We'll just have to pay it, damn it!" Dad barked back.

"What's this lawyer going to do anyway?" I asked. "I mean, Lee's guilty, right?"

"He thinks he can work out a deal for him involving payment of restitution in exchange for dropping the charge," Dad replied.

"Restitution?"

"Why yes, he knocked out one of the poor girl's teeth."

Lee's efforts his first semester of college to pursue a social life took another strange and embarrassing turn when he started hitting on a literature professor named Susan Brown. This was completely unrealistic and perhaps even grandiose, given his status as a lowly freshman and hers as an erudite professor. She also was much older than he. More significantly, she wanted nothing to do with him.

When he was home one weekend, we talked about this unrequited love affair. He was lying on the hospital bed which made it to the basement in our last move. He had a bedroom upstairs like the rest of us, but for some reason, he elected to stay downstairs. Even in sleep he was isolated from us as a result. His hands held the back of his neck, and he stared vacantly at the ceiling. On his lap lay a pen and a notepad containing some writing.

"Mom says you're interested in a teacher," I opened.

Lee shrugged and smiled bashfully. I doubt he even noticed the frown on my forehead since he was so preoccupied.

"What are you writing?" I asked as I pulled a chair next to the bed.

"A love letter to Susan," he replied wistfully.

"How did you meet this woman?"

"She's a teacher in a class of mine."

"Have you ever seen her socially?"

"Nope."

"Then how do you know she likes you?"

"I don't, I guess."

"Have you ever talked to her outside of class?"

"Yeah, one time I asked her in the hallway if she would like to have coffee with me."

"And what did she say?"

"No."

Lee shifted on the hospital bed, perhaps because our exchange had become uncomfortable. The bed squeaked several times as if it were protesting my questions.

"So what's the status of this little fling now?" I asked next.

"I think she's afraid of me."

My eyes widened. "W-why do you think that?"

"Her husband called and told me to back off."

"Husband? Jeez, Lee."

"I suppose it's pretty stupid to think she'd have anything to do with me, her being married and all."

I didn't respond, for the answer was so obvious it didn't warrant articulation. Finally, after the shock wore off, I asked my brother if he was still in Susan Brown's class.

"No, I withdrew."

"Okay, good. Now please, Lee, don't ever try to contact her again, not in person, in writing or any other way."

My brother ignored me and resumed writing the love letter. I then left the basement, shaking my head as I climbed the stairs. While I was very much concerned about what he had done, I felt sorry for him. He seemed so alone, and I could hardly blame him for reaching out to someone, even if it was inappropriate. Perhaps I related to this since, other than my parents, I had no other sibling, relative, or friend with whom I could share my experience. I was just a young kid struggling with the difficulties of junior high school while trying to cope at home with an unidentified phenomenon that even a trained professional would find challenging. And like Lee I was floundering miserably.

During the rest of Lee's first year of college, luckily for us he came home only sporadically. The Susan Brown obsession faded away, though I worried that there would be others like her. When we did hear from my brother, it always had to do with money. This included restitution for the co-ed's injuries, rent for a room on Bassett Street in Madison, and still more rent when he got an efficiency apartment on East Johnson Street. Despite the largesse of my parents, Lee did not work part time or contribute anything financially to his education. In addition, he attended few classes, took none of his exams, and failed all his courses.

At Christmas that year, I had another talk with him in the den. As usual, the only light in the room came from the floor lamp next to the purple couch. In the living room upstairs, I could hear Mom and Dad whispering to each other in subdued tones. I tried to ask Lee about school, but he barely responded. The same thing occurred when I attempted to address his non-existent social life. Finally, I gave up and rocked quietly in Grandfather's chair, while he gazed at the coffee table in a listless torpor.

After several minutes of uncomfortable silence, I tried another strategy to get him to open up. The Manson murders had occurred that past summer, and details of the grisly affair had unfolded in the media. So I asked him if he had heard anything about the incident.

"Yeah, his followers killed six or seven people, and they didn't even know them."

"That story keeps me up at night," I replied. "I wonder if that could happen here."

"You're so insecure."

"No, I'm not. It's easy to become afraid for yourself and your family after hearing about something like that."

"I suppose you're right. It was pretty bad."

"Pretty bad?"

My brother did not respond.

"Tell me something, Lee. What would you do, if Manson's followers broke into our home and tried to kill us?" I don't know why I asked him this. Maybe I thought it would bring out the hero in him, and he would say something about wanting to protect our family. I would then feel better, and we would have some common ground.

Lee pondered my question carefully for a few seconds, whereupon he answered calmly and quietly: "I would get out of here as fast as I could and take you with me, and let them kill Mom and Dad."

I said nothing, as my mouth froze open in shock. During this time, my brother asked me without any transition, "Do you have a girlfriend, Kenny?"

"W-why are you asking me that?"

"I just don't understand what your reason is for not having one."

"I don't feel like it, okay?"

After several minutes, Lee asked an awkward question: "Is the reason you don't have a girlfriend to do with Mom?"

"No!"

"You do understand that she is a very castrating woman."

"What?"

"Do you know what I mean by castrating, Kenny?"

"Look, if you think—"

"She wants to cut your balls off, so she can have you all to herself."

"That's a lie!"

"Well, you do defend her a lot. Just like a little momma's boy."

"Shut up, Lee."

"Why? Does the truth hurt?"

"No. Because it's not the truth, and you know it."

"I do?"

"Tell me something, Lee: why do you hate Mom so much?"

"Because she's been against me my whole life," he replied angrily. He then ran down a list of complaints about her, everything from not getting him to the dentist for a bad tooth to standing in his way on his driver's license. Some of them were valid, but they were not enough to cause outright hostility toward her, much less a desire for my parents to be dead. I was beginning to feel like Mark Leroux's sister again.

In the middle of this conversation, without explanation or lead up, Lee got up and rushed into the foyer, which was a half story below the living room where my parents' were conversing. The foyer's lights weren't on, so he couldn't be seen. I followed him there, but he stopped and only eavesdropped. His face displayed the same look he had during the kitchen-table row, one of fury and rage. "She's the one," echoed in my head, and I thought he would attack her at any moment. But he returned to the purple couch, luckily, and I sighed nervously as we both sat down.

"What were you doing?" I asked.

"She was talking about me behind my back again, Kenny."

"Come on, man."

"She was! I could hear her!"

"She was probably just expressing concern for your welfare."

"No, she wasn't! It was completely different than that!"

Frustrated, I left the room to get away from Lee and went up the back stairway to the kitchen. I was obviously concerned about what he might do to my parents, especially Mom. So I decided to look in the knife drawer. My plan was to remove any weapons in the house so that he could not use them. But in the indirect light from the adjacent living room, I determined the knives were already missing from the drawer! I searched the rest of the kitchen, all the while worried that my brother had taken them to another part of the house. Instead, I found them wrapped neatly in a dish-towel in the back of another drawer where Mom saved sundries.

She must have hidden the knives already herself, I thought, but what about other weapons? There were no guns in the house as far as I knew, and my parents weren't hunters and didn't really believe in firearms. Yet in the garage all manner of blunt instruments could be found. Indeed, anything in our home could be used to harm my parents, even my brother's bare hands.

I started to tell Mom and Dad about my conversation with Lee and his reference to the Manson murders, but ultimately decided against it. It would have only upset them further, and they likely wouldn't have done anything regardless. Maybe I was the one being paranoid and becoming mentally ill, a victim perhaps of my brother's projection. On the other hand, maybe I wasn't, and my worst fears would be confirmed.

I left my bedroom door open that evening when I went to sleep. I even turned the light on in the hallway outside my room. While lying awake, I listened carefully for my brother, in case something happened. I made sure the covers did not obstruct my hearing or cause me to misinterpret the sounds of the night: a sudden air current here or there, the scratching of a mouse, the settling of the framework or rafters, or even a noise from the outside that seemed like it originated inside. Since I couldn't always explain the sounds, I periodically lifted my head in order to discriminate them, only to put it back down when I confirmed it was something innocent.

At one point I was convinced I heard footsteps moving up the stairs rapidly. I even got up to investigate and charged into the hallway, but it was nothing. I went down to the basement, where I heard Lee snoring and determined it was a figment of my imagination. Eventually, daylight came, and I managed to close my eyes and go to sleep.

17

Slip Sliding Away

During 1970, Lee continued to live in Madison. Whenever he visited us, I would watch him carefully and stay awake at night in case he tried something. I also remained at home whenever he was around, did not visit friends, and monitored any potential weapons in the house. I know this sounds paranoid, but I had to do everything in my power to protect my parents. When Lee finally did leave, I would go from being extremely anxious and depressed to relaxed and happy the minute he walked out the door. It felt like I was high, actually. That's how good it was.

One weekend during this period, something occurred that convinced me beyond all doubt that Lee was extremely disturbed. I had gone down to the den to speak with him, and as I approached via the foyer, I could hear him whispering to someone. At first I thought a friend from the past had dropped by, but after turning the corner and looking to see who was there, I only noticed my brother. His face exhibited expressions that one would expect in a normal conversation—a smile, a grimace, or a frown. He even laughed out loud at times.

Thinking it would be best not to interrupt him, I slipped back into the foyer where I could not be seen. At this point the whisperings grew louder, and I could hear him saying something truly bizarre: "Can't cash the check without the money, but can't get the money without cashing the check." He said this Catch-22 over and over, each time laughing harder and harder at its absurdity. His saying this in itself didn't really bother me. The words were true after all because sometimes Dad would send Lee a check that he couldn't cash, as he lacked a checking account that had money in it in the first place. If my brother had explained this dilemma to my father at the dinner table, we might have all had a hardy laugh given the irony, but he said it to himself when no one was around. That was the scary part.

As I lay awake in my room that night, I could hear more of such self-directed conversation in the den. Later, it emerged from the basement. Sometimes I heard repeated bursts of laughter, as though a party were taking place, a party involving many people, a party to which neither I nor my parents had been invited.

As time went on, this occurred every time my brother came home, to the point where it became normalized. At the dinner table, Dad would ask him about how he was doing in his classes. "Oh, uh just fine," Lee would reply, whereupon he would return to his fantasized conversation. Someone might ask him to pass the milk. He would stop talking to himself for a moment, pass the milk, then resume doing it.

For several years after this phenomenon started, we sought no explanation for it from a professional of any kind and never once called Lee's attention to it. We just tolerated this strange and frightening display much the same as one might do when a family member has a facial tic or engages in some other idiosyncratic behavior. Why we did this, I do not know. We may have just been uninformed, but more likely it was just another example of denial. We just didn't want to believe what was going down.

In August of 1970, our family was invited to my father's sister's home in Salt Lake City. Several years before, in 1966, we had visited there for a family reunion. The reunion made us realize that Dad had family too, and we enjoyed the relationships that developed as a result, particularly since Mom had cut us off from her extended family.

Lee came along on our first trip, and we spent most of our time with my cousin, Mark, who was the son of my father's sister, Jessie, and her husband, Clayton. Their house had a pool table, air conditioning, and a sprinkler system, so we concluded they were rich. We relished the time we spent with Mark, playing pool, riding around in his pea-green Pinto, golfing, enjoying rides at an amusement park, and touring the Mormon Tabernacle.

My brother decided not to come with us the second time we went to Utah, but given his condition, this was fine with us. His talking to himself, face making, and laughing with no one around would have been too much for my relatives to handle. Mom let him stay at our house alone while we were in Salt Lake instead.

When we arrived at my aunt and uncle's home, I found out my cousin Mark would not be there for our visit. He had gone on a mission for the Mormon Church. Even so, I had plenty of things with which to occupy myself besides the pool table. Uncle Clayton took me golfing in the mountains and to various other events. He barbecued steaks in the backyard and let us sample his homemade ice cream.

Clayton was a caring man, not just an entertaining one. When we first arrived, I was sick to my stomach from airplane food. At 3 a.m., I didn't make it to the bathroom and vomited all over the floor near the bed where I was sleeping. Clayton helped me clean it up. He didn't swear at me like Dad or complain about the problem like Mom. He just asked me if I was okay and tucked me back in bed. As I went to sleep, I could hear him washing out the towels we used to clean up the puke in the laundry area sink. That was the kind of guy he was.

Besides doing things with Uncle Clayton, my Uncle Vern drove me down to his family's chicken farm in southern Utah. Instead of making me work, which he and his family did dawn to dusk, caring for 10,000 chickens, he fixed up an old scooter for me. I rode it around the countryside, even though at fourteen I didn't have a driver's license. I also got to go for a plane ride on the way back, as Mark's older brother Norm, who had a private pilot's license, rented a small Cessna and flew me back to Salt Lake City from an airstrip near Uncle Vern's farm. He even let me fly the aircraft a little in the mountains.

I had a great time to be sure. More importantly, I did not have to endure the struggles I had at home. So when it came time to return to Wisconsin, I did not want to go. We had already spent two weeks in Utah, and Mom was averse to wearing out our welcome. A stay of execution occurred, however, when my aunt and uncle invited us for another week. My parents agreed, so long as I could get someone to take my paper route, which I did. Still, the day came when we had to travel back.

Before we left, I ran to the back yard in tears. I didn't want anyone to see me crying, but my Aunt Jessie must have noticed I was missing and suddenly appeared. "What are you doing out here?" she asked.

"Nothing," I replied, while quickly wiping the tears from my face so she wouldn't see them. I then went back inside the house. The truth was this family offered me a warm, stable, and loving environment that I was unaccustomed to. Prior to this point, I didn't even know what a decent home looked or felt like.

Mom and I flew home from Utah, while Dad took the bus, as he had a morbid fear of flying. Thus, we arrived before him. When we got there, it was readily apparent that Lee had allowed the house to slip into a state of complete disarray. There were piles of dirty dishes in the sink and on top of the counters, numerous burnt pots and pans stacked on and around the stove, and clothes, mail, magazines, and cigarette butts strewn everywhere. Flies feasted on garbage not thrown away, but worse was the smell of cigarette smoke that mixed with that of rotting food. He himself was unshaven, had tangled and matted hair, and wore filthy clothes. He looked like a homeless person quite frankly, and I suppose in a sense the label fit him well.

We did our best to clean things up, collecting and throwing out all the garbage and rotting food, washing the dishes and pots and pans, cleaning the kitchen counters and table, sweeping and mopping the floor, scrubbing the bathrooms, and emptying the ash trays. While we did these tasks and more, Lee languished on the purple couch in the den, mindlessly raising a cigarette to his mouth with yellowed fingers, as though nothing were wrong. Every so often while Mom and I scurried about the house cleaning, he whispered a Catch-22 and loudly cackled. I had been in paradise and now returned to hell.

18

1971

The spring after our return from Utah, my parents urged me to visit Lee at his apartment in Madison. This was their way of having personal contact with him while keeping him at bay. I couldn't really turn down the proposal, since I wanted to help in whatever way possible. So at the age of fifteen, I became family emissary in addition to my other roles of psychologist and career counselor.

At the Greyhound station in Stevens Point, an agent at the ticket counter blared over a microphone that my bus would be departing from Lane Three. A menagerie of people exited the terminal and lined up at the bus's front door, where the driver took their luggage and punched their tickets. They included: a multi-generational Amish family; several young people, who I assumed were students; and two hard-looking vagabonds in their thirties.

As I waited for the bus to get rolling, I wondered what it must have been like for Lee to ride back after being pushed away by our family. Eventually, I convinced myself to stay strong and stop feeling guilty. We hadn't done anything wrong. We just did what we had to in order to survive. Anyone else would have done the same thing.

It took nearly three hours to get to Madison by bus, given stops in Plainfield, Westfield, and Portage. Along the way I had nothing to do. The bumpy ride and drone of the engine made me nauseous when I tried to read, so I gave up on that. The people around me stayed in their worlds, and I dared not enter them, for I had enough to worry about in my own. So I looked at the countryside instead.

My brother had instructed me to call him from the bus station upon my arrival in Madison. He did not have a phone, so he gave me the number of a pay booth near his residence. I waited at the bus station for the agreed upon time and dialed the number. He answered in a depressed and distant voice and told me to meet him at the Brat Haus on State Street.

With my backpack containing my sleeping bag and a few other necessities for the weekend, I trudged toward the capitol dome. It must have been a mile, as it took me twenty minutes to get there. At the Capitol Square, I stopped to rest on a bench. After five minutes I asked a passerby where State Street was, and he looked at me with disgust and continued walking. I tried another person, this time standing up to greet him, and he pointed across the Capitol grounds and snottily said, "It's over there, little guy."

Eventually, I found the top of State Street. I figured that the Brat Haus would not be far, so I continued walking block after block west without asking directions, expecting the place to appear at any moment. I passed a plethora of stores and various street people: a guy playing a flute with his instrument case left open on the sidewalk for contributions; a man preaching about Jesus; and a group of hippie-looking people sitting on the sidewalk in a circle while singing to the strum of a guitar. Some of the stores had boarded-up windows, presumably the result of being broken during the anti-war protests. Others were open for business, including a head shop, where I went inside.

I asked the person behind the counter whether there was another State Street on the other side of the Capitol, thinking that I had gone the wrong way. He sighed, looked at me like I was an idiot and responded, "No, there's only one." Before restarting my trek, I browsed the store's contents and saw bongs, hookahs, cigarette papers, and pot pipes. "Are these for marijuana?" I asked. The guy at the counter rolled his eyes.

About six blocks after the head shop, I saw a rustic-looking establishment with a red and white sign that said, The Brat Haus. In front of it, I saw Lee, dressed in a yellow shirt with vertical green stripes. Its collar was lower on one side than the other. It had obviously been worn several days in a row and had on it random coffee and food stains.

Within five minutes, we made it to Lee's apartment building and took an elevator to the third floor. As we went up, the only sound I heard was the motor humming and the whoosh of the door opening at our destination. The hallway beyond the elevator had about ten doors on both sides in either direction.

To the right and inside the front door of Lee's efficiency was a small kitchen counter and a single-tub sink that was full of dirty dishes. It stood next to a two-burner stove. In the corner, I saw a garbage can overflowing with discarded wrappers and empty jars and cans. They came from the same type of food Mom served us at home. Around the corner from the kitchen, another door appeared, and I asked my brother where it led. "A bathroom that I share with the guy next door," he replied. "Make sure you lock his door when you use it."

The rest of the apartment, the size of a small dorm room, resembled a prison cell in some ways. The walls were made of concrete blocks and painted a dull off-white. A twin-size bed with twisted blankets and a soiled pillow occupied the left side of the room, and a carrel-like desk stacked with Accounting and Economics textbooks took up half the opposite wall. Lee picked up an ashtray overflowing with cigarette butts from the dirty all-weather carpet in front of the bed and set it on the desk. "You can sleep here tonight," he said, pointing to the floor. "You brought your sleeping bag, right?"

I nodded as I looked around the room further. A small window faced the street, and below it was a heating unit. Nothing had been put on the walls, not even a poster or picture of a favorite person or place. I felt empty, not only because of the stark surroundings, but also because of the isolation I knew my brother was experiencing.

"I see you're taking a couple of business-related classes," I said cheerfully, picking up one of the textbooks.

"Yeah, two," Lee replied, while lying on his bed. "Accounting and Economics."

"Where are your classes held?"

"In a building about a half mile or so from here."

The distance took me aback. "Pretty big school, huh?"

"It does take some getting used to."

"So tell me something, Lee. When was the last time you made it to class?"

My brother lit a cigarette and blew out the first drag. "A couple of weeks ago," he said without concern or embarrassment.

"Seriously, Lee, you need to go to class or you'll flunk out."

"You were always the responsible one," he replied. "Still doing forensics?"

"I am, and next year debate."

"Debate? I once did that." He spoke as though it had occurred a lifetime ago, but really it had only been two years.

"You were the one who encouraged me to do forensics in the first place. Don't you remember my first speech? It was about the Middle East."

"Yeah right," Lee replied with a distant voice. He then lit another cigarette. An awkward silence enveloped the room, whereupon he started whispering to himself. I swallowed hard at the brazen display and felt like leaving, but I continued talking to him, hoping I could get him to return to our conversation.

"You could still get your degree, you know."

"That's true. Dad even suggested I declare academic bankruptcy and maybe get a degree in Accounting as well as Economics. After that I could go to law school," he replied. He then repeated this somewhat unrealistic notion in a formula over and over, each time giggling sarcastically: "Three years of Accounting, three years of Economics, and three years of Law." After finishing the refrain, he resumed making faces and talking to himself. The rest of our conversation went pretty much the same way, with him passing from our reality to a separate one and back again. This was what my big brother had become, a traveler between worlds, and I was powerless to change it.

For supper that night, we went to a cooperative on University Avenue to which Lee belonged. The arrangement entailed paying a reduced fee for a certain number of meals. The price was lower since the people involved contributed by cooking, doing dishes, and cleaning up. I paid for a single meal for myself, and together we ate. At the end of our time there, someone came by the table and reminded Lee that it was his turn to do dishes. So he gave me an extra key to his apartment and told me to meet him back there in an hour. I asked where I might go in the meantime. He responded in a fake gravelly voice, "The Nitty Gritty."

"You must have forgotten I'm only fifteen and can't go to bars," I replied, laughing. Lee smiled back. At least he was trying to be social, I thought, though I knew it wouldn't last long.

That night I barely slept. The hard floor beneath my sleeping bag at my brother's efficiency did not provide much comfort, and the noise from partiers at the Nitty Gritty across the street didn't help, either. I also continually worried about Lee. Literally, nothing had improved in his life, and there was no hope anything would. He was definitely sick, but I didn't understand why. I didn't know who to ask about it, though it was not my responsibility to do so. All I wanted was to go home as soon as possible and avoid such negativity. At the same time, I felt guilty about returning, for I knew the minute I left, my brother would have no one, except perhaps the imaginary people to whom he sometimes spoke.

The next morning Lee told me he would be moving to an apartment on Spring Street and asked if I could help transport his things. I agreed, and together we carried his limited belongings to the new apartment. It took several hours, given the place was a mile away and we were on foot, but we managed to get it done.

Afterward, we went to the Memorial Union. Built in 1928, it had ornate stone columns and a terrace in back that abutted Lake Mendota. In the basement was a gathering place called the Rathskeller, where Lee and I grabbed a table. He bought some coffee, and I got a Coke. Cigarette and marijuana smoke pervaded the air so thickly I almost missed the dimly-lit pub's colorful archways, marble-like pillars, and grand fireplace. A stranger at the table to our right passed my brother a joint, and he passed it to another stranger. "I guess they smoke pot out in the open here," I said ingenuously.

"No one cares, man. This is Madison," my brother replied.

Indeed, the environment was different than the one to which I had become accustomed in Stevens Point, a town more famous for its many bars than its counter culture. Though Point had a university, UW-Madison dwarfed it, not only in terms of its size but also with respect to its diversity of people. It was a different world, but this didn't matter much to my brother, for he had another one to go to anyway.

After having virtually no conversation with him at our table at the Rathskellar and watching him drag on cigarette after cigarette, I looked at my watch and realized I only had an hour to get to the bus station. At last, I had been given a reprieve.

"I have to go back soon," I announced. "Is there anything you need from Mom and Dad?"

"From them?"

"Yeah."

"Uh, tell Dad to send a check directly to my landlord for the rent." He wrote the name and address of the guy on a scrap of paper he got from the garbage and gave it to me.

"Okay, take care then," I said as I shook his hand.

"Yeah sure, Kenny," he replied without any enthusiasm, then returned to methodically smoking his cigarette.

In July of 1971, I attended Camp Tesomas with my Scout troop. Lee was staying at home more frequently by then, having lost his apartment on Spring Street. Because it had been some time since his last violent episode, I felt okay about leaving him alone with my parents. Still, in the back of my mind I worried about them, given his propensities.

The camp, located in the deep woods of northern Wisconsin near Rhinelander, was an inviting place compared to the ones I had attended earlier. It had a half-mile-long lake surrounded by stately white and red pines. Hundreds of acres of woods and walking paths offered plenty of opportunity to hike and reflect. During my time there, I thought about what it would be like to have my own family someday, one without delusions, violence, dysfunction, and sleeplessness, and a home where the knives did not have to be hidden. At the same time, I doubted I would ever take on the risk of a new family. A rerun of my current one would simply be too painful.

By the end of the week, I had completed Conservation of Natural Resources and Rowing merit badges, the last two I needed to become an Eagle Scout. The first one consisted of a lot of physical labor, building a nature area, and taking several tests. The other one taught me to do everything from feathering my oars properly to sculling a boat. I was proud that I could now row a quarter-mile straight without having to look behind me.

When I returned Saturday afternoon, Dad wasn't around, but I did speak to Mom about camp. She seemed unnaturally pleasant, as though she had something to hide. I mentioned to Lee the merit badges I had earned, but he ignored me. By supper Dad had come home, and I learned why things had been so awkward: his left eye was swollen shut and bruised black.

Mom and he spoke to each other in the kitchen as though nothing were wrong. I asked her what had happened, and she mouthed the words: "Lee hit Daddy."

I could hardly contain my rage. Dad was almost sixty-five and not a good sparring partner for my fully grown brother. Though my father had been violent with us in the past, he was still my dad, and I didn't want anyone to hurt him.

"Kenny, please!" Mom said as I stormed down to the den to confront Lee about it.

"Did you hit Dad?" I asked him, while clenching my teeth. I assumed his response would be laden with guilt, but instead he doubled down.

"He attacked me!"

"How hard did you hit him?"

"As hard as I could!"

I was a head shorter than my brother and physically underdeveloped. Even so I got in his face and stated, "Don't ever do that again! Got it?"

"I'm not afraid of you. If you touch me, you'll get the same."

"He's an old man, damn it!"

"The next time will be worse! You tell him that, okay?"

Later that night, I asked Dad what had happened. He told me that Lee had become convinced that Uncle Boyd, an engineer who designed giant drill bits used in the ocean, had stolen Lee's invention having to do with ocean nodules. Lee claimed he had already obtained a patent on this device. Of course, he didn't really have a patent or a viable invention, and Uncle Boyd wasn't stealing ideas from a person who had little or no technical knowledge. The so-called invention was just another grandiose get-rich-quick scheme. Despite this fact, my brother had called Uncle Boyd in the middle of the night and accused him of stealing his idea. This awakened Dad, and he asked Lee what was going on. My brother then hit my father in the face, causing the black eye.

19

Lee's Return from Berkeley

During my high school years, from the fall of 1971 to the spring of 1974, Lee moved to Berkeley, California, so things went better at home. I received my Eagle Scout at the age of seventeen in October of 1973, not twelve as Lee had demanded. He wasn't around for the ceremony, but this was okay, as it would have been unnerving, given his condition. My chief extra-curricular activity in high school was debate and forensics. This helped raise my grades. But it wasn't the only reason for my improvement. My brother's absence enabled me to thrive in school, I believe. With him gone things were less stressful since I didn't have to worry about his talking to himself, attacking my parents, or going off as a result of a paranoid fixation or ideation.

In Berkeley, Lee stayed at a dive motel called the California Terrace Inn. We occasionally received letters from him, and he seemed to be doing better. For example, he took a class at the University of California-Berkeley and aced his exams. He even sent us a blue book from one of them, and it was very apparent from his answers that he had lost none of his intellectual capacity.

One of them started off as follows: "A paradigm, as defined by Kuhn, is a scientific achievement of a broad nature which helps lay the foundation for further research. Such a paradigm does not eliminate debate, but drastically limits it. After the paradigm comes into wide acceptance, research efforts become directed toward what Kuhn called a process of paradigm articulation..." Lee went on for eight pages of abstract discussion, integrating this concept with scientific history and even the thoughts of ancient Greek philosophers. At the end of the essay, the professor wrote, "Outstanding answer, 18/18."

Unfortunately, my brother did not take any more classes at Berkeley. Instead he informed us that he had become involved in a term-paper business in which he wrote and compiled papers on every subject imaginable and sold them to university students for a pretty penny. When a student needed an A-level paper, Lee delivered. When a more modest effort was sought, he accommodated that as well. My brother didn't get rich doing this, but he earned enough money, albeit dishonestly, to pay for food, while Dad took care of his rent at the motel.

Toward the end of the summer of 1974, Mom called me out of the blue at my bakery clean-up job at the university food service in Stevens Point. When the phone rang, I was in the middle of scrubbing a donut-making machine with degreaser and had to remove my gloves first before answering. So I almost missed her call. She said Lee was back in town and would be picking me up after work in the family car. Since I hadn't seen him in a couple of years, I was quite excited. Still, I didn't know what to expect.

I met him at the curb in front of work an hour later. He had hair down to his shoulders, but it was neatly combed. He wore clean clothes too. I almost didn't recognize him, though he was driving my parents' car. "You're looking good," I said as I got in the front passenger seat.

"Doing all right, for now at least," he replied. Strangely enough, he spoke with a New England accent. So I asked him about it.

"Been hanging around with a guy named Kelly, and he comes from Boston."

"Because of that you completely changed the way you talk?"

"Hey, we're all creatures of our environment," he said, while not pronouncing his "Rs" and gesturing confidently with his cigarette. He sounded like a mobster from the forties.

I nodded reluctantly. "Who is this Kelly guy anyway?"

"A business partner. We were involved in a term paper gig until the fucker took off with our inventory."

"That was pretty shitty of him."

"Yeah, I should have sued him for stealing intellectual property."

"How did you get all the way back here?"

"Dad wired me the bread for a bus ticket."

"So what are your plans now that you're back?"

"Maybe go to school here or in Madison," he replied while tapping his cigarette in the car ashtray. "I could always go back to California and buy a houseboat in Sausalito and live there."

"Doing what?"

My brother cleared his throat. "I don't know. Maybe get back in the term-paper business as a sole proprietor since I got so much experience."

Lee's plan to buy a houseboat seemed like another one of his grandiose schemes. So I decided to question him about it in order to bring him back to reality, just like I had done so many times in the past. "How are you going to get a houseboat without any money?" I asked. "Your term-paper thing won't cut it."

"I could start a more lucrative business, I guess."

"Doing what? Ocean nodules or tropical fish?"

"Neither, unless I get the capital," Lee said, smiling.

"And maybe some training and expertise, right?"

"Details, details."

While Lee's newly acquired accent took me aback, his improvement in mood and affect heartened me. That night at the supper table the conversation was not stilted or fake, like it had been previously. He did not whisper to himself or contort his face while engaged in animated dialogue with persons not present. He expressed no paranoid ideas about Mom. Instead he and Dad talked for hours about Economics and what courses he might take in school. Mom just sat there, but she looked the happiest I had seen her in years.

When I went to sleep that night I didn't leave the hall light on or listen for Lee to charge up the stairs and harm my parents. I didn't check the knife drawer, either. As the days progressed we didn't usher him to the bus station in order to get rid of him. Without explanation he had snapped out of the ailment that had gripped his life so tightly, finally giving us a measure of hope.

Several weeks after Lee's return from California, he hooked up with an old friend from high school, an off-the-wall genius named Mark McKinney. Mark never attended college. He didn't need to, because he had a photographic memory containing every subject imaginable. I once asked him with the aid of an almanac to identify the highest point in an obscure province in Russia, and he not only gave the name, he also pronounced it correctly using a perfect Russian accent. After I closed the book, he told me the exact elevation in feet of that particular location. It was a waste of time to open the source back up to verify his answer.

Despite Mark's intellectual capacity, he often was completely irrational. He never applied for a social security number, for example, because he feared the government would know his whereabouts and possibly monitor him. He generalized about every minority group and absolutely hated all authority. He would draw negative conclusions about people based on virtually no evidence. In the student union, he once offered to spit in the University president's face for a nickel. No one gave it to him, for they knew he would do it in a heartbeat.

In addition to his reasoning problems, Mark was a social misfit. When someone would talk, he would often interrupt the person with a burst of anger and counter what had been said. He stood a good 6'4" and weighed as much as 350 pounds at one point. He had never shaved in his entire life, so he had a long, disorganized beard that matched his greasy dark brown hair that fell down to the middle of his back. He did not regularly bathe or use deodorant, and his smell would cause people to wince. He once grew his fingernails out four to five inches. Eventually he cut them off with the exception of a half-inch pinky nail that he used to scoop weed into the bowl of a bong. Often he spoke in a sing-song voice while swaying his head back and forth. For these reasons, my brother, who was also a misfit of sorts, related to him well.

Despite Mark's social ineptness, he did have a lot of friends. He was a regular at the bars in Stevens Point, and because of his disarming intelligence, became somewhat of a legend there. He also had a reputation for having good marijuana as well as LSD. Because of his anti-establishment disposition, he connected well with the counter culture, as minimal as it was in Stevens Point. And so out of the spirit of "peace and love," he took Lee under his wing and introduced him to people. It was the highlight of my brother's life.

During the time they hung out together, Mark involved Lee with countless women, and my brother would constantly brag to me about his sexual adventures with them, smiling during each detailed description. Every night he would borrow my parents' car, drive to the bars, and meet Mark. I, on the other hand, didn't particularly like this. For one thing, my brother would drink and drive, and for another he would often exceed the speed limit, racing to and from our house each night. When my parents' car was not available, he asked to use mine, but I had the perfect excuse: my old Chevy had a clutch and a manual transmission that he did not know how to operate.

Lee's sexual exploits did not go unnoticed, and Dad confronted him about them one night when he got back from the bars. "If you get any of these girls pregnant, you'll not get a penny from me!" he snapped. If we did something wrong, he would sometimes say this. If what we did was really bad, he would tell us we would someday go to "the penitentiary." I thought for sure that when my father said this, there'd be another row, and I'd have to play referee again. Yet my brother, having now obtained a renewed sense of self-worth, just laughed it off.

As he went down to the den to smoke a cigarette after the confrontation, I wondered if my parents had been right all along about him: his troubles were simply part of a stage that he would one day magically morph out of. It remained to be seen if this prediction would come true or be filed away as wishful thinking, for in his case the evidence was definitely not all in.

20

The First Commitment Petition

In the fall of 1974, I enrolled at the University of Wisconsin-Stevens Point. I had the grades to attend school elsewhere, but I decided to stay at home and maybe transfer later. For one thing, Lee was taking classes at UW-Madison, and my parents couldn't afford to send us both away to school. For another, I needed to be around, just in case he came home. However much he had improved after his return from Berkeley, I didn't want to risk the possibility he would regress and endanger my parents.

Unfortunately, by the spring of 1975, he did exactly that. He dropped out of school, came home, and resumed talking to himself all hours of the night. His appearance also went downhill, and he was noticeably withdrawn. I didn't know what had precipitated this significant development, but it was very noticeable. Needless to say, my family was dejected.

The feeling of disappointment changed to fear one night when Dad told me at the dinner table about another violent episode. "Lee was down in the den, and he must have thought Mom had said something negative about him," he started off. "So he came up to the kitchen and slapped her across the face. Then he choked her and threatened to kill her. If I hadn't been there, he might well have done so."

"Where were you when this happened?"

"At the kitchen table, and Mom was by the stove."

"Did you try to stop him?"

"Yes, but he threw me on the floor."

"Daddy's been so sore," Mom said sadly.

He must have been because he was nearly seventy at this point.

"Where's Lee now?" I asked.

"I have no idea," Dad said. "He stormed out of the house and went somewhere else."

"Did you call the police?"

"Mom said not to," Dad replied, shrugging.

I supposed I could have scolded my parents for this, but I didn't know if calling the police would have done any good. They might have just talked to my brother, like they did after the application-burning incident, and let him go with a warning. If they took him to jail, the judge would have released him in short order, causing my brother to become even more upset and possibly exact retribution.

As to other alternatives, I knew little about them. I was supposed to be enjoying college and having a good time with friends, not doing crisis intervention or being a security guard.

During the spring semester of my freshman year in college, I had a second job at Northpoint Restaurant in Stevens Point. My responsibilities included watching its parking lot and making sure people going to a nearby discotheque called Mr. Lucky's didn't park at the restaurant and take up spaces reserved for its patrons. The job worked out well since all I had to do was sit on a chair outside for several hours and wait for someone to violate the rule, which rarely happened. Thus, I had plenty of opportunity to read or study while making money at the same time.

The Monday after I spoke to Dad about the choking incident, the restaurant was closed, but I still had to work because on Mondays my responsibilities included mopping the floor. Since I was alone and had no one with whom to talk, my mind focused on the predicament I faced. Lee was acting out again, and if I didn't stay at home more and be around as much as possible to protect my parents, he might kill or seriously injure them. But if I did stay at home, I wouldn't have a life. Worse, I would expose myself to more anxiety inducing, violent events, not to mention endure sleepless nights due to my brother's constant cackling, talking to himself, and pacing back and forth in the dark. Simply put, I became overwhelmed in a refrain of "On the one hand, but on the other."

So I decided to do something about it by calling C.Y. Allen, a Communications professor at the University, who had served as my college debate coach the past year. I had spent a lot of time with him while preparing for and traveling to and from various debate tournaments around the Midwest. I had learned to trust him as a mentor. He also had the right balance of common sense, intelligence, and compassion. He had a soothing southern accent, having come from Kentucky like me. Finally, everyone referred to him as C.Y, which gave him an air of approachability.

When I phoned him, his wife answered, and she immediately put him on. "C.Y?" I asked, but my voice cracked before I could say anything more.

"What's a matter, buddy?"

"I-I think my brother has gone crazy, and I'm worried he's going to kill my parents." Since I hadn't broached the subject with him yet, I'm sure such words must have taken him aback. Even so he remained incredibly calm and reassuring.

"What has he done specifically?" he asked.

"He slapped and choked my mom and threatened to kill her. This isn't the first time he has done something like that, and it's not going to be the last."

"Is he home now?"

"No, he left, but he'll be back," I said. "He always comes back, and sooner or later he is going to kill them. I can't always be around, C.Y. I just can't!" By now I was in full tears.

"Where are you now?"

"At my job at Northpoint Restaurant."

"What makes you think your brother has lost his mind besides his being violent?"

I rattled off Lee's symptoms in staccato-like fashion.

"Are you yourself okay?"

"I don't know."

"Well, are you thinking about harming yourself?"

"No, no. I'm just worried about my brother and what he might do to my parents."

"Would it be okay if we met tomorrow morning and talked more at that time? I have something going on at home right now."

"I guess."

"How about Country Kitchen on the east side at seven?"

"Okay, I'll be there."

"Everything is going to be all right, buddy. Just stay calm."

"I'll try, but I can't make any guarantees."

I went to the Country Kitchen at 6 a.m. the next day and got a booth, even though it would be an hour before C.Y. would arrive. I nursed some coffee while I waited and reflected. For the first time in the long and sordid history of my brother's troubles, I might actually be getting him help. Maybe I would no longer have to rely on myself or my conflicted and ill-equipped parents.

C.Y. startled me when he sat down a few minutes before seven. I hadn't been paying attention to the front door and had been gazing out the window. "Feeling any better?" he asked.

"A little," I answered morosely.

"Maybe some breakfast will help. You can get anything you want. It's my treat."

I ordered corned beef hash and eggs-over-easy. It was my favorite, and frankly the only thing my stomach would tolerate given the circumstances.

"So your brother's name is what?"

"We call him Lee, but his real name is Merl Lee Farmer Jr. After my dad, you see."

"Is he in school?"

"Kinda. He takes classes at UW-Madison once in a while. He also got some credits at Berkeley and at the university here when he was in high school."

"How long has this problem been going on?"

"It started getting more noticeable when he was a senior in high school," I replied. "He was just depressed at first, but as time went on he got worse."

"And how old is he now?"

"Twenty-three."

"It sounds like your brother is very sick. Why haven't your folks done anything about it? It's been five or six years."

"I don't know," I said, staring down at my coffee. "Maybe they feel caught in the middle. On the one hand, they love him, but on the other, they fear him. Sometimes it works like that."

C.Y. nodded, and the waitress arrived with our food. "You look worn out, sweetie," she told me. "How 'bout some more coffee?" She gave us each a refill.

"Tell ya what I'm gonna do," C.Y said, loosening his collar.

"I'm open to anything."

"I know the District Attorney here, and I'll ask him if there is anything that can be done about a boy like your brother."

"I don't know, man. Can this be kept quiet?"

"Not sure."

"I don't want my brother to be treated like a criminal."

"Let me contact this guy and see what he says. Come to my office around ten, and by then I'll have talked to him."

At the appointed hour, I went to C.Y's office. He was just ending a conversation with someone on the phone when I arrived.

"Yes sir."

"All right then."

"You bet. I'll give him the information."

C.Y. hung up the phone. "That was the DA."

"What did he say?"

"That your brother is seriously mentally ill, and that there's a legal proceeding called an involuntary commitment that you and your parents can initiate that'll get him the treatment he needs."

"Commitment?"

"I know. I know. People hear that term, and they think 'Oh my god, a *commitment*.' It only means they require him to go to a hospital for a short time and get on meds designed to control his mental illness. Then he gets released to the community, and so long as he is compliant with his medication, he doesn't have to go back."

"You say hospital. You mean a *mental* hospital?"

"I'm afraid so."

"Well he isn't going to go along with that. There's just no way."

"He may not at first. That's why they call it an *involuntary* commitment. But later, once he's better, he may very well thank you for having gone ahead with it."

"No, no, no, you don't understand. He's going to hate my guts if I do this, and I'll probably lose the only brother I have ever had."

"Would you rather have him kill someone?"

"No. I just wish there was some other way."

"But there isn't, Ken. Not unless he gets treatment on his own, and from what you've been telling me, that's not an option."

I sighed deeply. "All right, so what has to be done for a commitment to take place?"

"Three adults, one of whom must be a family member, have to sign a petition stating that your brother is mentally ill and dangerous and give specifics on why they believe this."

"And then what?"

"I'm not sure of the details, but I assume the police will pick him up and take him to a hospital where he can be evaluated by some doctors. If they say he's sick, a commitment hearing will occur, and they'll get him a lawyer for it."

"A lawyer!"

"Yes."

"I don't know, C.Y. Maybe we should just forget about this."

"Look, do you want your brother to get help or not?"

"Yes."

"Then you've got to go through with this."

I stared at the floor pensively and nodded agreement.

The night of my talk with C.Y., I had dinner at my parents'. Lee was not present. As usual Dad was criticizing government economic policies at the kitchen table, and this time it was about Gerald Ford's Whip Inflation Now campaign. "He knows less about Economics than Nixon," he declared. "And Nixon didn't know much."

I decided to change the subject and get on with what I had planned to say. "We need to talk about something as a family," I opened.

Dad's babble came to an abrupt halt, and Mom backed up in her chair. It was as if they knew what words would come out of my mouth before I said them.

"I found out what we need to do to get Lee help."

"Well, I don't want to hear about it," Mom replied.

"Then don't listen," Dad said, his jovial mood now having shifted. "Whether you like it or not, something needs to be done."

"Mom, if Lee doesn't get treatment soon, he could kill you or Dad."

"That's a real fine thought, isn't it," my father said while glaring at my mother.

"I don't care what he does," Mom responded. "I'm not going to do anything to harm my own son!"

I breathed in deeply to gather myself before saying what I knew I had to. Finally, I looked in Mom's eyes and said in a quiet but firm voice: "We need to commit Lee."

"I won't do it!" she declared.

"We'll have to!" Dad snapped.

"Look, Mom, a commitment petition requires three signatures. If you don't sign, I'll just have to get someone else."

"If you do, I'll never forgive you!"

"But I don't understand why you're standing in the way of this."

"Because you'll *ruin* him!"

"Ruin him, ruin him, ruin him…" Those words still echo in my head today, nearly fifty years later.

On the evening of Sunday, May 11, 1975, Lee appeared at our house out of nowhere. We hadn't seen him in several days, and I thought he had gone back to Madison. He rushed inside and started hollering that the Black Mafia would arrive at any moment and kill us all. He didn't specify why this purported organization wanted to do this, but he was quite insistent that we leave the house immediately.

"Lee, honey, calm down," Mom replied. "No one is going to hurt us."

"They'll be here any minute! We need to get out of here!"

At this point, I could see my father pass by my bedroom door and rush down the hallway to the top of the stairs that led down to the living room. Lee must have been at the foot of them, though I wasn't sure, as he was out of my view. Dad told him that he was imagining things and to stop causing trouble. Lee then charged up the stairs toward him, for what purpose I did not know. So I went out in the hallway, but by then my brother had already latched onto my father with his hands. I pulled the two apart and got in between them like I had done in the kitchen row during the summer of

1969. The resulting physical struggle took the three of us down the hall and into the master bedroom. "They're going to kill us all, but you won't do a damn thing about it!" Lee repeatedly yelled during this time.

The three of us fell to the floor on the other side of my parents' bed. By then, Mom had made it up the stairs and was screaming. I was spread eagle atop Lee, trying to grab him and somehow restrain him. Dad was sprawled on the floor behind me, having been knocked down in the fracas. As I reached at Lee, he started crying hysterically. While he sobbed, he looked at me and pleaded, "Why don't you believe me, Kenny? Please just listen to me. We need to get out of here, or we're all going to die!" I hadn't seen my brother cry in years, and his pathetic voice made its way to the deepest part of my heart. He really believed what he was saying. In fact, he was so convincing, I believed it myself. But when no one broke into our home or brandished any weapons, I concluded it was all a delusion. It was at that moment that I knew that my dear, sweet brother, the guy who mentored and even fathered me when I was young, had truly lost his mind.

But somehow I had to get him out of the house. Self-preservation and protection of my family had taken over. By virtue of an adrenalin surge, I pushed, pulled, and nearly dragged Lee down to the den as he repeatedly screamed that the Black Mafia would soon kill us. I managed to open the door from the house to the garage, shove him through it, and shut it. I then ran upstairs to my parents' bedroom and told them to call the police. When I turned around, I saw my brother again, and now he was armed with a tennis racket. A scene from a horror movie seemed to be unfolding. In the haste of getting him out of the house, I must have forgotten to lock the door to the garage behind me. Lee swung the tennis racket at Mom's head but missed. I then wrested the weapon from his hands and pulled him back downstairs and into the garage again. This time I did a better job of locking the door.

My parents and I barricaded ourselves in Dad's office using an easy chair and locked the door. By then Dad had finally tried to call the police, but he hung up at Mom's insistence. I looked out the window, fully expecting to see Lee taking off with our family car, but it remained in the driveway. I listened for him to push in a door or smash a window in order to get inside, but I heard nothing. Apparently, he had taken off on foot, chased by the imaginary demons that now besieged his life. That night we slept in a motel.

Believe it or not, the latest incident did not immediately trigger a commitment petition, for Mom still refused to sign one. But on Tuesday, May 13, 1975, Dad got a hold of me after one of my classes at the Collins Classroom Center at the University. He was in an obvious state of worry and confusion. "Lee just came to my office and demanded the car keys," he said while out of breath.

"What?"

"He said he had gone to the bus station to return to Madison, and the Black Mafia was there. So he needed the car."

I shook my head. "The bus station in Stevens Point?"

"Yes."

"How did they know he would even be there?"

"I don't know, Kenny."

"Why do these people want to kill him?"

"He claims he overheard them talking about a drug deal."

"What did you do when he demanded the keys?"

"I gave them to him," Dad replied. "He was so upset I didn't know what he'd do."

"Did he take the car?"

"Mom said he came out to the house and got it."

"Is she okay?"

"Yes, but we need to do something about this. Are you still willing to sign that commitment petition?"

"Of course, but we don't have three signatures."

"We do now. A colleague of mine in the Economics Department was present when Lee took the car keys. He says he'll sign."

The next day, we met at the Portage County Courthouse, where we reviewed a commitment petition prepared for us by a female clerk who appeared to be in her fifties. Thoughtfully we read our accounts. Once satisfied with them, we signed the petition. The pen felt heavy in my hand, as I was unsure we were doing right thing. But I loved my brother, and this was an act of love at its purest.

21

The Preliminary Hearing

Shortly after the commitment petition was filed, a social worker at Portage County Human Services was assigned to Lee's case. Let's just say her name was Julie Larson, though that was not her real name. When I spoke to her on the phone, she sounded like she was in her mid to late twenties.

Julie pretty much confirmed what C.Y. Allen had said about the process, but provided a few more details. After the police picked Lee up, a preliminary hearing would take place. If the judge found probable cause at this hearing that he was dangerous to himself or others, he would be evaluated at Norwood, a mental hospital 30 miles northwest of Stevens Point in Marshfield, Wisconsin. A final hearing would occur within 14 days of his arrest, and if a jury trial was requested, 14 days of his request for that. If he was committed as a result of the final hearing, the initial period of commitment would be six months and could be extended on a yearly basis after that. During the commitment, he would receive inpatient treatment at Norwood, and thereafter outpatient in the community. The average length of stay for the inpatient part of his treatment was 35 days. If he didn't take his meds while out or comply with treatment otherwise, he could be put back in the hospital during the involuntary commitment period.

I asked Julie about Lee's right to a lawyer. She told me the public defender's office would represent him and gave me the number of that office. After talking with Julie, I made an appointment with the lone attorney who worked there in an effort to learn about the legal aspects of the case. I didn't go to a lawyer representing our family, because we didn't have one. No one told us we needed one, and if someone had, I doubt my parents would have spent the money on it. I didn't think to go to the District Attorney's Office since that office didn't seem to be involved.

The Public Defender's Office was located in a large old house near the Portage County Courthouse. The receptionist there directed me to a parlor where I saw someone sitting behind a desk. As I entered, Lee's public defender stood up, reached out his hand, and warmly shook mine. A tall man, appearing to be a little under thirty, he wore wire rimmed glasses and had light-brown hair that covered part of his ears. He smiled broadly and offered me a seat. Throughout our conversation he maintained a pleasant affect and never appeared strident or oppositional, something I didn't expect.

"I'm just trying to help Lee," I said right off the bat, already apologizing for my involvement in the case. "When you see him, will you tell him that?"

"Sure, uh, whenever he's picked up."

"Thanks."

"I assume you are quite close to your brother," the lawyer said. "This must be difficult for you."

"Yes, he's my only sibling," I replied. "He's all I've got besides my parents. So the commitment of him is the hardest thing I've ever had to do. He was everything to me growing up, you see."

I paused to collect myself, and after a few minutes of uncomfortable silence, the discussion turned to the cold, hard law and facts. During this exchange, the public defender mentioned a new court decision. It had just come down in the fall of 1972 and was called *Lessard v. Schmidt,* a federal class-action suit that had originated in Milwaukee. A woman named Alberta Lessard was picked up by the police and detained for observation at a mental hospital on an emergency basis. Without her presence or that of a lawyer, the arresting officers appeared before a judge a short time later. After only receiving their side and not hers, he ordered her confined pending an evaluation by two psychiatrists. There was no probable cause or preliminary hearing with the assistance of counsel. The psychiatrists then determined she was schizophrenic and recommended permanent commitment. Prior to a non-jury final hearing on the matter, the judge appointed a guardian ad litem for the woman, but not a lawyer. She was, however, present for that hearing. After it concluded, the judge committed her for a maximum period of 145 days. While the statutes provided for a right to a jury trial, she was not given notice of that right, which probably contributed to her not requesting one.

In overturning the commitment, the *Lessard* decision struck down much of the existing Wisconsin statute that had allowed this procedure to occur and established a new one. It included the right to counsel, notice of all hearings, a probable cause hearing within 48 hours of arrest, presence of the person being committed at all hearings, confrontation of witnesses face-to-face, cross-examination of them, and the privilege against self-incrimination. At trial, dangerousness, and appropriateness for treatment had to be proven *beyond a reasonable doubt*, the highest standard in the justice system. Years later, that burden was lowered to one of clear and convincing evidence, but for now it would be beyond a reasonable doubt. In short, a commitment case was now being treated more like a criminal one.

The trouble with *Lessard* was it did not become finalized on appeal until April of 1976, though it came down initially in October of 1972. Technically, it didn't even have to be followed yet, since it was now May of 1975. So the judge in Lee's case could have used the old procedures that did not afford as many rights. Moreover, new legislation, called the 1975 Mental Health Act, which included the rights announced in *Lessard,* was not effective until October of 1976, which was again after Lee's case. So the public defender and the judge faced a dilemma: follow the law as it currently existed or anticipate what it would be based on the dictates of *Lessard* and the new statute. If they used the existing rules, which really was the law, the case might be reversed in light of the new decision. If they didn't and followed the new procedures, the case might still be reversed, as they would be employing ones that technically did not exist yet. In the end, the *Lessard* standards and the 1975 statute were used in Lee's case, though really they didn't have to be.

Lee's lawyer also revealed to me another important legality that would impact his case immensely: the dangerousness standard of *Lessard* and the new statute required a recent, overt act or threat to do physical harm to oneself or others. A psychiatrist couldn't just offer an opinion that Lee was dangerous. There had to be a specific occasion in which he physically harmed himself or another person or overtly threatened to do so, and this had to be based on what people observed and not hearsay. Moreover, Dad and I couldn't testify about times in the past that my brother had become violent, no matter how many incidents had occurred, since the acts or threats had to be recent, meaning a short time before the commitment petition.

One other thing the attorney said was even more concerning: Lee would call the shots and not him. However cordial, reasonable, and nice this man appeared, my brother, a potential mental patient, was in charge of the decisions in his case, and that scared the hell out of me.

Lee didn't get picked up until Friday, May 16, when he called the Portage County Sheriff's Department and requested that it check on my parents' welfare. He told the police he was in Madison and that the Black Mafia had gone to Stevens Point in order to kill my parents. Since the police already knew from my dad that Lee had our car, they notified the University of Wisconsin Police and gave them a description of it as well as its license plate number. Thereafter, that agency arrested Lee on the detention order issued by the Portage County judge in conjunction with the commitment petition.

Since our car was impounded as a result, Dad requested I go to Madison and retrieve it from the UW Police Department. The next day I went there by bus and trudged over to its headquarters on campus. The officer on duty brought me to a parking lot where the car was located. Interestingly enough, strewn inside it were hundreds of our family's photographs.

In and of itself, this didn't concern me. The cops probably searched the vehicle during Lee's arrest, dumped the photos out, and made a mess. What did bother me was they had been stored in a green vintage cardboard box in a dresser in an upstairs bedroom of our home. The box and photos were now in our car. So Lee must have grabbed it from the bedroom and put it in the car before he left the house.

The photos depicted my brother and me wearing Halloween costumes, swimming in our plastic pool in Erlanger, celebrating birthdays, and making faces when Mom snapped shots of us in our Sunday best before church. Nearly every event from our childhood was included, and seeing the pictures caused me to well up. It seemed like my entire life with my brother was being played before my eyes like a movie.

What I did not understand was why he retrieved the photos. I could only speculate, but I wondered if he wanted to look at them and review our life together before the so-called Black Mafia had a chance to kill him. Perhaps his memory of this was just as important to him as it was to me.

On Monday, May 19, 1975, the probable cause hearing was convened in my brother's case, with Portage County Judge Robert C. Jenkins presiding. This was the next business day after Lee was arrested on Friday, May 16, so apparently this was considered to be within 48 hours for all intents and purposes though actually it was not.

Ironically, Jenkins had been the defense attorney for Mark Leroux, the young man who had shot his parents and burned down their house. I wondered if this would make him more sympathetic to Lee, given the parallels between the two young men, but then I realized Jenkins probably hadn't even thought about my brother's case enough to draw that connection. So I didn't worry about it.

Present outside the judge's chambers were myself, my father, and Julie Larson, but there was no sign of Lee or his attorney. Obviously Mom didn't attend, as she wanted no part of the proceedings. I specifically remember that no lawyer from the District Attorney's Office approached us, nor did one enter an appearance on behalf of the State when the hearing started. Moreover, no person from that office contacted me or Dad to prepare our testimony for the hearing. In effect, no attorney represented our family's interest or that of the public at this important stage. Finally, to my knowledge no one from that office participated in negotiations after the hearing, despite the serious physical threat my brother presented to our family and the community at large.

After I became a lawyer and had a chance to look at the statutes, I discovered why this may have occurred. While the 1975 Mental Health Act required that the District Attorney's Office participate in commitment proceedings and represent the public interest, this was not yet in effect. Under the existing law before that act, the District Attorney only became involved *if the judge requested it*. Judge Jenkins must not have made such a request. What was ironic about this was Jenkins used the 1975 Mental Health Act to protect my brother's rights, even though it wasn't in effect, but did not use that act to involve the District Attorney's Office in order to protect my family's interest and that of the public. If you are going to use new legislation, why not apply it for both sides?

While waiting for the hearing to start, Julie, Dad, and I talked nervously about everything but the case—baseball, my college classes, the weather, and even the history of stoplight development in Stevens Point. Though the conversation was pedestrian, the atmosphere remained tense, for soon the mysterious machinations of justice would take over, something that Dad and I respected but did not necessarily trust. Given what we had seen so far, we had no reason to, for everything seemed to be about my brother's rights and not our own. He had an attorney, and we didn't. We were responsible for investigating and proving things, not the police and prosecutor like in a criminal case, even though in many respects the case was treated like such a case. Most importantly, we had to live with the fallout, while everyone else in the system got to go home and return to a life of relative safety and normalcy.

At the scheduled time, the bailiff ushered us into the judge's chambers, a space the size of an average living room. Judge Jenkins sat behind a finely finished wooden desk, angled in a corner opposite the entrance. He wore a black bow tie, an expensive gray suit, and a crisp white shirt, but no robe. With his gray hair, tan complexion, and tortoise-shell glasses, he exuded a sophisticated and sagacious flair. Four wooden chairs stood in front of his desk, one already occupied by a stenographer and three other empty ones reserved for the witness, the main party (in this case Lee), and his attorney. The rest of us sat quietly in back on a leather couch while the judge perused the file. Significantly no prosecutor was present during the hearing. Soon the back door opened and two sheriff's officers in dark brown uniforms marched Lee in, followed by his public defender. They took their respective places in front of the judge's desk, who without further fanfare called the case.

While there could be no doubt the proceeding was judicial, it did not seem like a formal "due-process" hearing. Instead it resembled a discussion with the informal assistance of witnesses. We were not separated and heard one at a time, as we would be today. The clerk swore us in together, and Jenkins heard what we had to say in each other's presence. Further, he merely chitchatted with us directly without questioning by attorneys.

During the entire hearing, Lee sat quietly next to his lawyer. With the exception of an occasional sigh or uncomfortable shift in his chair, his behavior was quite appropriate. If the outcome had to do with how he acted in the hearing, I am sure the case would have been dismissed.

The person Jenkins spent the most time with was Dad, whom he told to come forward and sit before him. He first asked him about the tennis-racket incident at my parents' house and was particularly interested in the language Lee had used during the course of it. He insisted that my father detail every single profanity that my brother had employed. When Dad refused to say the word "fuck," he made him say it anyway, and my father's forced articulation of it sounded completely unnatural.

Next the judge focused on my brother's education. Dad emphasized that Lee had only earned 51 credits in six years of college despite his academic ability. He mentioned he had spent thousands of dollars on him, only to see failing grades and uncompleted coursework. At one point, Jenkins accused my father of being too "magnanimous" with my brother, as though getting tougher on him would have averted the problem. Apparently, the judge thought a mental health issue that trained doctors often struggle to treat could simply be resolved by better parenting. I wondered if he took our case seriously and considered it to be a minor family squabble.

This attitude got worse when he asked me about the tennis-racket incident. He quibbled with my statement, claiming I had exaggerated things. "You said you threw your brother out of the house," he noted. "You didn't really do that, now did you." Of course, I didn't mean that literally and probably should have said dragged, pushed, and pulled him out the door. But in my mind this was the same thing as throwing him out of the house. Given the intensity of the situation that night, it certainly felt that way.

"All right then," Jenkins finally stated, half bored. "I have considered the statements of the family and their additional testimony today. While I am not entirely convinced that Merl Jr. is mentally ill and dangerous, I do find probable cause that such conditions exist and will order his evaluation at Norwood by two psychiatrists. We are adjourned pending the result of such examinations and any further proceedings herein."

22

The Devil's Bargain

To travel to Marshfield and the Norwood Health Care Center, I took Highway 10, a two-lane road that snaked north from Stevens Point along the Wisconsin River, then west through the villages of Junction City, Milladore, and Auburndale. By May, the snow had melted, and farmers faced tough decisions regarding the planting of corn, soy, alfalfa, oats, and other crops. If they planted too early, their crop might be destroyed by excess moisture in the ground or a late frost. If they waited for warmer weather and the land to dry out, growth might not be completely achieved by the time it got cold in the fall, causing yields to be compromised. In the case of corn, if it were planted past the crop-insurance deadline, compensation from such insurance would be lessened in the event the fall crop was reduced. The result of the farmers' rolls of the dice was a hodgepodge of furrowed and seeded soil, fledgling plants, remnants from last year's harvest, and pools of water in low spots caused by the rains. Spring brought hope, but at the same time, it presented risk.

The countryside and the plight of farmers caused me to contemplate the risk-reward balance I now faced. The commitment proceedings offered Lee the opportunity to escape his demons, and our family the prospect of safety and security. Yet, the risks were high: Lee might never forgive me and even direct his anger and violence toward me; Mom would blame me for "ruining" him, and thereby heap upon me a suffocating avalanche of guilt; and the system might do little or nothing, given its bureaucratic indifference. Because the decision Dad and I had made was not clear cut, I felt the need to explain myself to Lee, and that's why I travelled to Marshfield to see him.

Norwood was on the edge of town in a quasi-pastoral setting, though today there is a residential area and business district nearby. The brown-and-grey-brick facility had been built in 1973 and was relatively new then. It did not appear like I had imagined a mental hospital to be—an old building with four or five stories that had metal bars on its windows. Instead it had two stories, and with its American flag waving on a pole out front, seemed more like a school than an institution for the insane.

Inside, I did not see nurses or orderlies in white uniforms. They were dressed casually, though they had name-tags that identified their status and function. Patients walked about freely and sometimes even signed out to travel into town, provided they had earned the privilege to do so and could be trusted. Given the surroundings, I felt better about my decision.

I identified myself to the receptionist by photo-driver's license and indicated I wished to see my brother. While the woman looked for his name and location, she told me to have a seat in the waiting area. I did so and paged through some magazines. Soon a young man wearing jeans with a set of keys hooked on his belt loop escorted me to a locked pod with patient rooms shooting off from a centralized area. Adjacent to the door of the room where we stopped, I saw a plastic name-tag holder that bore a paper slip scrawled with the letters, M-E-R-L. The room was empty, so the person who brought me told me to stay there while he found my brother.

After a few minutes, Lee arrived. He had combed his hair, tucked in his shirt tails, and shaved his face. "You look great," I said, already stating my case that this place was the best thing for him.

"Yeah, Kenny," he responded morosely. "But this isn't exactly a spa, you know."

"True, but it's not a prison either."

"The staff has control and likes to exercise it over people held against their will. Doesn't that make it a prison?"

"But you can earn privileges."

"Did they tell you that?"

I sighed in response. "Have the doctors been giving you any medication?"

"They've offered, but I don't have to take it, as I'm not committed yet. I'm only here for an evaluation."

"So do you think you'll win in court?"

"I don't know. My lawyer says things are stacked against me."

"Even if you lose, it won't be that bad. The social worker told me the average stay here is only thirty-five days."

"Do you believe her?"

"Why would I doubt her?"

Lee shrugged and went onto something else. He asked me if I had gotten him cigarettes. From my backpack, I dug out a carton I had bought, but he told me to check it in at the nurse's station. "Cigarettes are doled out as a means of positive reinforcement," he said. "Another means of control."

After a few seconds of uncomfortable silence, I attempted to explain why I had signed the commitment petition. "I never wanted to hurt you, Lee," I said solemnly. "But you just seemed so out of it that I didn't have any choice. If they can help you, it'll be worth it."

"The Black Mafia wants me dead, Kenny. You have this all wrong."

"Who are these people?"

"Criminals who want me silenced."

"Do 'they' know that you're here?"

"Not sure."

"Maybe you're better off then. Have you ever thought about that?"

Lee's eyes darted nervously around the room, whereupon he asked, "Did Mom convince you to do this to me?"

"She didn't say a thing. In fact she's been against this from the start."

"Uh-huh."

"Well, what do you think she's doing then? Employing me and Dad as her soldiers for her sick pleasure?"

"Maybe, I don't know."

I shook my head, realizing I would not be able to win him over, given his current state of mind. At least he had heard my side and a dialogue still existed. All was not lost.

Without warning, a nurse popped in and asked, "Merl, have you changed your mind about taking those meds?"

"No," he replied. "I have the right to refuse them and that is what I intend to do."

Shortly after my return from Norwood, Judge Jenkins set the commitment case for a final hearing and sent Lee and the petitioners a document that read as follows:

YOU WILL PLEASE TAKE NOTICE that a hearing will be held before me on the 3rd day of June, 1975 at 11:00 o'clock in the fore noon at the County Court Chambers, County-City Building in the City of Stevens Point, Wisconsin, to determine if you are mentally ill and in need of treatment, and whether such treatment should be provided in an institution because you are dangerous to yourself or others, or in some other manner or place. You are further advised that you are detained pending said hearing because you are probably imminently dangerous to yourself or others as follows: Physical attacks and threats to members of family and implied threats of harm to family; unpredictable and irrational behavior.

While this date slightly exceeded the time limit for such a hearing, this could have occurred because Lee and/or his lawyer agreed to it. On the other hand, it could have also been a mistake that no one caught, which sometimes happens in the legal system. Significantly, the notice advised that my brother had the right to a jury at the final hearing and attached summaries of the proposed testimony of witnesses, including myself, my father, his colleague, and two psychiatrists from Norwood.

The first psychiatrist, in addition to concluding Lee was mentally ill, stated: "Without indicated therapy, patient has potential factors in his illness to act in a manner toward others and/or himself that could be more threatening than his recent problems." Since Lee's "recent problems" included choking Mom and some other extremely violent acts, I wondered if this meant homicide. I really did. The other psychiatrist said that Lee refused to speak with him because he believed his report would be unfavorable. He wrote: "Past history obtained would indicate that Merl has a high likelihood of hurting someone."

After I finished reading the notice, Dad called me and mentioned another development that would make the final hearing moot. He said he had worked out an agreement with Lee and his lawyer. Under this agreement, Lee would receive treatment at the UW Medical School Hospital in Madison for a period of ten days on a voluntary basis, and the involuntary commitment proceedings would be dismissed. If Lee decided he wanted to leave, the director of that facility could file a new commitment petition within 48 hours of his request to do so. "Thank God we don't have to go to court" was my initial reaction. Thus, I went along with the proposal.

Based on my current professional experience in this area of law, however, we should not have agreed to this. In fact, no prosecutor on a commitment case worth their salt would have endorsed it since it would not allow Lee to be put back in the hospital if he later got off his meds or failed to comply with treatment in the community. Further, because of the recent overt act requirement our case might have gotten worse with the passage of time if we had to go back to court to pursue formal commitment. At this point, we had a good case based on several recent violent events. Why give that up?

Unfortunately, we did not have the benefit of my current legal experience. Nor did we have the benefit of legal representation or advice from the District Attorney's Office, at least to my knowledge. No one called me from there about it, and Dad never mentioned anything about talking to a representative of that office about the agreement. If the judge did appoint that office, the District Attorney definitely should not have agreed to this proposal for the reasons I just outlined. If the judge did not appoint it, then he was the one who screwed up in not doing so. In any event, someone dropped the ball. As a result, we succumbed to the pressure of not wanting to face Lee in court and air out our problems before a jury. Avoiding the wrath of Mom's opposition to the commitment was also a factor. In the end, we agreed to a Devil's Bargain since we were in a vulnerable position emotionally without having anyone to tell us the pitfalls of that bargain. More importantly, as will be described later, this agreement seriously endangered our family and the public at large.

Since there was no formal court-ordered commitment, our family—not law enforcement—provided transportation for Lee to the UW Medical School Hospital. The cops dropped him off in Stevens Point from Norwood, and we drove him to Madison from there. Because it might be dangerous for my parents to be in the car, given Lee's propensities, Dad had the colleague who had signed the commitment petition drive, and Mark McKinney and I rode along as security guards. The morning after the agreement was made we picked my brother up at the courthouse. I sat in the right front passenger seat, and Lee and McKinney were in the back.

The drive to Madison went off without a hitch. While Lee seemed apprehensive about his stay in the hospital, in that he would be required to follow whatever treatment regimen was prescribed, including taking anti-psychotic medication, he maintained an agreeable disposition. The only thing unusual that occurred was when McKinney, who by his nature was quite demonstrative, suddenly yelled "Splat!" He was describing what had happened to a friend who fell off a barstool. Dad's colleague didn't know this and nearly drove off the road.

At the end of the ride we escorted Lee to the medical school hospital, an old yellow-brick building on campus that looked far more foreboding than Norwood. When we told the admitting nurse what we were there for, she immediately said she knew about the situation. She then called someone on the phone and whispered, "Ward 2B."

What's that? I thought. *Code for "We have a live one"?*

Within a few days of Lee's admission to the hospital, the psychiatrist in charge asked us to come in for a "family therapy session." Of course this seemed absurd. While we certainly had dysfunction in our family, it would have taken more than a single counseling session to unravel it. My brother's immediate need was stabilization on some type of anti-psychotic medication. Nevertheless we went there, thinking that if nothing else, we would be able to learn about his condition.

I drove, as I didn't think Dad could handle Madison traffic. Mom agreed to come, but only because Lee had entered the hospital on a "voluntary" basis. She was very sensitive to the accusation that she had been behind the commitment and didn't want to be associated with any confinement accomplished against his will. Due to Madison's heavy traffic and the difficulty in finding a place to park near the hospital, we arrived twenty minutes late. Mom's limp didn't help matters, for we had to walk better than six blocks from our car. But we did make it to Ward 2B with enough time to get a better grip on the problem.

After grousing about our tardiness, the psychiatrist took us to a lounge that had worn-out-waiting-room furniture. As we walked down the long narrow hallway, I couldn't help but notice the chaotic and overcrowded conditions. Patients, family members, and staff milled about the confined area seemingly without function or purpose. Every once in a while, someone would scream or yell something, and throughout our visit it was necessary to speak loudly to be heard amongst the racket. The hallway itself had glossy-lime-green-brick walls and a thoroughly waxed solid-surface floor that gave the place the appearance of cleanliness. In the air I could smell disinfectant.

Once we got comfortable, the psychiatrist brought Lee into the lounge, who sat in the corner with his arms and legs crossed defensively. He had a pronounced scowl on his face.

"Since we don't have much time," the doctor said to my father, "I want to ask you something very important about your son right off the bat."

"What might that be, doctor?" Dad asked.

"When Merl was a little boy and had a nightmare, to whom did he go for reassurance?"

Lee really had no one to turn to as a child, and what he was experiencing now was in fact a nightmare. So perhaps the shrink had hit on something. Yet during the brief time we had for our session, the question was just too involved to pursue. "Honestly, I don't know," Dad replied, chuckling.

At this Lee abruptly stood up and moved toward my father, while the doctor got in between them. "You've got to listen to me," he said to Dad desperately. "They've infiltrated the hospital! They have me right where they want me! It's only a short time until they kill me!"

"What are you talking about?" Dad asked.

Lee grabbed him by the hand and led him to the nurse's station just outside the open door of the lounge. On the counter there was a vase containing some flowers. It had a card attached to it. "What does the card say?" my brother demanded angrily.

"Bradley?" my father replied.

"Bradley is a member of the Black Mafia! Now do you get it?"

Dad frowned, and the doctor escorted Lee back into the lounge. As he did so, my brother pointed his finger over his shoulder at Dad and screamed, "Those flowers are for my funeral! That's why Bradley sent them. It's a message!"

"I think we'd better end the session," the doctor said. "He's not in a good place right now."

Several attendants came and hauled Lee off, while he screamed, "It's a message! It's a message!"

Once we made it to the other end of the hall and near the exit of Ward 2B, where Lee was no longer privy to our conversation, the psychiatrist said the following to my dad: "Bradley is a catatonic patient whose family sent him those flowers. The flowers were never intended for Merl. The Black Mafia does not exist. Also your son refuses to eat because he believes this so-called organization has enlisted staff here to poison him."

"What's wrong with him?" Dad asked.

"He suffers from a severe mental illness called paranoid schizophrenia," the doctor said intensely. "Unfortunately in his case this disease makes him extremely dangerous to himself as well as the public. We will put him on medication, but we have to have more time than the agreed upon ten days to get him up to the right blood level, and he needs to be closely supervised in the community after that. That can only happen if there is a formal commitment order for an extended period that would allow us to return him to the hospital if he doesn't comply with treatment or decompensates. Whoever came up with this agreement wasn't thinking things through."

"But can't we file another petition if he is still having problems?" Dad asked.

"Not without a new overt act or threat. The last one is now stale since it happened a month ago."

"The tennis racket incident isn't enough?" I asked.

"No, especially given that in the interim he has had some treatment. It is no longer a *recent* overt act."

"So we have to wait until he does something else? What if he kills someone?" Dad asked.

"You should have continued with the original commitment petition when you had the chance."

"But no one told us!"

"I'm sorry. There's nothing I can do."

23

Breaking Away

Lee was released from Ward 2B in June of 1975 and initially lived in Madison. During this time, I attended summer school at the university in Stevens Point and resided in the dorms, because I couldn't handle the many haunting vestiges that existed at home. Eventually Lee moved back to my parents' house during this time. He then got off his medication and was arrested for disorderly conduct that involved my parents. They didn't reveal the details of the incident to me, but he must have done something significant for them to call the police. He then got back on his meds after he was released from jail and the charges were dropped. By then summer school had ended, and I decided to move back home for the fall semester.

Because Lee was taking his drugs, I got the opportunity to observe firsthand the effects they had on him. The psychiatrist prescribed Haldol and Cogentin. The goal of the anti-psychotic Haldol was to relieve him of paranoid thoughts and auditory hallucinations. The aim of Cogentin was to combat the deleterious side effects of Haldol, such as involuntary movements, body stiffness, and poor balance, the typical symptoms of tardive dyskinesia. The meds stabilized him well enough, I suppose. No longer did he laugh, whisper, or talk to himself. He did not express paranoid thoughts about the Black Mafia, Bradley, or Mom, and he avoided violent or threatening behavior.

At the same time he did not appear to be himself when I talked to him. He stared off into space for hours in the den, while rapidly alternating between sucking on a cigarette and tapping it on a coffee table ash tray. His legs were typically crossed, and his top one would rhythmically bounce up and down. When I made an effort to speak with him, he said little, and his voice was distant and passive. Effectively he had become a chemically lobotomized zombie, lacking in will, animus, or purpose. It was as if the person I had known growing up had died twice: once when he became psychotic and a second time when the doctors put him on those damn meds. But I rationalized this result based on a cost-benefit analysis. Which would I rather have: a sedated and soulless person or a violent and psychotic one? I just wanted my brother back when it came down to it, but that was not one of my choices.

By mid-October of that year, I had had enough of being at home again and wanted to move out. I had developed a close friendship with my college debate partner, Bob Loichinger, who lived in a house near campus with his dog and three other students. Bob asked me if I wanted to stay with him. I agreed to the proposition, but breaking the news to Mom would be difficult. I chose an afternoon when Lee was not around to tell her. The conversation started near the door to the garage.

"Bob says they have an extra room at the house where he's staying," I opened.

Mom limped toward me with a confused look. "What are you talking about?"

"Just that a room at his place might work out better for me since it would be closer to campus."

"Wouldn't it be cheaper to stay here?"

"Actually, I'll only have to share in the utilities until next semester, and with my two jobs, I think I can make it."

"I don't know, Kenny. We need you here."

"Look, I can't handle this place any longer."

"But you're the only one who can talk to Lee."

"I know that, but I need to have a life, and I can't be his keeper forever."

Mom nodded.

"Besides, I've tried to speak with him, and he just stares off into space. The lights are on, and no one's home."

"But you'll be giving up on him."

"I might be giving up on myself, if I stay here."

"Oh, honey."

"He's back on his meds now, so you and Dad will be safe. If he gets off them again, I'll come back right away. I promise. All you have to do is call."

I left the house, but Mom pursued me. In the driveway, my car's engine wouldn't turn over right away, so she was able to catch up with me. When it finally started, I rolled down the window.

"I still don't understand why you're leaving," she said.

"Because I need a new family," I blurted angrily. Obviously, my filter was not turned on.

Mom started crying. I got out of the car and hugged her, then left before I had a chance to change my mind.

Bob's place offered the usual accoutrements of off-campus student housing. It had furniture that wouldn't be acceptable at a Goodwill drop-off site. The living room had a sagging, worn-out couch that must have been thirty years old. Decorated with beer and food stains, and marred with cigarette burns, it looked like several generations had partied down on it. "Party down" was a phrase students used in those days, and it had a certain truth in it, for if you partied too much, you most certainly went down. A bong constituted the centerpiece of an old wooden coffee table in front of the couch. The only items of value in the room were the TV—on which we watched *Saturday Night Live, MASH* and *Monday Night Football*—and a stereo, which constantly droned Bob Dylan.

Our house had two bedrooms, each with bunk beds. Bob and a guy from Antigo named Crow had the larger room, and I stayed in the smaller one with a roommate who mostly slept at his girlfriend's. In addition, we had a cot in the hallway for a friend of Bob's from Manitowoc.

The kitchen was accessed by a long hallway that ran alongside the larger bedroom. It had no clean dishes or pots and pans in it. Instead of getting utensils from a cupboard, we obtained dirty ones from the sink and washed whatever we needed for a single meal. Likewise, we never swept or mopped the kitchen floor. Our shoes would stick to it, as it had on it months of food spills and dried beer from the last party.

While living at the house I was introduced to weed. I smoked it for two reasons: first, I wanted to fit in, something I had missed in high school; second, I needed an escape. As trite as that might sound, it was true. All my troubles dealing with Lee's mental illness and my family's problems seemed to vanish when I was high. Although we had a good time doing this and dope had its advantages, our use of it was not without a price.

A Friday night in November that semester was a good example. Crow and I had been partying down at the Square, an area of Stevens Point that had an excess of bars. The minimum drinking age in Wisconsin back then was eighteen, and this guaranteed a lot of business. Early in the evening, shots were served by pouring booze directly into customers' mouths because by then the bars had run out of shot glasses. By nine o'clock, everyone was drunk, including the bartenders. By ten, the fights started, and by bar time, patrons flowed out onto the streets and created a large crowd that didn't dissipate until the police started arresting people. After walking back to the house following several hours of such degeneracy, Crow and I decided to do some bongs of Columbian that one of us had managed to score at the square.

"I am fucked on my ass," Crow yelled out, before whooping at the top of his lungs.

"Yeah, this is really good shit," I replied. After taking another hit from the bong and choking on the smoke, I attempted to offer my own whoop, but it was significantly dampened by the resulting hoarseness.

Predictably developing the munchies, we stumbled to the kitchen, bouncing back and forth against the walls of the hallway. In the refrigerator we found nothing, but on a shelf above the stove, we eyed a package of popcorn. I washed out a kettle, and Crow put the kernels in it together with some vegetable oil. He then cranked up the stove and set the kettle on the burner. "Come on, let's see if there is any more weed left in the living room," he said.

We couldn't find any, so we sat around talking and forgot about the popcorn on the stove. Soon we started to nod off, for the weed and alcohol had taken their toll. After about twenty minutes, our slumber was interrupted, however. Smoke had started billowing into the living room from the kitchen. In the resulting cloud, Diane, a student who lived upstairs, appeared. She screamed: "What the hell is a matter with you clowns? You're gonna burn down the house!"

Without a word, we ran to the kitchen, where we learned just how close we had come to doing precisely that. Our popcorn had become a pile of unrecognizable blackened cinders, and only by virtue of Diane warning us did we not become cinders ourselves. Obviously, my escape from my family problems through the use of drugs wasn't working out very well.

By mid-December, the fall semester had ended. Bob and my roommates had moved out, and the rest of my student friends had gone home for the holidays. I guess I should have done the same, but by then home was no longer home for me. Solitude had become my friend, for it did not act irrational or unpredictable, and I could control it. When I did break down and go to my parents', I couldn't wait to leave, and when I got back to my student pad, I felt safe, secure, and calm.

One evening in this time frame, I decided to go to Bob's Food King around 7 p.m. for groceries. The streets were devoid of cars and students, and snowflakes gently fluttered down from the night sky. I imagined hearing them hit the ground, though in reality they made no noise. It was my way of filling in the blanks, something that I had become accustomed to lately.

When I got back from my wintery sojourn, the phone rang. "Hey man, what the hell you doin' there all alone?" It was Eric, a college friend, who must have felt sorry for me. He had called from a bar 67 miles away in Appleton and wanted me to come there and party down with him.

"I can't. I have no wheels," I replied. This was the truth, as my Chevy Impala had quit running.

"Hitchhike then."

"It's dark, man, and it's starting to snow really bad."

"So?"

"Okay, okay, I'll get there the best I can."

I relented because a voice inside my head told me I needed to be more social, however much I enjoyed my aloneness. It took me a half hour on foot to get to the outskirts of Stevens Point on Highway 10. As I stood next to the road, semi after semi and car after car whooshed by me and sprayed my face with snow, but I kept my thumb out. When I had just about given up, a car full of women stopped.

"We're headed to Oshkosh," the driver said as I hopped into the back seat and we began moving down the road.

"Is that where you live?" I asked.

"Yeah, we're strippers," she replied. "We stay there between jobs."

"Look I need to get to Appleton, and it's twenty-five miles north of there."

"Well, if you come to our place and help us unload our stuff, we'll drive you up there."

I concluded that I had little choice but to accept the invitation.

Everyone has to make a living somehow, I thought. Along the way to Oshkosh, I listened to stripper story after stripper story, which I must admit were amusing. One of them claimed she could partially tie her breasts in a knot. Even though I didn't believe her, I didn't ask her to prove it. Another demonstrated how she could braid the stem of a cherry with her tongue. A third threw a stuffed cat at me. I asked her why she had done this, and she replied, "That's my pussy. Don't you want it?" I laughed and nervously shifted toward the window.

After about an hour, we made it to the strippers' apartment in Oshkosh, and I helped them get their luggage inside. We sat around and smoked ditch weed, of which they had plenty. Eventually, I got bored and reminded the driver-stripper of her promise to take me to Appleton.

"We got other things to do now, honey. You'll have to take a cab or hitchhike."

I knew better than to argue with a pack of strippers. Besides, one of their biker boyfriends had come home, and I didn't want to mess with him. So in the snow-deluged night, I set off for a phone booth at the nearest convenience store.

"I know exactly where you are," Eric said loudly at the other end of the line. I could hear people laughing and talking and disco music playing in the background. "We'll be there in thirty minutes."

After Eric and his friends picked me up, we went back to the disco bar where they had been before coming for me. Because the place was packed, we moved sideways through the crowd to the bar, where we ordered some drinks. We then inched our way to a wall across from the dance floor. There, a strobe flickered on and off our faces. The music was so loud we couldn't talk, so we decided to head to Eric's friend's apartment, where the partying started in earnest, again in the form of weed. Eventually, my eyes became heavy, and I passed out on the couch.

The next morning I could see Eric stretching his arms and yawning. "Did you sleep well?" he asked.

"I guess, but frankly I don't remember much from last night."

"Don't worry. You didn't do anything stupid."

"That's good," I replied, though that was certainly a possibility.

"Listen, I have to go to Point today. So if you want, you can catch a ride with me rather than hitchhike."

"Thanks, man."

By noon, I was back at Bob's, and I slept the rest of the day. When I woke up, it was Christmas Eve, so I went to my parents' house. I did this out of obligation rather than the holiday spirit. Obligation will get a person to do a lot.

Lee was home, and I spoke to him in the den. Eventually, we got on the subject of pot and drugs, and I told him how often I had used, figuring it would be a way to relate to him. Instead, I received a word of caution. "Yeah, weed," he said. "I can take it or leave it. I suggest that in your case you leave it."

My first reaction was, "He's telling me how to live my life even though he's the one who's messed up?" But then I thought about it for a second and told myself, "I'm glad he still sees me as his little brother."

24

Lee's First Involuntary Commitment

By the start of the second semester of my sophomore year of college, Lee had gotten off his meds again. I knew this because he had resumed talking to himself, grimacing, and even laughing out loud with no one around. I didn't know for sure why he did this, but I suspected he was hearing voices. Worse, he was still expressing delusions about the Black Mafia wanting him dead, even though this organization did not exist, and there was no such threat.

Since he lived at my parents' house, it was very possible he would come home one evening and rant about this evil force, just like he had done the previous May. Given I wouldn't be around, he might even be successful in attacking my parents and choosing a weapon that would be more menacing than the tennis racket. So when Dad asked me if Lee could stay with me at my place near campus instead of theirs until my brother found one for himself, I readily agreed. I had no other choice.

By then, I had a new set of roommates, and amazingly enough, they acquiesced in Lee sleeping on the couch in our living room. I didn't tell them what was wrong with him, because if I had, they never would have gone along with the arrangement. But they figured it out soon enough. All they had to do was look at his disheveled appearance or watch him during one of his episodes of conversing and laughing with imaginary people.

Obviously, Lee's stay didn't last long. While my roommates never expressly complained about him, I could tell they were very uneasy about his presence. Who wouldn't be, given his overt symptoms? But there was more to it than that. The very reason I had moved away from my parents' house was to distance myself from Lee and the intolerable situation he created. Yet now that problem had followed me and haunted my daily life.

So I sat down with my brother one evening in the living room of my student home to discuss his departure. Ironically, Bob Marley's song *Guiltiness* played on the stereo as I worked up the guts to tell him the truth: I wanted him to leave. When I did, he told me that Dad had given him rent money, and that he would be out of my place soon. I was relieved he was so agreeable.

Within a day or so Lee was gone, he having found accommodations at a rooming house two blocks away from my place, which was good because I could monitor him. The three-story brick home had been built in the thirties and fallen into disrepair, but the landlord had recently refurbished it and put in several sleeping rooms. It also had a good-sized living room, kitchen, and dining area. Stone steps flanked by concrete wing-walls led up to a porch and the front door. My brother's room was on the second floor and had a window that faced Division Street, a major thoroughfare in town. When I would check on him, I didn't even have to ring the front doorbell to get inside. The house was unlocked 24-7, and visitors pretty much walked around there unescorted. The common areas seemed very open as well, resembling a lounge at the student union or some other sitting area on campus.

Not long after Lee moved, I visited him at his new abode. After I made it up the stairs, I noticed the door was unlocked and half open. I peeked inside his room, but he wasn't there. As I turned to leave, I saw a long object leaning on the wall near the doorway. It was a shotgun! Lee had never hunted in his life and otherwise had no legitimate need for such a weapon. Had he obtained the gun to commit suicide? Worse yet, did he get it to defend himself against his imaginary enemies from the Black Mafia? What if he thought that his housemates were part of this organization and started shooting them? I remembered how he had acted in Ward 2B of University Hospital in Madison and what the psychiatrist had said about him being so dangerous. I wondered if we ever should have gone along with the ten-day agreement. If we hadn't done so, maybe Lee could have been put back in the hospital after he got off his meds and before this happened. But that was then, and this was now. People's lives were at stake. So I entered his room in order to do something about the shotgun.

I considered taking the gun with me, but feared that this would alarm the people in the rooming house when I left. Further, it would have been awkward to carry it back to my place on foot in broad daylight. I was also not familiar with firearms, having not owned one, so I didn't know how to check if the shotgun was loaded. I spotted on the floor a full box of shells, however, which told me this was not the case. I put the box in my jacket pocket, hoping this would resolve the problem temporarily until something could be done.

As I scanned the room for other shells or possible weapons, I found a recent receipt for the purchase of the shotgun from the Sport Shop. Apparently, someone at that store had sold it to Lee, despite his unkempt appearance and bizarre behavior. I don't know if a background check was made or even required, but if the shop had done one, it wouldn't have mattered. Lee was not a convicted felon and had not yet been involuntarily committed, and thus he was not subject to any firearm prohibition. The earlier involuntary commitment petition had been dropped in favor of a voluntary ten-day stay at Ward 2B. Even if the employee who sold it to him otherwise knew for a fact he was mentally ill and had a history of psychiatric treatment, Lee could legally own a firearm!

When I located the receipt for the gun on the floor, I also discovered some disturbing notes in my brother's handwriting. One of them said: "*I live in The Death House, conveniently located across the street from a funeral parlor. Behind it is the woodshed, the traditional symbol of child punishment.*" I looked out the window and saw the funeral parlor and a woodshed in back of it. Both were located just as Lee had described, across the street. I broke into a cold sweat.

Back at my student home, I immediately called Dad and told him what I had found. "We need to file another commitment petition as soon as possible," I pleaded. "Otherwise he may kill somebody or himself. It's only a matter of time until he gets more ammunition."

"But three petitioners are required, and Mom won't sign," Dad replied. "This goddamn legal system would sooner allow people to be killed than to violate its technicalities!"

He was absolutely goddamn right, but there was no time to discuss social or political issues. We had to act and act fast, for this was a matter of life and death. I told Dad I would do whatever it took to find another petitioner, and he promised the same.

After speaking with my father, I literally ran to the student union in a desperate attempt to find someone who knew Lee. At one of the tables near the food line, I found his friend Mark McKinney and told him what had happened. Even he was shocked, but he hadn't seen my brother lately, and he said he preferred to stay out of it when I asked him to sign the new commitment petition. McKinney did say he knew some people who stayed at my brother's rooming house and would check on whether they had seen anything unusual. After I returned to my place that afternoon, the phone rang.

"Is Ken Farmer there?"

"Speaking."

"My name is David Hetrick. You have a brother who lives in the same house as I."

"You're familiar with him, then?"

"Yes, and that's why I'm calling. A friend of a friend told me that a commitment petition is brewing."

A little unsure of David's feelings on the issue, I nervously acknowledged this and explained the need for three signatories.

"I'm willing to help," he replied.

"You'll sign the petition?"

"Yes."

"And say he's not all there?"

"Without any doubt, your brother is a very disturbed, and I can testify about how he has acted while at the rooming house."

"Thank-you, God," I told myself.

The next day we filed the commitment petition. McKinney decided in the end to sign it, so we had four petitioners. This time the clerk seemed more familiar with the situation and efficiently prepared the paperwork. I told her about the shotgun and the writings. Dad talked about Lee's erratic behavior at home and his being off his meds. McKinney went into my brother's irrational ramblings around him, and David Hetrick mentioned Lee pacing the floor at the rooming house and talking to himself all hours of the night. While no discrete recent overt act or threat was described, the possession of the shotgun hopefully was enough.

Within a couple of hours of filing the petition, Dad called me at my house and said that the Portage County Sheriff's Office had taken Lee into custody at the student union. "Did they get the shotgun?" I asked desperately, just in case my brother would somehow get out on a technicality.

"Yes, they took it from his room with the assistance of the landlord."

Despite the fact Lee needed to be committed, I still had sympathy for him. It was undoubtedly embarrassing for him to be arrested in front of other students at the union. I imagined the police walking out of the rooming house with the shotgun in tow and the shocked faces of people who lived there. However necessary the legal process was to get my brother treatment, I wanted it to end, even though I sensed it was just the very beginning.

I have no memory of being at my brother's probable cause hearing on the new commitment petition, though I learned later from Portage County Sheriff's Department records that it occurred on January 21, 1976. I don't know if my brother waived the hearing or my dad simply testified together with the cop who retrieved the shotgun. At any rate, probable cause must have been found, for the matter was set for a final hearing. Lee requested a jury trial for his final hearing through his public defender. It was scheduled February 13th, two days before my twentieth birthday. The police records referred to it as a "sanity trial," though sanity or lack thereof was a defense in a criminal case and had nothing to do with civil commitment.

The days leading up to the final hearing were not made easier by my roommates. They were aware of the proceedings, but didn't really understand the emotional fallout of having to betray my only sibling, who for so many years had done so much for me. Thus, for the most part they offered little sympathy or understanding. Instead, they squabbled about who took whose food, weed, or beer, and focused on looking cool and getting laid. On the other hand, they were college kids, and weighty matters such as someone mowing down people at a rooming house with a shotgun were not on their radar.

Besides my father, I mainly spoke to three people in the days that led up to trial: Julie Larson, the social worker at Human Services; the District Attorney, whose office Judge Jenkins finally appointed, and Lee's public defender. While I spoke to him quite a bit after the first petition was filed, I didn't speak to him much after the new one. He told me that since my brother's case was now being tried, his role would be less as a counselor and more as an advocate.

Julie Larson was a little more open, as she strongly believed that my brother should be committed. Yet even she was not very comforting. She stated that proving the case would be difficult, for possessing a firearm, believe it or not, may not be considered an *overt* act or threat of violence, in spite of my brother's writings and paranoid thoughts about the Black Mafia. He hadn't shot, threatened to shoot, or pointed the gun at anyone, even though he had likely purchased the weapon to do precisely those things. I hadn't gone to the law school yet, but already I knew the law was an ass!

The evening before trial I paced back and forth at my house and worried about the glaring proof problem regarding the absence of an overt act. My roommates were out partying, so they weren't around to talk about the case. If they had been, I doubt they would have even understood the issue. Fortunately, Julie Larson called and gave me some late-breaking news.

"Guess what," she said pleasantly.

"What?"

"Your brother hit a nurse at Norwood!"

"Well, that's hardly good news."

"Don't you see? We now have our overt act. Aren't you happy?"

"Not really."

"Well, I think your brother is asking for help. On a subconscious level he probably knows he needs treatment, but he just hasn't come to terms with it yet."

"If he wanted help, he should have just agreed to the commitment in the first place."

"Maybe he will now."

"I doubt it. That's not how he operates."

I didn't sleep at all the night before my brother's trial. Performance anxiety was something I would later suffer as a lawyer, but nothing matched this, not in the countless jury trials and other proceedings I later endured. As I tossed and turned in bed, I first tried to think of positive things, figuring that this would relax me so I could sleep. Then I attempted to blank my mind out entirely. I even repeated a mantra and breathed meditatively, but the same result occurred. Finally, dawn came, and I got ready.

At the courthouse, I checked in with the bailiff, an overweight sheriff's officer who had seen his better days, and he told me witnesses had been sequestered and to follow him to a conference room where I would be kept until I testified. This is done in all trials to assure that those who haven't testified won't be influenced by those who have. It is always possible otherwise that a witness who has already testified will tell another witness what they said, and the latter will then adjust their testimony in order to be consistent.

Since it might be a while, I asked the bailiff if I could go to the bathroom before being confined in the conference room. He told me I could, luckily. As I was washing my hands, I heard my brother's voice outside in the hall. Figuring the guards might permit him to come into the bathroom, thereby causing an awkward confrontation, I slipped inside a toilet stall. Through the crack between the door and the stall's frame I could see my brother as he walked in.

He stood impatiently at the mirror and fussed with his hair. As I waited for him to leave, I could hear his desperate breathing. I felt terrible, for he was facing the weight of the legal system, and I was part of that weight. I wanted to come out and defend him and make his troubles go away, but I knew that such an effort would only make it more difficult to restore his mental health. *Why has life given him such an awful cross to bear?* I asked myself. Sadly, I had no answer.

Back in the sequestration area, I didn't see Dad, because he would testify first. David Hetrick was scheduled after lunch, as well as the psychiatrists from Norwood. The only other witness in the room was a forlorn-looking young woman, who was with her husband. I assumed she was the nurse whom Lee had hit. She was not that much older than I was.

I considered introducing myself to her and striking up a conversation. Perhaps I could apologize for what my brother had done to her. But I decided not to bother her any more than she had already been. Further, I didn't know if her husband would be angry at me, given that I was Lee's younger brother. So for over an hour I uncomfortably sat in a chair at the other end of the conference room without speaking to anyone, while she whispered to her husband not ten feet from me. After the bailiff called out her name, and she left to testify, I never saw her again.

Just before the lunch break, the bailiff escorted me to the courtroom. I felt like a condemned man being led to the death chamber. He swung open the door to the courtroom and told me to walk up to the clerk to be sworn in. As I made my way down the center aisle with pews on either side, I saw the six-person jury seated along a wall on the left and to the front. They appeared to be sizing me up as a witness already. I opened the swinging wooden gate that protected the area where the judge and lawyers sat, approached the clerk, and raised my right hand without being told. "Do you solemnly swear or affirm that you will tell truth, the whole truth, and nothing but the truth, so help you God?" she asked. They were words I would hear over and over in my career as a trial lawyer.

"I do," I replied.

"Come right up here, young man," Judge Jenkins said, pointing to the witness stand that rose a step or two above the main floor.

I quickly did as told, turned around, and faced the stage on which my role in the play would be performed. Around me were the actors: Judge Jenkins was to my left, perched on a dais above me; Lee and his public defender were seated behind a table to the left of the gate; and the prosecutor stood next to another table to the right of it. In the gallery were my dad and Julie Larson. The jury was now on my right since I faced outward.

The District Attorney took me through the events that led to the second petition. He asked me about Lee's laughing and talking to himself and pacing the floor all hours of the night. He didn't go into any overt acts that had occurred prior to the first commitment proceeding, since they weren't recent. I assumed the nurse from Norwood had already given him what he needed on that topic anyway.

I wasn't asked to identify the shotgun in court, though I recall testifying that I had observed it in Lee's room as well as the shells. The DA may have introduced the gun through the sheriff's officer who recovered it from the rooming house, but I am not sure. It was also possible this was kept out of evidence since the cop probably seized it without a warrant. My testimony about finding the shotgun wouldn't have been affected by this technicality, however, as I was a private citizen, even though I had entered Lee's room without permission. Searches by private citizens aren't protected by the Fourth Amendment. Then too, this was a civil proceeding in which that amendment didn't necessarily apply.

The prosecutor also had me testify about the writings I had found on the floor. After I identified them and my brother's handwriting, Judge Jenkins admitted them into evidence. I was then asked to read the notes out loud to the jury. But before I could utter a word, Lee stood up and yelled, "I HATE YOU!"

I felt as though a knife had been driven through my heart and wanted to run out of the courtroom. With those three ugly words, my relationship to my brother seemed to wash away. I had already betrayed him by signing two different commitment petitions and testifying against him in the trial, but revealing his private writings went too far. This was his way of making me pay for that transgression in the most dramatic and painful way possible.

But I didn't back down. Instead I looked at him and yelled:

"WHY CAN'T YOU UNDERSTAND I'M JUST TRYING TO HELP YOU?"

Judge Jenkins told Lee to be quiet. He also suggested I do so in no uncertain terms. Fortunately, we both complied, for the last thing the court needed was a mistrial. The time limit that governed when a trial had to occur would likely be violated, if there were a retrial. Also, there was nothing in the commitment statute that even authorized a retrial after a mistrial, much less specified a time limit for one.

Once the commotion ended, the prosecutor again asked me to read the writings aloud, the first being Lee's statement that he lived in the death house, and the second about the woodshed. As I read the latter passage, I wondered whether the use of the words "traditional symbol of child punishment" to describe the shed was an allusion by Lee to Dad's physical punishment of us as children.

But before I could dwell any longer on the symbolism, it was Lee's lawyer's turn to question me. He really did not have many avenues to pursue, but he tried his best. Even though his duty was to represent my brother, I am sure he felt conflicted. On the one hand, he probably knew it was in his client's best interest to be committed and get treatment. But on the other, his role was to do what my brother wanted. A lawyer is often faced with this dilemma, whether it is in the context of representing a mentally ill person or a criminal defendant, whom he or she knows is guilty. In each instance the attorney represents his client's desires and nothing else. In order for the system to function for the benefit of everyone and for the truth to come out, sometimes lawyers have to advocate a position with which they personally disagree.

In cross-examining me, Lee's lawyer first took a stab at his pacing the floor and talking to himself at night. "Isn't it a fact that during at least part of the time you describe, your brother was a student?"

"Yes."

"And isn't it also true that students sometimes stay up late and study?"

"Yes."

"They might even recite out loud in an effort to memorize things for examinations, correct?"

"True, but usually they do so with the lights on."

The sharp retort caused Lee's attorney to abandon this line of questioning and go on to something else.

"Now your mother has been difficult with you and your brother at times, right?"

"Yeah, you could say that."

"Maybe even a little ornery?"

"Yes, but it wasn't always that way. She did a lot of good things, too. She…"

My voice cracked, and I couldn't speak. I wanted to tell the jury about Mom's physical handicap and the wonderful, beautiful things she had done to overcome it, but nothing came out of my mouth. To describe accurately and completely her efforts to raise us would have taken a lifetime. So instead of going into the details of her struggle, all I could say in finishing my sentence was she made "nice meals." It was a vast understatement of the contribution she had made to our lives for which I still harbor deep regret. If I could do anything over in the trial, it would have been to say a heck-of-a-lot more about the positive things she did.

As I returned to my student home after my testimony, I felt ambivalence. I was relieved it was over, but worried about what would happen to my brother if the jury committed him and whether treatment would do him any good. My legs ached from the stress of the trial, and I was tired from lack of sleep. After I got back, I took a well-deserved nap. A couple of hours later, the phone rang, and it was Dad.

"Well, the jury committed him," he said. "The judge required five of six jurors to agree, but they all did. It's pretty hard to get six people to see eye-to-eye on anything, so I guess we should feel good."

"Did Lee show any reaction?"

"No. He just talked with his lawyer a little bit, then the bailiffs took him away."

"Did Julie Larson say where he'd go?"

"Yes, Norwood."

"Even though that nurse Lee hit still works there?"

"She quit, Kenny."

"What?"

"I tried to get her phone number, so I could call her and ask her to reconsider, but they didn't have it."

I let out a long sigh and shook my head. "W-what about Mom? Did you tell her?"

"Yeah."

"What did she say?"

"'Such a waste.'"

"Lee's life, or the commitment?"

"Both, I think."

PART III

Coping with the Fallout

25

We Never Have to Worry About Kenny

Lee's first commitment could hardly be deemed a success. Human Services sent him to Norwood for about thirty days, then placed him at my parents' house, despite the threat he presented them. There wasn't much choice, given the lack of group homes and halfway houses that might have fit his needs better. Mom and Dad's limited ability to supervise him would have to do instead. During this period, the psychiatrist experimented with different meds and dosages. Each time he changed the meds, it took a while for my brother to get to blood level and for the drugs to work. Sometimes Lee wouldn't take the meds at all, perhaps frustrated or impatient about their side effects, and this would in turn delay their efficacy once he started taking them again.

Occasionally, in this time frame Lee would leave my parents' house for parts unknown. They eventually would hear from him when he needed money for rent at a dive hotel. At other times, my brother would go homeless entirely, and Dad would wire him money via Western Union or send him a check at General Delivery at the Post Office in the city where he lived so that he could survive. In time, Lee would encounter the police. They then would release him to Human Services, who in turn would put him back in Norwood. Once they stabilized him there, they would let him out, whereupon the drill started over. It was the classic revolving door of hospitalization, release, and hospitalization again.

I learned these sordid details from my parents and to a lesser extent Lee, not his social worker. I don't believe any representative from Human Services spoke to me a single time after the commitment trial, despite the fact I had offered on multiple occasions to discuss my brother's history growing up and my family's general level of dysfunction. While I am sure these people were busy with other cases, you would think those responsible for my brother's care and treatment would have wanted to know his background. A single call would have been enough. Since I had put my relationship with him on the line in the first place by getting the commitment process started and testifying against him at his trial, I was very disappointed in this lack of response. Effectively, I was blown off.

I remember telling Mom and Dad about the communication problem I had with Human Services, and they said they had trouble with this as well. The system only spoke to them if it was absolutely necessary and only on its terms. As a result, sometimes my brother would just show up at their doorstep with little or no notice when he exited a treatment facility or was AWOL from a program. Given his proclivity for violence, this was quite scary.

Some of this may have had to do with privacy concerns. My brother was an adult, and despite his mental infirmity, was not determined to be incompetent. So he could decide for himself whether information was released, and Human Services really didn't have to tell my parents anything without his permission. If this had happened under today's Health Insurance Portability and Accountability Act (HIPAA), the same result would have occurred. Unless Lee signed a waiver or there was an imminent threat to my parents' safety, they would have learned nothing. Still, these privacy concerns had little to do with calling me back and *receiving* information, as this wouldn't have necessarily involved Human Services divulging anything to me about Lee. Then too, I had to wonder if the privacy-protection justification was being used more as a sword than a shield for Lee. If the social workers didn't have to talk to me, they could spend their time on other things, and this was the perfect excuse.

Because of the revolving door of treatment, the general lack of structure and supervision of my brother in the community (few halfway houses or group homes), and the serious problems with communication, his initial commitment seemed like a failure, and I wondered if our effort in pursuing it had been worth it at all. Yes, there was some progress to the extent he was medicated on and off and even hospitalized at times. This was better than nothing, but that's not saying much. We had lost a family member due to a horrible disease, and I had little confidence that the system, which was all we had to rely upon, would be able to bring him back into our lives.

During the first few years of my brother's commitment, I was in my junior and senior years of college and lived in an apartment above the Public Square in Stevens Point. We called it "the Penthouse" since it had an excellent view of the Square's debauchery. Like the previous place I had lived in college, it had stained carpeting, trashed furniture, and the smell of stale cigarette smoke. The bathroom had two side-by-side toilets. I don't know who came up with this idea, but it was very convenient, since two guys coming back from a night of drinking could empty their bladders at the same time. Every so often, one of them would vomit in Toilet One while another would urinate in Toilet Two.

I didn't drink much beer or alcohol in this part of my life, but I did continue smoking weed as an escape mechanism in response to my brother's mental illness. My friends said weed was harmless. They even suggested it would enhance my learning experience by opening up my mind. They were wrong, of course, since by the time I had come down from a high, I had forgotten any enlightenment I had achieved. Further, my concentration was affected negatively, and I couldn't read or write as coherently. I felt tired, anxious, and confused. As a result, I dropped a class, quit working one of my jobs, and generally grew depressed.

I remember a teacher I had for Western Political theory took me aside one day and asked why I had not been coming to class.

"I didn't know attendance was required," I replied. "I'm getting my papers done and receiving good grades on them. So what difference does it make?"

"Because you're missing out on the collegial exchange," the professor emphasized.

I laughed not because I didn't appreciate the concept, but because I hadn't heard anything collegial spoken the entire semester. But I promised I would do better.

"And one other thing," the teacher said.

"What's that?"

"Try not to come to class high."

Ouch.

In light of my own mental health concerns, I decided to go to the University Counselling Office. Initially, the counselor there gave me a Minnesota Multiphasic Personality Inventory (MMPI) test. After discussing the results, which really didn't show anything other than I was consistent in my answers, we talked about my problems with school, depression, and stress. We didn't directly get into my use of dope. I didn't want to admit to having done something illegal, so I talked around it. Back then, the use of marijuana was far more taboo than today, and I didn't know what her response would be. Plus, I trusted my friends for advice on the subject more than someone in authority.

"What do you think the reason is for your changed outlook?" the counselor asked me once I explained my issues with school. "You otherwise were doing well and seemed to be really on top of things."

"I don't know. That's why I'm here, I guess."

"Sounds like you had a lot on your plate, what with your two jobs and full-time course work," she continued. "I think you did the right thing in cutting back."

"My brother wants me to be a lawyer," I replied. "But I'm not sure I can hack it. If I can't deal with college, how can I handle law school?"

"You don't have to decide what you want to do in life right now," the counselor declared. "Besides, kids your age often go through this. They pursue one thing, change their minds, and try something else. Some call this an identity crisis."

"Yeah, right," I replied sarcastically. "An identity crisis."

That was all I got out of the session at the counseling office. Effectively, it was garbage in garbage out, but this was my fault since I didn't tell the whole story.

A short time after my appointment, I went to my parents' house for dinner. Lee was not around, so we could speak frankly. Dad and I initially sat around the table and discussed my classes. Mom, who was also present, did not participate in the conversation, likely because she didn't make a habit of studying Machiavelli or Plato. Dad, on the other hand, knew such subjects well. Even though he was incompetent with respect to the mundane, he was comfortable with the sublime. I was just glad he and I finally had something to talk about. Our bond was also enhanced by having to work together on Lee.

As the conversation progressed, Dad transitioned into something more contentious. "One of your professors told me you've been cutting classes lately," he said. "Do you realize how much your tuition costs?"

"Yes," I replied bluntly. "But I pay for my room and board."

"You could be staying here and paying nothing," Dad said as he passed the bread.

"No offense, but I prefer not to."

Mom frowned and got up to get something from the stove,

but Dad continued with his dress down. "You just make sure you attend class, or you'll not get a penny from me."

"You paid when Lee was in school and didn't go."

"He needed our help," Mom said, having returned to the table.

"And I don't?"

"There is no point in arguing about this," Dad said.

"Yeah, there is. You've shelled out a fortune for him and little for me. I have lived in town or at home to save you money and worked two jobs, while he has done nothing."

"But he's mentally ill," Mom said.

"I'm glad you finally acknowledge that."

"Now, Kenny."

"It's all about him, isn't it? Lee. Lee. Lee. That's all I ever hear."

"Because you are different than he is," my father replied.

"Daddy has always said…'We never have to worry about Kenny.'"

"Maybe that's the problem," I said.

"I don't understand…what do you mean?" Mom asked.

"You are so obsessed with Lee, you've forgotten about me."

"I told you to be careful about that!" Dad barked.

"A mother is always to blame," Mom said, looking pensively at her plate.

"Oh, stop being a martyr, honey."

"You're just as much to blame as I am, Merl."

"What are you talking about?"

"When Lee was a child…you never did anything with him."

"That's a lie."

"Well, you never took him fishing."

"Stop!" I shouted. "This is about me."

"All right then," Dad growled. "Say what you have to say."

"I started seeing a counselor."

"Oh no!" Mom replied. "We have enough to worry about without that."

"Maybe it'll do me some good."

"Well, I don't want you talking to anyone…especially about Lee."

"I haven't!"

"What have you said then?"

"Just that I missed some classes and whether I still want to be a lawyer. I can't decide right now, so she says this could have to do with an identity crisis."

"An identity crisis!" Dad replied, laughing. "These goddamn psychologists don't know what they're talking about."

"You're right. There's more to it than that."

"God all Christ! What is it now?"

"He's trying to tell you something, Merl. Be quiet!"

"All right then, go ahead, talk," Dad said.

"I-I've been smoking too much dope."

"What?"

"I said I've been smoking too much dope! In case you didn't know, your perfect little child isn't so perfect."

"Just cut it out then!" Dad hollered.

"It's not that simple."

"Yes it is. Just cut it out!"

I could see the conversation was going nowhere, so I went up to my room and smoked a cigarette. I found a pot pipe in my pocket that had plenty of resin in it and considered scraping it off and smoking it up. But for some reason I looked around my room instead.

Atop my dresser, I saw the trophies and medals I had earned in public speaking contests as a teenager. I even noticed a picture of me at my Eagle Scout Court of Honor. Mom and Dad flanked me in the photo. She wore a dark green dress, her Sunday best, and discretely covered her paralyzed right arm. The dress had on it a yellow corsage the scoutmaster must have given her. My Eagle medal was pinned on my scout shirt, and my sash with all my merit badges was angled neatly across it.

I remembered Mom sewing the merit badges on that sash, as well as my rank patches on the front pocket of my Scout shirt. She threaded the needle by holding it in her teeth and closing her right eye so she could focus on the needle hole. Carefully she guided the thread through the hole using her good hand. While still holding the needle in her teeth, she crossed the thread with the other end of it and formed a knot that she carefully pulled tight. Next she brought out a merit badge or patch and precisely positioned it on the sash or shirt pocket, whichever applied. While holding it in place with her little finger, she used the thumb and forefinger of the same hand to stick the needle through the badge. A single stitch took several minutes and a merit badge or rank patch an hour. She did this twenty-two times for each of the twenty-two merit badges I had earned and five more for the ranks leading up to Eagle. She exercised the same diligence in clipping out newspaper articles about National Honor Society, Badger Boys State, and Debate and Forensics, again with her one good hand.

Realizing how important I was to her and how proud she was of me, I threw the pot pipe in the garbage and gazed out the window. As I did, a single phrase crossed my lips: "We never have to worry about Kenny." I decided at that point to live up to that mantra and use dope considerably less. Eventually, I stopped using altogether, especially when I attended law school, but this was the impetus that made that possible.

26

Family Hero

Despite all the obstacles in my life in college, I graduated with honors. I even managed to receive an Albertson Medallion, an award given to a dozen or so graduating students for scholarship and leadership. My grades were high, but my law school entrance exam score was mediocre since I couldn't sleep for several nights before the test. As a result, I didn't get into the University of Wisconsin. So I moved to Kentucky, the state in which I was born and partially raised, and got admitted into the University of Louisville.

Even though this law school had an average academic standing, it was not like college, and I found it quite difficult. I distinctly remember my first class. The professor called on someone, and the student did a good job answering his questions. *Wow, he is smarter than I am,* I thought, but maybe it was just the luck of the draw. Then the professor called on another student, and she was smarter than the first. A third person was called on, and he was smarter than the second. I came away from the class feeling humbled and wondered if I even belonged.

Besides having more ability than the students in college, law students were also more motivated. They always completed the assignments and were well prepared. They did not cut classes. The administration made sure of this by making us sign a roll sheet that was passed around at the beginning of class. If you missed more than three times, you received an F. It didn't matter if you had pneumonia, for there was no such thing as an excused absence. There was only an absence.

With the exception of legal writing, each class only had one exam per semester. You either made it on that test, or you didn't. The school enforced a straight C curve, which put a lot of pressure on us. Under this system, half the students, all of whom had decent grade-point averages in college, would get Cs. If you had less than a C average by the end of the second semester, because you had screwed up on one exam the first semester, you flunked out. A couple of third-year students told me that first-year students would sometimes take their final exams while seated on a toilet, as they had such persistent diarrhea from the stress that they couldn't take them anywhere else. Given how things had gone my first semester, I actually believed them.

But it was more than fear that motivated me in first year law. Mental illness had robbed my parents of their number one son, and I was all they had left. So I developed a new identity: let's just call it Family Hero, a role a dysfunctional family member takes on to compensate for another member's malfunction. In my case, it was a variation of, "We never have to worry about, Kenny."

Contracts was taught by the most feared instructor in law school: Professor Jacqueline Kanovitz. She didn't have a law degree from Harvard or Yale like some of the male instructors, but this didn't matter, since being a genius trumps an Ivy-League education any day. Instead she went to the University of Louisville where she managed to obtain the highest grade-point average in the history of the school. Since it was founded in 1846, this was no small accomplishment. She often spoke in abstractions as she stormed around the classroom, ending each statement with a staccato-like pronunciation of a student's name as she snapped her index finger randomly on the roll sheet to find it.

"When a promisee has an independent obligation to perform the promise of the promisor, can the promisee claim estoppel against the promisor, Mr. Bailey?" "Is an offer that has a total price for a group of goods sufficiently definite for a valid contract when the components of the group are variable, Ms. Jensen?" "Does an offer that demonstrates an objective intent to be legally bound transfer the power of acceptance to the offeree even though that offeror has a contrary subjective intent, Mr. Green?"

The answers could be found in the endnotes after the main case in our book or perhaps in another source altogether. When a student seemingly gave the correct response, Kanovitz would launch into a long-winded tirade that presented a different point of view based on the Uniform Commercial Code or Williston's Restatement on Contracts, a reference that could only be found on a dusty shelf in the law library. Occasionally, I couldn't even find it there, since other students had already checked it out by the time I arrived. But this did not matter, for we were responsible for learning the law, regardless of how and where we found it. It was our problem and not our teachers'.

I don't think we covered more than 150 pages of the Contracts casebook the entire first semester, thanks to Kanovitz's painstaking review of it and reference to outside sources. We bought our books new, but the pages already taught in class were soiled and dog-eared. So much that we didn't even have to know the page number where we left off. All we had to do was look at where the wear marks stopped.

"The holding in the current case is contradicted by one we previously discussed having similar facts," Kanovitz proclaimed one day in class. "What is the name of that case, and how are its facts distinguished from today's case thereby justifying the different holding?"

Since this professor was so meticulous in covering the cases, the reading assignment never matched what we went over in class. Even though she hardly ever finished the actual cases assigned for a given day, she always gave us more to read, further exacerbating this disconnect. We had actually prepared the case in front of us the week before, and the one she wanted us to distinguish three weeks before that, which seemed like a decade ago in law school time. Because she had taught the class a zillion times and knew all the cases, she could not relate to this problem. Then too, she had a bottomless pit for a memory.

In response to the question, I scrambled through my casebook, while she approached the roll sheet for a victim. I selected a case that seemed to hold the opposite of the current one, quickly scanned it, and found a fact that justified its different holding. Kanovitz glared at me as she looked up from the roll sheet, then quickly turned her face away and called out, "Mr. Page!"

Whew! A stay of sentence.

"Uh, Lucy v. Zehmer?" Page quietly replied. It was the same case I had found, so maybe I had been right all along.

"That has absolutely nothing to do with our discussion," Kanovitz snapped. "I don't understand how anyone who has been in law school this long could possibly give such an answer!"

I gulped.

About six weeks into law school's paranoid grind, the legal writing instructor gave us an assignment. We were to construct a memorandum advising a lawyer about the legal pros and cons of a client's proposed course of action. It had to be based on three cases that the instructor gave us and no others from independent legal research. Significantly, he told us our writing needed to be as concise and direct as possible. "The fewer words the better."

I spent hours on the project, reducing complex legal propositions to one or two terse sentences. My memorandum was five to six pages long, though it could have been twenty. I applied with exactness the Uniform System of Citation, a style manual used in law school that prescribed how to cite every case, parallel case, treatise, statute, comma, colon, and ellipsis. We called it "The Blue Book."

The grading of the assignment had significance since Legal Writing was the only class in which we were evaluated based on what we did during the entire semester, versus a single, comprehensive exam at the end. The memo was worth ten percent, the next three assignments fifteen percent each, and the final one, a full-blown brief, forty-five. A bad grade on the first exposition would not cause a student to fail, but even with perfect scores on the rest of the assignments, he or she could not receive an A. So there was pressure.

The teacher handed back our memos by calling out names one at a time. My memo received a grade of two on a scale of five. I had nearly flunked. The only note on my paper indicated that I had not fully and thoroughly applied the cases to the facts. Of course, this was directly at odds with the teacher's clear instruction that we be as brief as possible. The highest grade I could now get in the class was a B, and it might go down from there.

That night I decided to call home for the first time since law school had started. I used a phone booth in the lobby of the dormitory for the Kentucky Baptist School of Nursing. I had rented a room there on the first floor, along with several other male grad students. Female nursing students stayed on the second and third floors.

Mom answered the kitchen phone. I could hear her yell at Dad to go upstairs to his office so he could participate in the conversation on the other line. A pause ensued, whereupon I heard a thud. "You dropped the phone, you old fool!" Mom called out.

After some rustling sounds, Dad came on and said, "Hello, Kenny? How's law school?"

I spewed out a long-winded explanation about everything from the method of teaching to the nature of the coursework. No doubt both my parents' heads were spinning.

"What about your marks?" Dad asked.

"We don't get them until the end of the semester because there's only one exam."

"For the entire grade?"

"Yep, but we did get one assignment back in Legal Writing."

"How'd you do?"

"I got a two on a five scale, which would be like a D."

"Uh-huh."

"I'm not sure I'm cut out for law school, Dad."

"Well, just do the best you can," he replied. It was nice of him to be so supportive and understanding, but I knew that that approach wouldn't be enough, for family heroes have to do more than the best they can. They are, after all, doing the work of more than one person.

Preparation for final exams my first semester of law school was particularly intense. I compiled outlines in each class, memorized them, and reduced them to checklists. I obtained all available tests previously administered in my classes from the library reference desk, as did most law students. The actual exams would not pose the same questions, but I practiced over and over writing answers to those asked in the past. I even timed myself to make sure I could think and write quickly enough.

To say I was driven during the exam period would be an understatement, but the source of that energy was not just my desire to be a family hero. It was also Lee. I could hear his words as I studied: "Be an Eagle Scout at twelve. Memorize everything you need to know for Tenderfoot for your first scout meeting and come back later, so I can test you. Read *Little Men.* When you get done with that, read *Little Women.* You want to live in a tract house like this all your life? Some punk at school told you that you aren't good enough for forensics? Prove him wrong. Now research your speech. Do it and do it now!"

My first exam took place in Contracts, of course. It had five lengthy fact-patterned-essay questions that were to be answered in an oversized blue book that had about twenty-five pages. We got three hours to get it done. As was the case on all my exams, I immediately wrote down a checklist for the entire subject on a separate piece of paper before starting. That way I wouldn't have to worry about forgetting anything I had memorized. After that, I read each question and jotted in the margin prompts that the checklist inspired. The prompts succinctly described in a word or two the legal issues involved and helped me organize my response.

Question 1 concerned a remodeling contract in which a company was supposed to install a Turkish bath in someone's home. After reading the question, I didn't write any prompts in the margins and thus spotted no issues. I read it again, but I still found absolutely zip to write about. If I messed up this part of the exam, I would get an F, for it comprised 20 percent of the grade. So I started to panic. After taking a few deep breaths, I calmed down and answered the question the best I could by reciting some basic contract principles and applying them to the facts. This was nothing more than a feeble effort to show I knew something despite the fact I had completely missed the point of the question. Fortunately, the rest of the exam went better, but my response to Question 1 was pure bullshit, and I knew that Kanovitz would rip it to pieces. After the exam, I prayed I would at least get a D in the class and make up for it with good grades in my remaining courses.

By the end of the examination period, I was exhausted, but I did do a better job on the rest of the exams besides the one in Contracts. Instead of partying and getting drunk like the other law students, I drove to a White Castle near campus and ordered six sliders. This seemed like a more sensible way to reward my efforts, even though it was hardly healthy.

Within a week of my last final, the law school sent my grades to my residence in Louisville. I nervously opened up the envelope.

I got a C in Contracts and Bs in the rest of my courses including legal writing, enough to make the law review, given the curve. I couldn't wait to tell my parents, so they could feel proud. More importantly, I couldn't wait to tell Lee.

After I went home for the holidays, I told everyone in my family how I did in my first semester of law school, and they were all pleased. Lee wasn't the slightest bit jealous or morose about my success, and he congratulated me on making the law review. Still, I rambled on and on about my classes with anyone in my family who would listen. I had become so immersed in school that I couldn't think about anything else. Even Lee, who wasn't exactly Mr. Social, claimed I was a machine. "Law, law, law, that's all you ever talk about," he said. I read my parents the entire first draft of an article I had been assigned to write as part of my law review candidacy, believe it or not. Though they listened politely, by the end of the reading, they had both fallen asleep. Frankly, I had turned myself on in law school and couldn't find a way to turn myself off.

Eventually, I managed to leave behind my obsession and transition into Christmas. My parents, due to their age and ever-growing feebleness, went outside the house very little, with the exception of going to a rerun of *One Flew Over the Cuckoo's Nest* at Lee's suggestion. So I bought the presents. Among other things, I got Mom a book on soap operas, Dad a World Almanac, and Lee, *A Brief History of Time* by Stephen Hawking.

After everyone opened their gifts just before supper on Christmas day, Lee retrieved his ones for me. The first was a paint-by-number picture of a horse by a fence that he had made at Norwood in occupational therapy. The second and third ones were books he must have found around my parents' house at the last minute: an old accounting text and *The Fountainhead* by Ayn Rand. The pages of the books were dog-eared and stained with coffee. Though the gifts weren't wrapped and hardly amounted to much materially, they were all he had to offer. So they were special to me.

The meal came next. "Mom's made ham, baked potatoes, and corn pudding," Dad announced.

"I'm sure it'll all taste fine," I replied.

"I see the Packers aren't doing very well," Dad continued as we ate. "Looks like they're going to have a losing record."

Lee said nothing and finished his food as quickly as possible. In fact, he said little during the entire meal. Mom just stared at her plate and consumed nothing.

"It's not the Glory Years anymore," Dad went on, again with faux pleasantness.

"Remember when we had Bart Starr, Lee?" I asked.

But he gave no answer, for the days of us tossing the football around in the back yard and pretending to be legends had long since passed.

"When Starr played, we always knew we were going to win," Dad declared.

"May I be excused?" Lee abruptly asked.

"Well, of course, honey," Mom replied.

Lee left the table and went down to the den, then returned, apparently having forgotten something. "Did you get me my cigarettes?" he asked Mom angrily. I thought Dad would blow up given the hostile tone, but he said nothing. Instead, Mom immediately got up, rushed to a cabinet above the refrigerator, and pulled out a carton of Salem menthols. As she handed it to Lee, she anxiously told him she would buy him more the very next time she went to the store.

After we cleared the dishes, I asked Dad why everything had been so phony at dinner and Mom had been so deferential. Did something happen with Lee? I posed the question under my breath, so that my brother could not hear me from the den.

"There was another commitment proceeding this fall called an emergency detention," Dad replied.

"What was the emergency?"

Dad just shook his head and stared at the floor.

Mom then changed the subject and asked in loud, pleasant voice, "Would anyone like some ice cream?" It seemed like an attempt to divert Lee's attention from what we had been discussing, just in case he was listening.

I moved to a seat directly across from Mom. I hadn't gotten a chance to look at her directly since my mind had been so focused on school, but for the first time I noticed she was wearing her hair in bangs. She had never done this before in her entire life. Even in the pictures taken before I was born, her hair was always brushed to the side.

"When did you decide to change your hair?" I asked.

"You might as well tell him," Dad said sharply.

"Just don't worry about it!" Mom replied.

Instead of pushing the point further, I went down to the den to talk to Lee. There he occupied his usual position on the purple couch. I got out a Winston light from my pocket, and he pulled out a Salem. I lit both cigarettes with my Bic lighter.

Lee took a drag and looked at me squarely. "I hit Mom," he said, implying he had done so only once. He then looked down at the coffee table in shame.

I honestly didn't know what to say or do. Perhaps I should have demanded more details from him or lectured him or even punched him out. But he looked so pathetic sitting there, staring at the coffee table and nervously tapping his cigarette on an ashtray. It would be like kicking a skinny, mangy dog that had just bitten me, so I didn't respond at all.

Later during the holiday break, I reconnected with my former roommate, Jon, who was one of the guys from the Penthouse. We decided to visit Lee at his low-income apartment, an independent living arrangement Human Services had put him in.

After my brother let us in, we noticed the place was completely dark, save some ambient light from outside. I asked him if we could turn the lights on, and he indicated that the fixtures did not have functioning bulbs. When I questioned why he had not purchased new ones, he did not respond. Instead, he just sat on the couch and smoked a cigarette in the dark. The tip of it glowed orange every time he inhaled, revealing his unshaven face and unkempt hair.

Jon tried to engage Lee by talking about a Billie Holiday album that we could see on the coffee table with the assistance of a nearby streetlight. He even offered him a joint to get him to open up, but my brother declined and continued smoking his cigarette, then another, and another. Around us, we could see what appeared to be notebook pages, books, over-filled ashtrays, and cigarette butts and general garbage on the floor, though we couldn't be sure of the identity of such items in the dark. After about thirty minutes of trying to get Lee to open up and not getting a response, we decided to leave.

On the way back to my parents' house, Jon said, "Wow, I knew your brother had mental issues, but I didn't realize how bad they were. He just sat in the dark the whole time and hardly said a word. It was really creepy, man."

In the past I had told Jon about Lee, but I wasn't sure he completely comprehended the problem, nor did any of my other friends. Now he seemed to get it, or at least part of it: my brother had a condition that drew him so inward that he could care less about sitting in the dark in his own apartment, even in the presence of guests who had come to see him.

The next day I bought Lee some light bulbs and took them to his place. I knocked on the door, but he wasn't home. Since the door was unlocked, I opened it and put the light-bulb box on his kitchen table. Perhaps I should have just left them outside the door, but I didn't think it mattered. I came back later and took him to my parents' for supper. Afterwards, I told him more about law school. He seemed to enjoy my description of what it was like, but then without warning switched topics. "I want my property reassembled," he said firmly.

"What are you talking about?" I asked.

Lee did not respond, but I figured it had something to do with my going into his apartment to leave the light bulbs. I had invaded his space, regardless of my good intentions. From his perspective, I had done the same thing when I took the shotgun shells and the writings from his room at the Death House in 1976. He must have never gotten over it.

"All right, I admit I went into your apartment without you being there," I said. "But I didn't take anything. I just left you some light bulbs because your place was dark, man."

Lee just stared at the floor. I wondered if he had even heard me.

"Look, I'm sorry, okay?"

Lee nodded, then went back to the subject of law school and asked me to identify my courses. I answered Property, Contracts, Civil Procedure, Torts, Legal Writing, and Constitutional Law. In the middle of my response, he glared at me and asked pointedly, "Have you learned anything about *trusts*?"

"A little in Property, but most of that comes in our second year."

"Uh huh," he replied as though he didn't believe me.

Likely this involved the same paranoid thinking that Mom had pursued with Aunt Mell and the tapestry years before. He must have thought I was plotting to deprive him of his share of my parents' estate through a trust. Actually, setting up one would have been appropriate, given his irrational business schemes and general irresponsibility. In fact, his having access to money might have even harmed him. But I knew little about trusts and frankly wanted to stay out of it.

Rather than get into it with him on this topic, I decided to move onto something else. I asked him if Bradley and the Black Mafia still bothered him.

Lee shook his head no and responded with something very cryptic: "I'm protected on all sides."

As bizarre as this reply was, I tried to apply it to my own situation. "Am I ever going to feel protected on all sides?" I asked myself. "Not in a million years," I responded. "There's just too much riding on me."

27

Shame

The phone rang at my Mom and Dad's house about twenty times when I called to let them know about my law school graduation ceremony. Sometimes it took Mom a while to answer, as she had to negotiate her way from one part of the house to another with her bum leg. Her advancing age made the problem even worse. As for Dad, he never answered calls. He had lost some of his hearing. In addition, the ringer on the phone in his office upstairs didn't work properly, and he had never bothered to get it fixed.

I probably should have called sooner, but I had too much on my mind with exams and didn't get around to it until the last minute. Besides, I was unsure whether my parents wanted to attend my graduation because they rarely ventured out of their routine, much less travelled far from home. Mom stayed at the house unless she went to the grocery store, and Dad left only when he went to the Emeritus Professor Office at the university.

By now I lived in a bungalow in Louisville's Clifton neighborhood with a doctoral student in theology, a medical student, and a down-on-his-luck unemployed guy who occasionally paid rent using questionable sources of income. He claimed he was a Vietnam veteran. I say "claimed" because his current age would have made him sixteen during that war.

The house had no air conditioning, and in early May the weather in Louisville had already turned hot and humid. Despite weekly spraying of insecticide, cockroaches were everywhere, even inside the kitchen clock that had stopped functioning due to a nest they built in it. Since the heat would continue to be insufferable that summer, I had already set up a study table in the cellar for my bar exam prep. In addition to being cooler, there would be fewer cockroaches down there, thanks to the skinks that occupied the walls in that part of the house.

Mom finally answered the phone with a dreary hello.

"Hi, it's Kenny."

"Oh my goodness…we haven't heard from you in so long."

"Been studying for exams. You know. Law school."

"Is everything all right?" Mom asked.

"Yeah. Pretty tired, though."

"Hold on. I'll get Daddy. Merl!"

After a few minutes I could hear him pick up. We exchanged greetings, and I told him about how happy I was to be done with law school. Then I mentioned the graduation date.

"May ninth? Why that's next week," Dad replied.

"Sorry for the short notice, but I was wondering if you and Mom wanted to come to the ceremony."

"In Louisville?"

"Yeah. Where else would it be?"

"But how are we going to get down there?" Dad asked.

"We could drive…but I can't manage the highway," Mom said, pausing after the first phrase before continuing to the second.

"Well, I'm not going to drive all the way down to Louisville, and that's all there is to it," Dad said. "I'm seventy-six years old!"

"Oh, Merl."

"You'll just have to fly, and I'll take the bus!"

"Not sure if that'll work," I replied, thinking about the complications of my feeble mother trying to negotiate several busy airports. "How 'bout I come up there, drive you down here, take you back to Wisconsin after the ceremony, then return to Louisville?"

"But that would involve four trips," Mom said.

"That's okay. I'll make it."

"Are you sure?"

"Yeah."

"Well…if you are willing."

"What about Lee?" I asked.

"We haven't heard from him lately," Dad replied.

"I guess that settles it then," I said. "He's not coming."

"But he's never been to any of your graduations," Mom pleaded.

"I'm not sure it would be a good idea for him to come. He might do something in the car on the way down or back," I said. "And where would he stay? You two can use my bed, and I can sleep on the couch, but otherwise there won't be enough room. Besides, my roommates don't know what he's like. And then there are my classmates. They won't understand, and I won't have a chance to tell them."

Mom sighed. "It seems like you're making excuses."

"Maybe so, but that doesn't mean the excuses aren't valid."

"What's the real reason, Kenny?" she then asked.

I paused, not knowing what to say. "I-I guess it's because I'm embarrassed about him."

"You shouldn't feel that way…since he's done so much for you."

"Honey, just stop it!" Dad said.

"Look, Mom, he isn't around," I replied. "So why make an issue of it?"

"Because he's your brother!"

Graduation went pretty smoothly, and I made the trip between Kentucky and Wisconsin multiple times so my parents could come.

After the bar exam that summer, I stayed at my parents' house while awaiting the results, which didn't come back until late October. I didn't particularly like being there, since by then Lee was home. Most of the time, I hung out with Mark McKinney and my college friends and stayed away. I probably should have included my brother and brought him along, but I was just too ashamed of him. I do remember one conversation I had with him at the house though that is definitely worth repeating.

Lee had a filed a number of law suits against institutions where he had been incarcerated. He asked me to look at a federal judge's written decision on one of them in which he claimed he had been denied his right to date women. The rules of the place prohibited male patients from dating female ones and vice versa. He claimed this deprived him of a liberty interest without due process in violation of the 14ᵗʰ Amendment to the Constitution and Section 1983 of the Civil Rights Act. The judge actually took the suit seriously and almost denied the motion to dismiss. But eventually she caved, noting that Lee hadn't actually provided the names of any specific women at the facility who had agreed to date him. I'm sure the suit was very entertaining to Lee, but it was upsetting to me. *Now he's filing frivolous law suits, for Christ sake*, I thought. *Is there anything else he can do to drag us through the mud?*

The second decision Lee asked me to review dismissed a law suit he had filed against Sentry Insurance and its CEO, John Joanis. Sentry was a major employer in Stevens Point, and Lee had applied for a job there. Needless to say he was not hired. So he claimed the company had discriminated against him in violation of the Americans with Disabilities Act of 1980. Of course, this was absurd, as he had no qualifications, let alone a favorable employment history. Yet I might be looking for a job there as a lawyer. With my law review experience, maybe the company's legal department would consider me. Further, the position would be in my hometown, an ideal situation for me.

After looking at both cases, I confronted Lee about them in the den. "I understand being forced to stay in a hospital is a pain and boring at times, but couldn't you have found something better to do with your time than file frivolous lawsuits?"

"What do you mean?"

"Well, the dating case was one thing, but the employment discrimination suit was another. You have no experience or training in that area and no work history."

"They should have at least considered me, and they didn't because I'm mentally ill."

"Okay, but there is one slight problem."

"What's that?"

"I just graduated from law school and have no job. Did you ever stop and think I might be able to get one at Sentry?"

"No."

"Did you ever consider that since you sued the CEO of that company, they would automatically not hire me?"

My brother looked down at the coffee table. For several minutes he did not respond. Realizing I had hurt him, I finally said, "Look, Lee, Sentry may not have had an opening anyway. So just forget it."

"Sorry, Kenny. I didn't mean to hurt your job prospects."

"We all make mistakes. Just try to be a little more careful, okay?"

But Lee didn't do that. In total, he filed thirteen law suits all of which were dismissed. His defendants included: Portage County Human Services; the 51.42 Mental Health Board; the Department of Vocational Rehabilitation; the State Public Defender's Office; the State of Wisconsin; the University of Wisconsin; the United States of America; and Dad. Interestingly enough, he did not sue me. Apparently, I had been given favored nation status, a small consolation in the grand scheme of things.

Fortunately, Lee's suit against Sentry Insurance and John Joanis didn't affect me, as I got hired at the Louisville Public Defender's Office, where I had interned during law school. I was glad to get a job in the city where I had lived for three years and at an office with which I was familiar. The job also had the benefit of keeping me far away from my family and Lee. As bad as that sounds, it was part of the calculus. You see, if they were out of sight, I could keep them out of mind.

I started at the PD's Office in December of 1982. My first assignment was juvenile court. Most of my clients came from two impoverished neighborhoods: the West End, which was mostly black, and the Portland neighborhood, which was mostly white. Nearly all my juvenile defendants were male and came from fatherless homes. Many had committed armed robberies, assaults involving firearms, rapes, and attempted murders. The ones who weren't waived to adult court ended up in Camp, and Camp was no summer resort. It was a generic term for a system of locked institutions around the state that used behavior-modification techniques, some good and some not so good. They were successful in turning kids into yes-sir-no-sir automatons. It was difficult to believe, when I visited my clients in such facilities, that they had committed serious felonies since they were so respectful and well behaved. But after they went back to the same desolated and poverty-stricken homes from which they came and caught a new charge, my naïve attitude about them took a course correction.

The white Portland neighborhood had shot-gun-style homes with no garages, vacant lots overgrown with vegetation, and crumbling sidewalks. The businesses, aside from the paint factory, catered to the poor: dollar stores, plasma centers, and drive-thru liquors. Every shop had bars on its windows, and some had fences topped by razor wire. At night, it was best not to travel in that area on foot unless you had a gun. Most of my clients from there were "paint heads," so called because they used paint to get high rather than drugs. They would spray it in a sock or a paper bag and inhale it. Trouble was it lowered their IQ, not to mention their impulse control, which in turn caused them to become violent.

The major benefit I received from working in juvenile was

that it gave me perspective on Lee and offered a healing process of sorts. However dysfunctional and violent my background had been growing up, it was not as bad as that of my clients. I may have had it worse than a lot kids my age, but at least I had two parents who gave a damn and expected me to achieve something besides a delinquency or criminal charge. Second, my family experience enabled me to empathize with my clients. I knew what it was like to feel short changed, live in fear, not want to go home, and long for escape from ugly trappings. In short, my background made me a better lawyer.

After work one day in juvenile, I decided to go to the local courthouse watering hole known as Legal Street, which was conveniently located below the Public Defender's Office. There I met up with my supervisor, a guy named Bill Carley. Bill had for many years dealt with adult criminal cases and defended more than his share of ones involving the death penalty—too many, in fact. Eventually, the chief public defender put him in juvenile for an extended mental health break that turned into a permanent one.

"Kenny Farmer," Bill said as I strolled up to the bar. "How the hell are ya? Did you kick some ass today?"

"Not really."

"Want a drink?"

"A rum and Coke maybe."

The seasoned public defender beckoned the bartender with his hand, then turned back to me and asked, "So are you learning a lot?"

"Mainly about kids with shit backgrounds," I replied glumly.

"Someday one might face the chair, so mind them well."

"You've had some clients like that, right?"

Bill handed me my drink. "A few."

"What was it like?"

"Let's not talk about it."

I frowned and swallowed some of my drink.

"Look, if you want to learn about stuff like that, don't talk to me. Talk to Goyette."

Dan Goyette was the head public defender. He had hired me, and I knew him well.

"He handles the worst of the worst, man, murder cases nobody wants. Usually, they involve insanity or mental incompetency defenses."

Bill ran down a list of Goyette's clients, every one of whom I had heard about in the news at one time or another as they were so notorious. Among them was a mentally ill man who stabbed his parents to death and left a grisly scene at their home. That case made me think about Lee doing the same thing to Mom and Dad. Another concerned a paranoid schizophrenic who walked into Lincoln Federal Bank in downtown Louisville wearing a stove-pipe hat due to an obsession with Abraham Lincoln. Once inside he randomly shot and killed multiple patrons with a pistol. This brought me back to the day Lee had the shotgun at the rooming house. He could have done something similar to his roommates. What was weird about this conversation was I never mentioned my brother to Bill, though this would have been the perfect opportunity. In fact, I never told anyone in the office about him, for I wanted to keep my prior life completely behind me.

During the rest of my time in juvenile, I tried to do some dating, which was difficult for me, for I was hopelessly behind in that department. In high school, I hardly dated at all, as I suffered from delayed puberty. I don't think my voice started changing until I was nearly eighteen, and I never hit a growth spurt until I was well into college. I am not sure why this delay occurred. My suspicion is it had to do with the stress I endured as a result of Lee, the worst of which occurred in my early teens. It could also have been a medical problem, but I never found out, as Mom refused to send me to a doctor about it. Regardless of the reason, I lacked confidence as a result. By the time I graduated from law school, I had had no serious relationships, and I didn't even attempt to have one while pursuing my legal studies because I figured it would disrupt them. So at a time when most people my age were already married, I was just starting to date.

Legal Street didn't work for me when it came to women despite the fact Bill Carley was always trying to set me up there. All I did was meet people from work, and I really didn't feel like getting involved with them for that very reason. Things changed for me when a fellow public defender told me he had met some eligible females at a Jaycees meeting. So I went to one, even though I had absolutely no interest in this organization. In time, I hooked up with a woman from that group named Tina. She was an attractive brunette, who worked in sales. We did the dinner thing, the party thing, and the movie thing, and we seemed to get along fine.

I remember showing a photo of her to my parents at Christmas. Prior to this time, I had a hang up about discussing women with them, though this really didn't matter, as I never had a steady relationship anyway. But I did want to overcome this fixation, so one night at dinner I just plopped the photo of Tina on the kitchen table after abruptly announcing I had a girlfriend. My parents had very little reaction one way or another. So I took the photo down to Lee, who was in the den on the purple couch. I wanted to rebut his earlier accusation that I was a momma's boy, but when I put the photo on the coffee table, he too had no reaction, which was strange since he was the one who had made such a big deal over my not having a girlfriend in the first place.

On New Year's Eve that year, Tina and I and another couple went out to eat at a five-star restaurant in Louisville. I had never been to an eating establishment where everything was ordered á la carte and the waiters opened wine bottles tableside. I was pretty much a hick. Despite feeling out of place, I truly enjoyed myself, as did Tina.

Unfortunately, this was last time I ever saw her. Without warning or explanation, she ghosted me and the relationship died away.

I ruminated over the loss of Tina for several weeks. Eventually, I decided to pursue counseling over this and other issues I had with my family. A social worker from juvie gave me the name of a therapist. I don't remember much about the guy, but I do recall several sessions with him that offered some valuable insight into my situation, particularly in reference to my efforts to distance myself from Lee and my family. In our first conversation, I mentioned the feelings of rejection I had over Tina and women in general. I'll never forget his response. He asked, "How will you know when your problem is solved?"

I shifted in my chair and responded, "When women are attracted to me, I guess."

The therapist nodded as he took in my answer, then looked up at me. "How will you know when that has happened?"

"When they give me as much attention as I give them."

"How will you know that?"

"When they call me or initiate a conversation."

The therapist repeatedly asked the same type of question on all my struggles whether they had to do with this issue or Lee. At the end of the litany, he observed the following: "So often in life we dwell on problems, but we hardly ever talk about solutions. By knowing when a problem is solved, we are better able to understand that problem and do the things necessary to set it aside. If you think in terms of solutions, you will find them. But if you think only in terms of problems, you will find them instead."

After the session, I listed on a sheet of paper all my problems. Under each one, I wrote the solution and precisely what it would look like. The list included having a normal family someday and in general having a grounded existence. In that moment of reflection, I advanced my personal development the most I had ever done in my life.

In one of my last sessions with the therapist, I asked him what, in his opinion, I was doing wrong with women since none of my relationships worked out, including the one with Tina. By then he had learned quite a bit about me. "Do you ever mention your family to the people you date?" he asked bluntly.

"I just tell them my parents live in Wisconsin and that I go back there once in a while."

"That sounds strange, Ken. Most people talk about their family in more detail once a relationship develops."

"Well, I don't."

"Even if you are serious about someone?"

"Absolutely. If I told someone I dated about Lee or my family, she would want nothing to do with me."

The therapist frowned and asked me to tell him why I felt so strongly.

"Look, my house growing up was like *The Munsters,*" you know the TV show.

"And which character were you, Ken?"

"Marilyn, the normal one," I replied.

"I'm beginning to understand now. You are embarrassed about your family because it is a little different."

"A little? It was worse than that."

"Tell me about that. What was it like?"

"If I saw my brother or my parents on the street in public, I would cross to the other side to avoid talking to them and being seen with them."

The therapist cleared his throat. Perhaps he was shocked by my answer. "I appreciate your honesty, Ken, but I do have an observation about this."

"What's that?"

"You need to get over your shame. By not even mentioning your family to a girlfriend or introducing them to her, you give the impression you aren't serious."

"Better that than be humiliated."

After several seconds of awkward silence, the therapist asked, "So what are your intentions about returning to Wisconsin? Do you plan on doing that soon or are you going to stay on the other side of the street the rest of your life?"

"One of these days I'll go back, I guess."

"Do you ever tell your dates that?"

"Come to think of it, I do sometimes."

"So let me get this straight. You don't tell the women in your life much about your family, but you also tell them you might return to Wisconsin."

"Yeah, so what's the big deal?"

"Well, it's kind of like you're camping out, Ken."

"Camping out?"

"Yes. Here today and gone tomorrow."

"And not available in between?"

"I'm afraid so, my friend."

Things began to crystallize for me. I had distanced myself from my family and Lee because I was ashamed of them. This in turn made me appear like I was unavailable to women and averse to commitment. "So this is the problem, but how will I know when it is solved?" I asked myself. "When I no longer camp out," I answered. "And how will I know when this has occurred?" "When I finally can introduce a woman I am dating to my family without pain or embarrassment," I told myself.

I filed away for future reference what I learned in therapy. In the meantime, I buried myself in my work. Ironically, my next assignment at the PD's office was the Mental Health Division, where I defended people who faced commitment.

I could have easily gotten out of the transfer, given my background, but I said nothing to my boss about it. I also really wanted to do commitment cases. I felt guilty about participating in my brother's and by zealously representing people like him in court, perhaps I could compensate for such guilt. My assignment in mental health lasted six months, and I represented hundreds of mentally ill people. I can't go into the individual cases, because the rules of ethics and confidentiality preclude me from doing so, but I can talk about my experiences in general terms.

What I remember the most about commitment cases was doing jury selection. Typically in this process, lawyers and their clients sit at a table while facing prospective jurors and take turns asking them questions designed to reveal their biases. If a serious one is exposed, a lawyer can request a juror be struck for cause by the judge. In addition, even if the bias doesn't arise to this level, the lawyer can still use the information learned in exercising a fixed number of peremptory strikes that each side gets. A preemptory strike is one that requires no justification.

In this part of a commitment trial, I would always ask if any juror had an experience with mental illness, either they themselves or a family member. I did this because I didn't want anyone on the jury to be sympathetic to the prosecution. Perhaps a juror had tried to commit someone in the past and had a tough time at it and would be more prone to vote for commitment, someone like me. Since I was opposing commitment as a defense attorney, I didn't want such a person on the jury.

In the eleven jury trials I had in the mental health unit, not one person ever raised his or her hand reference my question on having a personal experience with mental illness. This was the case despite the fact the incidence of the disease was quite high. To me this provided perfect evidence of the stigma associated with the problem. If I had asked prospective jurors if they or someone in their family had heart disease or cancer, many of them would have responded affirmatively. This was not the case when it came to mental illness.

Later in my lawyer life, I mentioned this to a colleague whose specialty was prosecution of commitment cases. He said that he had had the same experience earlier in his career, but he also noted that over several decades, more and more prospective jurors would raise their hands and open up about the subject. In fact, he indicated that today the vast majority of them raise their hands. Things have definitely changed for the better on the problems of stigma and shame, but we still have a long ways to go.

After my six-month stint in the Mental Health Division, I went to the adult unit. The name seemed appropriate, for that was where a public defender grew up. We handled over a thousand cases a year per lawyer, and at any given time we each had about two hundred pending. From the middle of 1984 to the end of 1986, I defended hundreds of felonies, including four in which the charge was murder. Two of the murder cases went to trial, one involving the death penalty and one not.

As you can well imagine, there was not much time for a social life in the adult unit, save an occasional Happy Hour at Legal Street. There were too many cases and too many trials. I didn't have a girlfriend or pursue one. As a result, I didn't get a chance to apply what I had learned in therapy about camping out or make more progress on the issue of shame with respect to my brother.

In February of 1986, I turned thirty, which for me was a depressing rite of passage. I had done well in school and in my job, but nothing else, and found myself in a Catch-22 pattern. In order to succeed in my career, I had to devote a great deal of time to it, but in order to succeed socially I had to spend a lot of time doing that. Yet if I spent time doing social things, I may not be as successful in my career, in which case I wouldn't be respected socially.

Just before I went home from work on my actual birthday, a friend of mine at the office and his fiancée invited me over for dinner. He lived in a second-floor flat on the near eastside of Louisville. I didn't have anything else planned, nor did I have much on my calendar of significance the next day. So I agreed.

After climbing the stairs and knocking on the door, I was met with a chorus of people yelling, "Surprise!" Before me were eight co-workers, all bearing broad smiles. I hadn't had a real birthday party since Mom had broken out the animal-patterned plastic table-cloth when I was seven. The party my colleagues threw wasn't a big one, mind you—just cake, appetizers, and a few gag gifts. But at the end of it, my eyes welled up as I thanked everyone.

Later that year, the couple who did the surprise birthday party got married, and the groom asked me to stand up in the wedding. I wasn't the best man, but at least I was a groomsman. It was a great honor, one that I never had before or since. You might think such an experience would have encouraged me to stay in Louisville. Instead it made me think about getting on with my own life. I grew up in Wisconsin and always wanted to return. Now it was the time to do so and try less camping out.

By Christmas of 1986, my friend Jon, who was also a lawyer by now, told me there was an opening at a District Attorney's office in Manitowoc, Wisconsin, a town about a hundred miles east of Stevens Point. I applied for the position and got the job.

28

Distancing Light

My move to Manitowoc and the "dark side" in early 1987 shocked me more than I thought it would. As a prosecutor, I had to fix holes in a dike versus poke them. I now had the burden of proof beyond a reasonable doubt and the responsibility of convincing all twelve jurors of guilt. I could no longer appeal and get a new trial if a judge made a mistake, for even if I had succeeded, the defendant could not be tried again given the double jeopardy clause of the Constitution. Further, I was expected to win all the time, versus once in a while as a public defender. Simply put, I was no longer the underdog.

The change in my physical surroundings was also significant. Louisville was a big city beset by big city problems: poverty, urban blight, neighborhoods that needed to be avoided even in the day, muggings, armed robberies, torture crimes, murders, and forcible rapes. Don't get me wrong. The city had many safe areas and plenty to offer, but being a public defender heightened my awareness of society's underbelly. When I lived in Louisville, I would actually show out-of-town guests the location of sicko crimes our office defended versus historical sites or museums. That's how much my job affected me.

Manitowoc, by contrast, had about 35,000 people. I worked in an office only having three attorneys and a couple of secretaries versus a large staff. Instead of taking the bus through crappy areas where a murder or an unusually sordid offense had occurred, I drove to work while relishing a view of Lake Michigan. It took me ten minutes versus forty-five, and I even got a free parking space, something unheard of in Louisville. The biggest case I dealt with involved a series of home break-ins in which a gang of juveniles stole liquor. I spent the majority of my time prosecuting drunk-driving, operating-after-revocation, speeding, truck-regulation, and salmon-snagging offenses. I laughed when I had to speak to a farmer about his ticket for leaving mud on a highway.

About three months into my employment at the Manitowoc DA's Office, I received a case that was a little different than those I had prosecuted so far. I had just come to work and hadn't even hung up my jacket before I noticed a new file on my desk. Inside it was an involuntary commitment petition.

Since I had done such cases as a public defender, I didn't think it would be a problem and breathed easily as I read the facts: a mid-twenties white male going through a major bout of dysthymia had repeatedly threatened to commit suicide. Perhaps I could see to it that his family's interest would not be minimized in the way ours had been in Lee's first commitment attempt. But as I reviewed the statutes, I couldn't get my mind off my brother's case. The number of petitioners required, for example, got me thinking about Mom not wanting to sign various commitment petitions and our desperate attempts to find other signatories as a result. I could hear her crying at the dinner table, "You'll ruin him!" and Lee yelling in court, "I hate you!"

The problem got worse when I saw phrases in the law like "recent overt act or threat" and "imminent dangerousness," language not used in Kentucky commitments. The words reminded me of Lee's violence—the beatings of my parents, the assault of the nurse, his screaming "She's the one" in the kitchen, the tennis-racket incident, the hiding of the knives, and the shotgun discovery.

Such an emotional flashback didn't happen to me when I worked in the mental health unit in Louisville. For one thing, the system was procedurally different. For another, I was able to put distance between myself and Lee's case, both temporally and physically. That occurred years ago and 550 miles away, I would tell myself. But now I was far closer and distancing was more difficult.

Somehow I managed to represent the State and get the guy committed after a jury trial. Fortunately, I didn't get assigned another case like that as a prosecutor. If I had, I probably would have declined to do it. Even though I was nearer to Lee and my family than I had been in Kentucky, I still needed space. I call this distancing light: close enough to be available if needed by my family, but not too close.

After I moved to Manitowoc, Portage County Human Services put my brother in the Winnebago Mental Health Institute near Oshkosh, Wisconsin. Mom asked me to see him, and since the facility was only sixty miles from where I worked and half way to Stevens Point, I decided to visit him on my way home.

The place was built in 1873 on Lake Winnebago, hence its name. One of the few nineteenth-century psychiatric facilities left in the country, its original building was an old-style asylum called the Northern State Hospital for the Insane. It warehoused anywhere from 500 to 1000 patients during the years of high hospitalization of the mentally ill. The old building was eventually demolished in the sixties and replaced by a series of smaller, more modern units. By the time my brother went there and community-based treatment had gained currency, the population at Winnebago had been reduced to a couple hundred.

Upon my arrival, I looked around and was impressed by the facility. Its grounds felt like a large lakeside park with many areas to walk, mature trees, and manicured lawns. I found Lee's unit quickly, and the staff permitted him to go with me and roam around outside without restriction.

Our conversation was easier than in the den at home. When I asked a question, he responded appropriately and did not ignore me or travel to a different world. His appearance seemed better too, with his clothes clean, hair organized, and teeth brushed. Perhaps he was up to blood level on his meds, having been supervised in a structured setting.

At the same time I knew from professional experience that institutionalization, whether for juveniles or the mentally ill, often improved a person's condition superficially. I remembered how polite my delinquent clients had become, for example, only to return to serious crime once released. The real test for Lee was not his ability to do well while confined, but rather his performance once out. And in that regard, he had a poor track record.

"Why did they hospitalize you this time?" I asked him as we strolled about.

"They got sick of me," he replied. "One failure after another in independent living."

"Maybe relapse is a better way of putting it. Ever consider that?"

"Yeah, relapse," Lee said, smiling at the euphemism.

"How long will you be here?"

"They gave me six months." He spoke of his institutionalization as if it were a sentence. Maybe he was right.

"Have you been marking your time on the wall of your cell?" I asked.

"No, Kenny," Lee replied.

We continued making our way around, but in silence. Finally, my brother asked: "So what brought you back from Kentucky?"

"I guess I thought it would be better to be closer to home. Home is home, after all." I didn't go into my struggles with camping out, for with Lee I always tried to evince an image of having my act together. Ever since the day he demanded I make something of myself at his card table in his room at our house on Lorraine

Street, I projected perfection whenever I was around him since I carried not only my own banner but his as well.

"Where are you working now?" he next asked.

"At the prosecutor's office in Manitowoc."

"Oh, so you're one of them."

"Yeah, but I'm hardly the enemy."

"But you're part of the structure that put me here."

I didn't want to argue with him and didn't take the bait. "So why don't you take your meds when you're on the outside? Better that than stay in places like this, right?"

"Because I want to control my own life and not turn it over to somebody else."

"I wouldn't take it so personally, Lee. You just have some messed up brain disease, the same as cancer or another medical condition. You would take drugs for them, right?"

"You have your lines down well, don't you?"

I shrugged. After we walked further, we sat on a bench and listened to the birds and the rustle of the wind through the trees. It reminded me of the time we'd spent together in the woods as kids in Erlanger, when we'd walk home from school together, when he told me about snapping turtles and snakes, and when he took care of me. Our roles had long since reversed, but I yearned for the day things would change back. "So how do you occupy your time here?" I finally asked, bringing things back to reality.

"I'm writing an autobiography."

"Really. What's it called?"

"Research."

"W-why do you call it that?"

"Because my whole life has been an investigation."

On this note, we returned to Lee's unit. He said he didn't want to be late for fear he would lose points in the behavior-mod system. We shook hands at least, and he thanked me for stopping by. I don't think my brother ever wrote his book, but as I travelled to my parents' house from Winnebago, I pondered the concept of "*Research.*" *In a way that is what we all do,* I thought: *look for answers that never seem to come.*

As a child I stayed at friends' houses in order to avoid my own. I did this as long as possible, turning play days into play nights and play weekends. This pattern of avoidance continued long after my formative years—in college, in law school, and even after I moved back to Wisconsin from Louisville. I could count on one hand the number of nights I stayed in my room at my parents' house following my return.

Curiously enough, nothing had changed in it as the years passed by. The bed was in same place and made up with the same bedspread. The desk had the same books atop it, and the dresser the same accoutrements, though years of dust and cobwebs had accumulated on them. Sadly, my parents never ventured into my room, not even to clean it. It was as if they didn't want to disturb anything just in case I moved back. Yet I never did.

Whenever I was in Stevens Point I stayed with a friend named Dean, sometimes at his apartment and sometimes at his parents' house, where he lived when he became unemployed. I had met Dean in the student union at UWSP during college. We had a lot in common. We enjoyed sports, had similar majors, wanted to go to law school, and sometimes partied together too much. We went to Las Vegas after my first year of law school. While he didn't go on to law school after college, he unselfishly praised my efforts to do so and was always excited to hear about my career.

When I came to Stevens Point to visit, the routine was the same. I would pick up Lee from the mental hospital, a group home, or a low-income apartment and drive him to my parents'. We would have dinner and open the presents if it was Christmas. After a short time, Lee would march up from the den to the kitchen and abruptly state, "I want to go back now." I would then drive him to his current residence, breathe a sigh of relief, and return to Dean's.

Often Dean and I would watch football and basketball together on TV. After I returned to Wisconsin from Louisville, we would attend the local college football games, one of which I remember well. We were losing, and I had grown frustrated and started whining about the poor quality of play.

"On offense we don't block, and on defense we don't tackle," I told Dean angrily.

"Look, they're not the Packers!"

"It's still college football, and they need to play better."

"You're used to watching bigger time sports and expect too much."

"But I want my teams to win, not suck."

"Why are you so negative all the time?"

"I'm *not* negative. I'm just pointing out the facts. We suck!"

Dean turned his head away from me and looked across the playing field. "You're the one who sucks."

"What?"

"You do a lot of things I just don't understand."

"What do you mean?"

"Like how often you stay at my house. My parents were wondering about that, you know."

"I thought it was okay."

"Whatever. It's just strange that you never sleep at your own home."

"If you thought that was a problem, you should have said so," I replied.

"Yeah, right."

"Okay, forget it then. I'll go somewhere else."

The argument clouded the rest of the game. Afterward, I dropped Dean off and stayed at my parents' the rest of the weekend, something unheard of for me. During this time, I felt horribly guilty. Mom had cautioned me about hanging around other people's homes too long. Her words still echoed in my head: "Don't wear out your welcome," and "don't be a burden."

Two weekends later, Dean's parents invited me over for dinner. He and I went about our business together as if there had been no falling out. When I was alone in the kitchen with his mom, however, she and I had a heart-to-heart conversation.

"You boys have become good friends over the years," she started off.

"True enough."

"I want you to continue that."

"So do I."

"I know the two of you had an argument at a ballgame a few weeks ago, but try not to let it ruin your friendship. Sometimes people say things that are hurtful and really don't mean them."

"True."

"You are like a brother to Dean," she said. "And a son to me."

I nodded.

"I don't completely understand your family situation, but I know it has been difficult for you."

"I could tell you more, but—"

"You don't need to explain, Ken," Dean's mom said, putting her hand atop mine. "I get it."

I started to choke up.

"Just remember one thing, if you don't mind my saying."

"What's that?"

"If you ever need a place to stay, no matter the reason, you are always welcome here."

In February of 1988, I got a job as a prosecutor at the Dane County District Attorney's Office in Madison. Though I liked Manitowoc, the town wasn't very big, and I didn't have many opportunities for dating. For a while, I didn't go out with anyone in Madison, either. But then I met someone through a case I had. She worked in law enforcement. Divorced, she had two kids and a dog. I'll say her name is Barb, though that is not her name.

At first we lived together at a farmhouse fifteen miles outside of Madison, but after several months I purchased a house near Oregon, a bedroom community south of Madison. She and her dog and her kids moved in with me. We had a decent relationship at first, the details of which have little to do with Lee, so I won't describe them. The day that marked the beginning of the end of our time together had everything to do with him, however.

I had just returned from work, and Barb was seated on the couch in the family room. She didn't seem happy. "Uh, a woman called and asked for you," she said.

"A woman? I'm not involved with anyone except you."

"No, no, it was an older lady."

I immediately knew it was Mom, as she was the only elderly woman who had my phone number. The trouble was I had been living with Barb for almost a year and hadn't told my parents about her.

I called Mom back, and she said a young woman had answered when she called. I tried to explain, but she interrupted me and said, "Well, I don't approve!" Then she abruptly hung up.

"So who was it?" Barb asked.

"My mom."

"You mentioned your parents lived in Stevens Point, but I never got to meet them. You said you had a brother too, but you never introduced me to him, either."

"I didn't get around to it, I guess. Someday maybe."

"And when is that going to be? Sometime in the next decade?"

I had a sickening feeling in the pit of my gut. I had done many things with Barb's parents; heck, we even travelled across the country together. And yet I couldn't imagine her meeting Mom and Dad, much less Lee. So I faced a dilemma. If I didn't introduce her to my family, I would risk jeopardizing our relationship. But if I did, I would feel shame. In the end, I chose the first alternative.

Eventually, Barb and I broke up. While this was not the specific reason our relationship failed, I believe that my inability to introduce her to my parents didn't help. Obviously, "distancing light" wasn't working for me, and I was still camping out.

29

Acceptance

In the spring of 1988, my parents finished building a small home for Lee on an adjacent lot they owned. They called it, "The House Down the Hill," since relative to their place that was exactly where it stood. They built it so they could keep an eye on him, and at the same time, protect themselves from his assaultive behavior. If he wasn't at their house, there would be less chance something could go wrong, and if he needed anything, he was not far away. It was my parents' way of "distancing light."

The mental health authorities supported this venture, as my brother could be supervised without taking up a slot in their system. I believe they may have even paid my father rent using Lee's social security money, though I am not entirely sure. Even if this didn't happen, my parents would have paid for it anyway, since it would give him a sense of independence, not to mention more personal space than at a group home or halfway house. Thus, in many respects this was a win-win for all involved.

Physically, The House Down the Hill was a prefab and nothing special. I doubt Dad spent much money on it. It had a garage, a living room, a dinette, a kitchen, and two small bedrooms, but nothing else. Its basement was not finished. It had no curtains or blinds because Mom didn't want to spend any money on them. If I were to guess, I would say it had maybe twelve hundred square feet.

As to my interaction with Lee, nothing changed just because he stayed in a different house. Instead of encouraging me to go to the den to talk with him, Mom would tell me to go to The House

Down the Hill. And just as I did at my parents' house, I would dutifully comply, and he and I would have the same kind of conversations we used to have when he sat across from me on the purple couch.

I remember one such visit well. It occurred when I came home for Christmas in 1988. After trudging through the snow-covered driveway and climbing the stairs to the entrance of the small house, I rang the doorbell. I could see Lee sitting in an easy chair through the living room window. As usual he was smoking a cigarette and staring off into space. He didn't bother answering, though I rang the bell several times. After about five minutes, he let me inside, but only when I started pounding on the door. He barely said hello when I entered and quickly returned to his easy chair and resumed smoking his cigarette.

The living room was a mess of books, papers, and cigarette butts; the kitchen and dinette teemed with dirty dishes and rotting food; and his bedroom was heaped with soiled clothing. Though the place was near my parents' house, its appearance wasn't any different than all the other independent living arrangements my brother had been in. Nothing had really changed.

I earnestly tried to engage Lee in conversation, but I just couldn't reach him. Whether I spoke about work or things we did together in the past, he didn't interact with me. While he exhibited no dramatic symptoms of schizophrenia, such as hallucinations, or carrying on conversations with imaginary people, he continued to have other problems—withdrawal, lack of sociability, and flat affect. He seemed to be somewhere else during the entire visit and simply didn't care if I was even there. As a result, I effectively spent twenty minutes talking to myself, and when I got tired of this solitary exercise, I left. Obviously, The House Down the Hill experiment had failed.

Two days after Christmas, Dad called me at my home near Oregon, and my suspicions were confirmed. "Lee tried to commit suicide," he told me matter-of-factly. "The sheriff's officers found him when he didn't answer our calls."

"How did it happen?"

"He swallowed some pills, I guess."

"Where did they take him?"

"St. Michael's. I assume they pumped his stomach there, but they didn't say."

"Where is he going once he gets out?"

"Norwood," Dad replied with resignation. "After that I have no idea."

In the days succeeding this call, I drove up to Stevens Point. As I did so, I worried if I had set my brother off when I spoke to him at Christmas. Maybe I spent too much time talking about my job, and he felt bad about his lot in life relative to mine. On the other hand, maybe he was just giving in, like a terminal cancer patient. Maybe he was better off dead anyway. Many thoughts entered my brain, and I can't say I was proud of them.

I had supper at my parents' that night. Lee was not there, as he was already in the mental hospital. We went over his involvement in the system: his sporadic response to medication and many placements. By then he had probably been in ten different independent living situations, numerous hospitals, halfway houses, group homes, and programs. Mom, the very person who had opposed treatment in the first place, kept saying that the doctors should try something else, perhaps adjust his meds or put him on a different level of supervision.

During our discussion, I was seated directly across from her at the kitchen table. I knew full well from my professional experience and personal history with my brother that the same result would occur no matter what was done. Deciding to be frank, I looked Mom straight in the eye and asked her, "When are you going to accept the fact that Lee is always going to be mentally ill no matter what is done?"

"Never!" she snapped. She then sobbed. It was the deepest I had ever heard her cry, and I hated myself for having spoken the truth.

Through a large bay window in our living room one day, the summer after Lee's suicide attempt, Dad and I watched Mom in the front yard while she cut the grass. She insisted on having an electric mower because she couldn't pull the starter handle hard enough on a gas-powered one. Neither of us went outside to assist her since we knew from prior experience this would upset her. She limped as she mowed a row of grass, then stopped and grabbed the power cord with her only usable hand and whipped it out of the way so she could mow another row without running over it. The tedious process went on for some time with us just staring at her and not saying a word.

The front yard had a circular driveway. Sometimes people would try to turn their cars around in it, and Mom didn't like this. So she blocked its two entrances with rocks, thereby serving notice to them not to use it. Most of the rocks were the size of grapefruits. Some were larger and very difficult to move with one hand without rolling them on the ground, but somehow she managed.

When she finished blocking the entrances, she put more rocks on the edge of the streets by our lot, this time to warn motorists not to drive on the lawn, even though they had never actually done so. All told, her project took several years, but she did it anyway. If we moved these obstructions in the slightest way, she would get angry. When parking any vehicle, we always used the driveway that went directly to the garage so as to avoid the circular one that she had so meticulously blocked.

After Mom stopped cutting the front lawn that day, she yelled at the neighbors about staying off our property. They had built their house too close to ours, and she was obsessed about it. Dad had bought most of the land that surrounded our house, but didn't buy the lot that the neighbors built their home on. As a result, Mom felt the need to guard the property line that separated our land from theirs, as she had done with all the other property lines at all the other houses we had lived.

With Dad following me, I descended the stairs that led to the foyer and the front door with the intention of going outside and calming Mom down, as I had done so many times in the past. I didn't tell him what I was doing. I didn't have to; he just knew. As I started to open the front door, he grasped my arm in order to gain my attention. "Just let it go," he said calmly.

"But—"

"Look, sometimes she just gets irrational, and there's nothing you can do about it."

I nodded, and we both turned and slowly made our way up the stairs to the living room and resumed what we had been doing before the episode had begun. I had learned something about acceptance that day, and amazingly it came through Dad. Hopefully, I would be able to apply that concept moving forward and not allow the bad characteristics of my family to define me and instead marshal the good.

30

Getting at the Truth

After a couple years at the Dane County District Attorney's Office in Madison, I earned several weeks' paid vacation. I decided to use it on a trip to California since I always wanted to go there but never got the chance. My first cousin B.A. or Boyd Ashby Wise III (son of Uncle Boyd or my mother's brother) lived near San José with his own son, Bryan. B.A was kind enough to allow me to use his home as a base of operations for my exploration of the California Coast and San Francisco. Though he would be on a business trip at the time, Bryan would be around and available to hang out with me.

One morning during my trip, Bryan mentioned he had some letters and other documents pertaining to my mother's side of the family that I might be interested in looking at while he was at work. I was excited about the prospect, so he rummaged through a closet and brought out several large cardboard boxes containing them. "Let me know if you find anything interesting," he said as he marched out the door.

I started going through the boxes immediately. The first thing I noticed was the sheer volume of weekly correspondence that took place in Mom's generation. The letters were yellowed and primarily written in fountain pen, though some were constructed on manual typewriters. They had an old, musty smell, and the dust from them sometimes rubbed off on my fingers. The prose was articulate and flowery, reminding me of a lost art. Much of the subject matter was mundane—a wedding, a birth, an illness, or the day a son or daughter would come home for the holidays.

But one letter from Aunt Mell to Uncle Boyd, written in the late 1930s, caught my undivided attention. "Dear Boyd," it began. "I have devastating news. My doctor has diagnosed me with *paranoid schizophrenia*."

I dropped the letter back into the box and stared at it like it was a piece of spoiled fruit. *Lee's condition may be genetic!* I thought. If true, no one in my family was at fault. There was no judgment or moral responsibility involved, and we could all feel better. Also, since the condition was genetic, it was physical, the same as diabetes or a myriad of other biological maladies. Thus, it might even be curable. Nice and simple, right?

"Not so fast," I told myself. For one thing, I wasn't sure Aunt Mell had schizophrenia. Long after the letter was written, she was able to teach at Illinois State University. This was not consistent with the schizophrenic I knew, who never held a job, much less taught college classes. So I wondered whether my aunt had been misdiagnosed. She also could have had a milder form of the disease or some other diagnosis that had similar symptoms.

If she did have schizophrenia, the next question was whether she got it from a gene, and whether Lee in turn contracted it from a similar gene since the two shared a common ancestor. What about Mom's paranoia? Did she have the same schizophrenic gene, adding even more credence to the theory that Lee's condition was genetic since his line of descent from Mom was direct? What about myself? Why didn't I get schizophrenia? I had the same ancestors. Was I just lucky?

Not to be lost in this analysis were environmental factors that could have contributed to Lee's problem or at least exacerbated it— Mom's irrational anger and paranoia about her relatives stealing things and the neighbors setting foot on her property, Dad's lack of involvement, explosiveness, and physical abuse, and the eccentric and dysfunctional nature of my parents in general.

In the end, I concluded that the riddle regarding a genetic

origin of my brother's schizophrenia could not be solved. The truth was the cause of Lee's mental illness didn't matter anyway. The treatment was the same, and we had to cope with the fallout regardless.

By the mid-1990s, Mom's physical condition had become unmanageable for Dad at home. She could hardly talk. I didn't know if this had to do with the brain condition that caused her paralysis before I was born, or an age-related illness such as Alzheimer's or dementia. Frequent urinary-tract infections also caused her to need assistance in dealing with her bodily functions. More and more often she fell due to issues with balance.

Because she could not make it up and down the stairs any longer, Dad turned the den into a bedroom. Their bed was the hideaway feature of the old purple couch that Lee had sat on during our heart-to heart discussions over the years. While a bathroom existed in that part of the house, it became increasingly difficult for Dad to get Mom there. The bottom line was she had to be put in the Portage County Nursing Home.

For about a year, Dad daily drove to that facility in order to see her. He could only do so during daylight hours, as he could not see well in darkness even with his glasses. He himself was in his eighties. When I visited Mom, he was always there with her. As mean and angry as he had been when I was a kid and as many arguments as Mom and Dad had both at home and in public, he had become a shining example of loyalty, compassion, and rationality.

Obviously, the situation was hard on Mom. She prided herself in being able to walk and do everything others did despite her disability. So when the nursing home confined her to a wheelchair due to the frequent falls, it was difficult to watch her pull herself around using the handrails along the walls. But as was the case with her all her life, she adapted and overcame.

When I was at work one day during this period, I received a call from one of Dad's colleagues. "A friend of your dad's wants to speak you," said the receptionist at the DA's office in Madison. "May I put him through?"

The colleague was a long-standing friend of my father with whom he regularly had lunch, so I immediately took the call, despite a mountain of work on my desk and several trials set for jury the following Monday.

"As you know, Merl and I go to Hardee's for lunch," he said. "I hadn't seen him in a while and couldn't reach him by phone. So I became concerned and went over to your parents' house to check on him."

I cringed at the prospect of bad news. "W-was he alive?"

"Yes, but he was very sick."

"Where is he now?"

"St. Michael's Hospital. I called an ambulance."

"What's wrong with him?"

"A variety of things. They said he had a urinary tract infection. He may have also had a minor stroke."

For years I had let things go with Mom and Dad. I figured the longer they had their independence, the longer they would live. I had engaged in benign neglect with them, the same as I had often done with Lee. But now I could no longer put off reality, and I dropped everything I had scheduled that day and rushed up to Stevens Point to check on Dad's condition.

I had never seen my father sick my entire life. When I went to the hospital and learned his location, I hesitated to see him. I didn't want to spoil my Ever-ready-battery image of him. A nurse's aide entered his room before I did and started cleaning him up, so I waited in a nearby lounge. I could hear Dad cry out in pain as she worked on him. The reality of my father's possible demise hit me, and I broke down. An orderly stuck his head in the lounge and asked if I was okay. I lied and told him I was fine.

After the nurse's aide finished, I quietly slipped into Dad's room. His face appeared drawn, his mouth gaped from fatigue, and his mop of white hair seemed more disheveled than usual. He hadn't shaved in several days, and his white whiskers added to his already pale look. Still, he recognized me and with a wince managed to utter the following: "Someone needs to get to the son-of-bitchin' nursing home and make sure Mom's okay." It was quintessential Dad, all right.

"I'm more concerned about you right now," I replied.

"I was fine, until that goddamn nurse washed my scrotum. It was already swollen from infection. I don't understand why they don't teach these medical people common sense."

I smiled, but the seriousness of the situation prevented me from doing so broadly. "I didn't know you were sick," I said. "Why didn't you call?"

"I didn't want to bother you. You got enough to do with those criminals."

I rolled my eyes. "How long will you be in the hospital?"

"I don't know. A few days probably, but I need to get out of here and pay the bills. These doctors don't have a right to tell me what to do."

"Don't worry, Dad. I'll take care of things until you get better."

"Just get over to the nursing home and see Mom."

After doing what Dad had instructed and telling her what had happened the best I could, I went to my parents' house to check things out. I hadn't been there in a while and wanted to see if there was anything I could clean up or fix. As usual the place was unlocked, and I was able to enter the den through the inside garage door. I winced at the sight of soiled blankets and sheets on the purple-couch hideaway where Dad had been sleeping. I immediately balled up the mess and threw it into the garbage. The odor made me wretch.

In the laundry room I saw mounds of dirty clothing strewn

across the floor. I could see the instructions I had taped on the washer for Dad: "1. Put clothes in; 2. Put soap in dispenser; 3. Pull out dial on right and turn to wash; 4. Push dial in." Obviously, my efforts had been ignored. As much as Mom had been dependent on Dad, he had been dependent on her.

The living room reminded me of a hoarder's home, with stacks of bills, mail, and newspapers filling every item of furniture with the exception of Dad's easy chair. The moss-green carpeting was now stained black from years of foot traffic.

Upstairs I found more evidence of neglect. On the desk in Dad's office, there were envelopes that contained numerous uncashed checks in substantial amounts. They came from the proceeds of bonds that had been retired in the wake of reduced interest rates. Judging by the dates on the postmarks, I concluded the money hadn't been reinvested in months. I gathered them up, together with all the unpaid bills, and put them in a metal box that I would later bring to Dad. I didn't know where he would be after his hospitalization, but I speculated I would have to handle his financial affairs in the near future.

As I went through things more, I came across Lee's last involuntary commitment petition, the one that had put him in Winnebago in 1987. It itemized by date his extensive treatment history and police contacts. In all there were nineteen incidents in the Stevens Point area alone, six that involved checks on his welfare or loitering, three in which he was a victim of a theft or burglary, two concerning threatening letters he had written, one for a fire at his apartment where he had left food cooking on the stove and forgotten about it, and seven assaults. There were probably a dozen more involving my parents that were never reported. Lee had lived at eight addresses in Stevens Point alone, and this didn't include residences in other cities or his stays at Norwood, a Milwaukee halfway house, the Rock County Mental Health Center, and the Winnebago Mental Health Institute.

Regarding the assaults, the victims were a local cop, a social worker, the nurse at Norwood, and Mom and Dad, of course. The report missed the tennis racket incident and the shotgun scare at the Death House, and it did not include the assault of the female UW-Madison student. It was a trip down memory lane to be sure, and the memories were not good.

Very significant was the entry about Lee's battery of Mom that I had learned about the Christmas after my first semester of law school. It said that she had suffered severe head and facial injuries and had to be taken by ambulance to St. Michael's Hospital where she was treated for several days. Yet Lee had told me, "I hit Mom," implying a single blow. This wouldn't have put her in the hospital and caused the multiple injuries described. But he wasn't the only one that minimized the assault. My parents had only described it to me that Christmas as "another incident with Lee," though Dad did say it resulted in an emergency detention.

The most intriguing part of the assault, however, was its date: September 26, 1979. I had called home about my bad grade in legal writing in early October of that year, which would have been right after that, but neither Mom nor Dad mentioned the assault at the time. Not until Christmas did they even tell me their minimized version of it. They had shielded me from this horrific event while I was in school, so I wouldn't be distracted and diverted from my goal. In fact, they had dealt with the most violent thing Lee had ever done in the history of his mental illness without my assistance. I was no Family Hero. They were!

At my home in Oregon, Wisconsin, I kept a box of letters and documents that had been given to me by a friend of the family after Grandmother's death. Since they contained information about my mother, her siblings, and my grandparents, she thought they might be of interest to me someday. I am not sure what prompted me to go through the records, but I noticed the box on a shelf in a closet after I had gotten back from another trip to California in 1996 and was in the process of putting my luggage away.

Like the box at my cousin's, it contained yellowed, crumbling letters. In one of them, written when my mother was in her early twenties, Grandmother referenced an injury to Mom's head that she had received during the course of a date while attending Brenau College in Gainesville, Georgia. There also was a release of liability. It was executed by Grandfather to the father of a young man named Frank. In exchange for $5,000, all liability was waived for any injuries Mom had suffered at his hands!

After learning about this, I phoned Uncle Boyd's ex-wife, Lura Jane Cottingham, formerly Lura Jane Wise. Boyd had died several years before with Alzheimer's disease, and she was the last living contemporary of Mom other than Dad. So I asked her about the incident.

"Frank was a West Point cadet. No one knows specifically how he hurt your mother but they were on a date," she replied. "He must have hit her head or thrown her down, causing her to hit something hard. He may have even sexually assaulted her, but I am not sure. But I do know one thing—afterwards she was paralyzed."

"Who was this guy?"

"Someone your mother dated before she met your father."

"Uh-huh."

"They brought her to the guest house by ambulance, all the way from Georgia."

"It must have been horrible."

"Indeed. She was sick for a long time and her rehabilitation was quite difficult."

"I can't even imagine it."

"She had to learn to walk again and write with her left hand. She was born right-handed, you see."

"This explains why her handwriting changed. I remember

seeing old letters of hers in which the slant was normal, but later it changed to backwards."

"She was a straight-A student before this happened and very attractive. She could have done anything she wanted until fate took her down."

"Fate is such a terrible monster."

"She had you boys despite the fact the doctors told her not to."

"I feel grateful for that, but I don't understand why she didn't tell us."

"That doesn't surprise me," Lura Jane said. "Your mother was a very private person, and she likely didn't want anyone's charity, certainly not yours."

"She never drew a dime of disability."

"Well, you are lucky to have been raised by a woman with such strength. Most people would have given up."

In the days that followed my conversation with Aunt Lura Jane, I contacted the doctor in charge of my mother's treatment at the nursing home. I asked him about the nature of my mother's lateral paralysis and how it came about. He responded that it was the result of an old cerebral accident or stroke. I told him about the assault by the boyfriend that caused her head to be severely injured. He indicated that sometimes after a traumatic brain injury a stroke can occur. Regardless of the physical mechanism of the paralysis, it was pretty clear from Lura Jane's description it was related to the assault, for only after that did Mom's disability appear.

After speaking to the doctor, a number of thoughts entered my head about the relationship that Lee and I had with our mother. If we had only known what had happened to her, our attitude toward her might have been different. We probably wouldn't have talked back as much, Lee might have thought twice before assaulting her, and we might have understood her better.

Though I felt remorse over Mom, I was also angry and bitter. *$5,000 in exchange for a life of misery?* I asked myself. *Grandfather must have not given a damn about her to accept such a pittance. Probably just worked it out with the guy's father over a cup of coffee—a swap among good old boys. The fucker who did this should have gone to prison or been sued. Mom had so much promise, and it was all dashed because of this guy. No wonder she felt short-changed. She was! What about me? What about Lee? Were we not affected by this man's thoughtless behavior as well?*

I wanted to find the creep who did this and tell him the results of his action. I looked up his name on the Internet, but he was dead. His obituary said he had become a high-level army colonel and was buried at Arlington National Cemetery. I vowed I would spit on his grave if I ever found it.

I dropped onto the couch in my living room and stared at the ceiling. I imagined Lee hitting Mom over and over in the face. This must have caused her to flash back to the earlier assault by Frank. How painful it must have been emotionally for her, not only because her own son had beaten her, but also because this assault had exposed a nightmare from her past. Yet, even after the severe battery by Lee, she remained on his side. Perhaps she was like any other domestic violence victim that I had seen in my career: caught in the middle of conflicting emotions and loyalties.

But I wondered if there was more to it than that. And then it came to me. Everything Mom had going for her when she was young and vibrant had been taken away by something beyond her control. Wasn't that what had happened to Lee? He had so much promise and was so gifted. Yet it all got flushed down the toilet due to schizophrenia. Did she not relate to him in her own special way? Was this why she was his most ardent defender?

My reflections about my mother continued for several days, but my focus became more philosophical. I had been a prosecutor for years and responsible for meting out judgment, more so than actual judges since plea bargaining decided the fate of most defendants. I knew as a result of that experience that there was a reason Lee pummeled Mom's face: mental illness and to a lesser extent Dad's physical abuse of him when he was young. There was a reason for Mom's paranoia and territoriality: her becoming paralyzed as a result of an altercation with a former boyfriend. And there was a reason Dad had been so angry and explosive: likely a significant authority figure in his life had treated him that way and possibly the loss of his mother at the tender age of eight.

With these thoughts in mind, I considered some principles that might guide my life going forward: be careful what you do or say to people in all the relationships you have, whether they involve a significant other, a friend, a defendant, a victim, or a co-worker. A single act or statement not only may affect the receiver of it, but also other people with whom that person later has contact and with whom they in turn have contact. Indeed, it might even affect the next generation.

A case in point was my mother. In a moment of anger, someone hurt her and caused her to be paralyzed. This affected how she raised her children. That act may have also exacerbated Lee's problems to the extent that Mom had modeled paranoia for him. Perhaps both of their issues in turn impacted my desire to have a family. I camped out, after all, and never had children.

Another thing occurred to me that was even more profound. In as much as the wrong we do or say may affect others negatively, the right we do can affect others positively, and like the wrong, can do so geometrically. We can touch people's lives for good as easily as we can touch them for bad, and that too can affect succeeding generations.

Soon after my conversation with my aunt, I drove to Stevens Point to see my parents at the Portage County Home. After his release from the hospital and subsequent rehab, Dad had decided to stay in the same room as Mom, even though he really could have been in a less restrictive environment. I considered this to be a tremendous sacrifice, as I didn't like being in the nursing home even as a visitor. To me, it was the ultimate expression of his love for her.

When I arrived at my parents' room, I could see my father sitting on the edge of his bed. His sad, sagging eyes stared into nothingness. Mom lay on her bed, propped up by pillows. Saliva dropped off the bottom of her chin onto a bib tied to her neck. Her eyes did not focus, and I doubted she even knew I was there. In the background, a cable news station on the portable TV that I had bought them droned on and on about an airline crash.

I rapped on the large wooden door, and Dad jumped. "Hi, I'm here," I said pleasantly.

"Come in, come in," Dad replied.

"But there's a stop sign here," I said, pointing to a banner than stretched across the door opening.

"Oh, that's just for the idiot down the hall. He keeps wandering into our room like it's his property."

I detached the banner and went inside. Surrounding Dad were pieces of notepaper filled with mathematical equations. The last time I was there, I had taken him to a bookstore and told him he could buy any book he wanted, and I would pay for it. He chose a study guide on College Algebra, amazingly.

"Showing off?" I asked, as I picked up one of the pages of equations.

"Just making sure I haven't forgotten anything."

I smiled, then changed the subject. "Listen, there is something I want to talk to you about."

"What's that?"

"Well, I was going through a box of letters and documents that I got from a friend of Grandmother's family, and one of them was a release executed by the father of a man named Frank."

Dad nervously glanced at Mom, who was staring off into space and obviously unable to comprehend our conversation. He then looked at me sheepishly and said, "So you know."

"Yeah, I talked to Aunt Lura Jane about it. Frank attacked her on a date and caused her paralysis."

"She didn't want you and Lee to know."

"But why?"

"She said it wouldn't make any difference."

"Maybe she was right."

"Why do you say that?" Dad asked.

"She was just as good as any other mother despite her paralysis," I replied, proudly.

"No, you're wrong, Kenny. She was better."

After my visit with Dad that day, I went to see Lee. By then he resided at a group home in Plainfield, a small town south of Stevens Point. After I had asked for him, one of the workers yelled up the stairs, "Merl, someone's here to see you."

Years before, when my brother was first committed, I had told Julie Larson, the social worker at Human Services in the beginning of his involvement in the system, that he preferred his middle name Lee and that that was what we called him in our family. Unfortunately, with few exceptions, the caretakers and system actors called my brother Merl. They probably just looked at the formal name on the file and used that. Maybe they didn't trust mental patients on this issue, for they might be delusional about their own identity. Regardless, for years I thought it was a terrible indignity that people in the system couldn't even get my brother's name right. I wondered what else they didn't get right. Eventually, I got over it though, reasoning that you can't fight city hall, even when it comes to your name. Perhaps my brother had come to that same conclusion, as he never corrected his caretakers, at least when I was around.

Lee came down the stairs quickly, despite an overhanging gut that now characterized his appearance. At forty-five, his hair had gone gray, and he had dark shadows beneath his eyes. He wore a plaid flannel shirt that was not properly tucked in. I hadn't seen him in a while and noticed for the first time he had sunken cheeks and no teeth. I thought about all the money my parents had spent on braces for him.

"What happened to your teeth?" I asked.

"They pulled them out."

"Did that need to be done, or was it a matter of administrative convenience?"

"It may have been cheaper than to have them fixed."

"Do you have false teeth?"

"Yeah, but I don't use them."

"Can you chew anyway? I was thinking about taking you somewhere to get something to eat."

"As long as the food is soft."

We drove to a truck stop near the main highway, where he ordered a hamburger. To eat it, he would take a bite and mash it with his gums, then swallow it with the assistance of water. I didn't eat anything, as I was too grossed out. Instead I sipped a Coke.

While Lee ate, I brought up the subject of Mom's paralysis, thinking it might spark reconciliation and rid him of his rage against her. "I found some records about Mom," I said. "Do you know how she became paralyzed?"

"No."

"A person who dated her in college assaulted her."

I assumed Lee would react emotionally upon hearing the news, but I was wrong. Not one bit of anger, sadness, or concern crossed his lips. His mental illness or his meds must have muted his emotions. Even so his callous indifference angered me since he had caused her to relive the experience that resulted in her paralysis by assaulting her. Moreover, he had lied to me about it by implying he had hit her once, and I wanted to make him account for that lie.

But before any venom could spew from my mouth, I remembered what I had told myself about words and actions affecting other people. I also thought about what Dad had said about letting things go when Mom was getting into it with the neighbors.

"So Lee, when do you need to get back to the group home again?"

By early 1999, Mom's condition in the nursing home had deteriorated. Several problems—the brain injury and attendant stroke, her long-term confinement in a bed, and possibly Alzheimer's—caused her to have oropharyngeal dysfunction (difficulty in swallowing). Frequently, she would choke when eating and eventually didn't eat at all. As a result she lost considerable weight and weakened substantially. The doctor called me and said she had been admitted to St. Michael's hospital, so I came up from Madison to see her, figuring she would die soon.

When I got to her hospital room, Dad was already there. Someone must have given him a ride from the nursing home. He occupied a chair in the corner. Before we had a chance to talk, the doctor came in, and Dad stood up to greet him. When he did, he slouched more than usual and frowned noticeably. The vicissitudes of life had clearly taken their toll—the loss of his mother at eight years old, the torment of having a schizophrenic son, and the unimaginable responsibility for a paralyzed and now bed-ridden wife.

"For a variety of reasons, Lillian's body has given up, and you are faced with a serious decision," the doctor told him, while eyeing Mom as she lay inert on the hospital bed. Her face, drawn and pale, had the texture and stillness of granite, as though she had already died.

"Is there anything you can do?" Dad asked.

The doctor sighed. "Well, if she doesn't eat, she's going to die from starvation or the inability to fight infection. I could put a feeding tube in her stomach—"

"Oh, don't bother," Mom stated abruptly. She hadn't spoken in at least a year, so we were taken aback. Even more amazing was her ability to comprehend the situation. She had used the phrase many times in the past, usually when she played the role of martyr. But this time it was her way of saying uncle.

"I can't let her starve," Dad replied to the doctor, disregarding Mom's protest. "Put the tube in her."

"The most it will give her is a year."

"Better that than nothing," Dad said.

I gave my father a ride back to the nursing home. On the way, he babbled about how long he had been with Mom, and I made every effort to console him. "I just"—Dad paused to gather himself—"can't live without her." I had never seen him cry before and cringed at the prospect of this happening. The man who had whipped us with a belt and hit us with his fists actually had a heart.

In late summer of 1999, my father's niece called me and told me she was compiling an album about our family's history that included stories she had found and a good deal of genealogy. She asked me if I would talk to my father about his memories growing up out west, and in particular, any details he knew regarding his mother's death in 1915. She wanted to include them in the album.

I obliged her request, and the next time I visited my parents in the Portage County Home, I engaged my father in a conversation about the topic. When I brought it up, he laughed and said, "That's because my niece is Mormon."

"Why do you say that?"

"Mormons want to do baptisms and other religious rites for the dead."

"Yeah, I've heard about that."

"You know what I say?"

"What?"

"Leave the dead alone."

His cynical response did not surprise me. While he had been baptized in the Mormon Church himself when he was eight, he didn't practice its faith. In my earlier conversations with him, he didn't express any faith in God. He once told me he was a naturalist, meaning he believed in the wonders of the natural world versus anything supernatural.

Despite his lack of interest in his niece's effort at family history, I questioned Dad further about his background. I was curious about it in general, but I also wanted to see if there was anything in it that might explain his explosiveness and physical abuse of Lee and me as children. Perhaps a parent or other adult had done that to him.

"So you mentioned at one point your mother died when you were eight. Do you remember much about that?"

"I just know she was taken to LDS Hospital in Salt Lake and died there."

"Why did she die?"

"I'm not sure, Kenny."

"You were the oldest, right?"

"Yes, I had two younger brothers and a sister who was just a baby at the time."

"So you were probably the most connected to your mother among your siblings since you had spent the most time with her."

"Maybe."

"Who raised you after your mother died?"

"A foster mother named Adeleine for a while, then my father, followed by his brother, Uncle Jim."

"What was your foster mother like?"

"Oh, she was pretty strict."

"By strict, what do you mean?"

"Oh, I don't remember much."

"What about your Dad, was he strict?"

"I can't really say, Kenny. In those days everyone was, I guess."

"What did your Dad do for a living?"

"He was in the sheep business."

"Did he make much money at it?"

"Sometimes, but if the lambs died in the winter, we were poor."

"What about Uncle Jim? What was his role in your upbringing?"

"He was in the sheep business, too. For a while, my brothers and I stayed with him on his ranch in Idaho."

"How did he treat you?"

"Okay, I suppose."

"So when did you graduate from college?"

"1937."

"You would have been thirty-one. How come it took you so long?"

"I had to work my way through school. Uncle Jim helped me some, but I paid him back every penny. And then there was the depression."

"So after you graduated what did you do?"

"Taught high school, then went on to get my Master's in Economics."

"At the University of Chicago, right?"

"Yes."

"How did you get there from Utah?"

"By sheep train."

"Sheep train?"

"Yeah, you could buy a ticket and ride in the caboose."

"So how did you meet Mom?"

"After I served in the Navy in World War II, I finished my masters in Chicago, and we met there. Somebody set us up. Later we married, and you and Lee came along."

While I had learned a great deal about my father, I wasn't getting anywhere in my attempt to discover the origin of his explosiveness. I didn't want to ask him directly, for he would never tell me the truth. In addition, time and the failing memory of a man ninety-three years old had probably buried it. One thing did come through loud and clear in our discussion, however: my dad had had a hard life growing up, which could explain why he was so hard on Lee and me.

31

The Death of Mom and Dad

On October 12, 1999, a friend of mine at work found me near the lunch counter at the Dane County Courthouse in Madison. I typically grabbed a sandwich there around noon, so he knew where I'd be. "Someone called the front desk about your dad and wants you to call back right away," he said. My heart froze.

I raced upstairs to my office and dialed the nursing home number. After several line transfers, a representative having knowledge of the situation came on. "Your father had a heart attack and has been taken by ambulance to the hospital. It happened right after he ate lunch in his room. He vomited on himself and then collapsed."

"Was he able to say anything before he lost consciousness?"

"Yes, he did actually."

"What was it?"

"'Take care of Lillian.'"

Lillian was Mom's first name.

As I drove north to Stevens Point, I called the emergency-room doctor. "I am not getting much of a pulse," he said. "I note from the chart your father has a 'Do-not-resuscitate' order. We can do chest compressions, but I doubt it will do any good."

"Just let him go," I said.

Though Dad was ninety-three, I hadn't prepared myself mentally for his death. I was much more focused on Mom, who was far worse off. Every Saturday morning for the last several years I had gone to the nursing home and picked him up. We would go to his post office box and retrieve the bills. I would prepare the checks for his signature and balance the checkbook. At the bank we would transfer funds to cover the expenses, deposit pension and social security checks, and purchase certificates of deposit from the proceeds of retired bonds. Afterward, we would go to lunch and return to the nursing home.

With two notable exceptions, Dad had it together the entire time I dealt with him: once when he blew up with me about the checkbook being out of balance, and another time when we sold the family home because it could not be insured very inexpensively due to it being unoccupied. In that regard, Dad had signed the closing statement, but later denied it and called every bank and lawyer in town to complain. This had more to do with him not being able to come to terms emotionally with selling the family home than any lack of mental acuity, however. He had bought it for Mom to keep her from going back to Kentucky, after all.

As I neared Stevens Point, I called the doctor again, and he confirmed that Dad had died. I stopped at the nursing home, so I could tell Mom. She did not appear to be in distress, though likely she had seen the EMTs take Dad away on a stretcher. She had gained weight and grown healthier because of the feeding tube. Still, she had not spoken since our discussion with her doctor at the hospital, and most of the time when I saw her she seemed unaware of my presence. Even so, I decided to tell her about Dad on the off chance she would comprehend.

"Mom," I said quietly, standing next to her bed apprehensively. "Dad died."

She didn't say a word, so I wasn't sure if the news had sunk in. Then, without a sob or the slightest movement, a solitary tear rolled down her right cheek. I kissed her forehead, and her simple expression of grief turned to a smile.

Next, I called Lee at the Plainfield Group Home. "I have some bad news," I told him. "Dad had a heart attack and passed away today."

"Okay, thanks for letting me know," Lee replied with no inflection in his voice whatsoever. It was as if I had told him his zipper was down. He had had the same reaction when he learned about the cause of Mom's paralysis. I repeated the events in more detail, hoping to stir him, but he remained disengaged. Finally, he hung up on me.

Disappointed and even numb, I went into autopilot and took care of the business end of death. I arranged for Dad's funeral in Stevens Point and burial in Danville, where I knew my mother would later be buried, for it was her wish to be laid to rest by her parents. I notified Dad's attorney, who had set up a complicated estate plan in order to care for my mother and brother. I even went to Dad's banker and let her know. She told me: "I watched you come in here every Saturday with your dad the past several years. Before that, I dealt directly with him, and he told me about the situation at home and what you had gone through. I want you to know there is a special place in heaven for you."

I thanked her, but deep down I knew the compliment was undeserved. I had walked on the other side of the street too many times, and I had distanced myself from my family way too much to be considered a saint. I had an excuse, though: I needed to maintain my sanity so I could keep my parents proud.

Dad's funeral was relatively small. It was held in a large room at the funeral home across the street from the Death House, the place where Lee had possessed the shotgun. Perhaps thirty people attended: colleagues from the university, several relatives, my friend Jon and his mom, Dean and his folks, and eight or ten of my co-workers from the Dane County DA's Office.

Before the ceremony started, a nursing home aide brought Mom to the funeral parlor in a reclining wheelchair. I rolled her up to Dad's casket, which drew the attention of everyone in the room.

A blanket draped her upper torso and lap. Her head fell slightly to the side, her mouth gaped, and her eyes stared at nothing. Dad being dead and lying motionless before her didn't seem to register. Bringing her there may have been a mistake, and I felt bad for having done so, but I wanted to give her an opportunity to see him one last time.

Lee arrived with an attendant from the Plainfield Group Home, clean-shaven and properly dressed. He spoke with my friends, Dad's colleagues, and Norm, a cousin from Salt Lake City. They didn't know much about my brother's illness, so when they asked him what he did in life, it felt awkward. What was he supposed to say? I'm a paranoid schizophrenic? In characteristic inappropriateness, Lee told each person the same thing: "I have read the Harvard Classics." Indeed he had, but it saddened me that this was all he had to offer.

Several of Dad's fellow professors spoke at the ceremony. Before they talked, I requested the coffin be left open, though the funeral director said this would violate tradition. I told him I wanted to feel like my dad was present for the remarks. His colleagues talked about his stellar academic background and his professorial appearance. I did not speak myself, as I didn't think I could hold it together. Fortunately, Lee didn't speak, either.

As I flew down to Kentucky to bury Dad, I reflected on his loss. When I was young, I had little or no relationship with him. He was a stern disciplinarian and didn't measure up with younger, more active fathers. Yet things changed for us as I got older. I was able to converse with him about great philosophers and deep theoretical concepts. When Lee had become mentally ill, Dad emerged as a rational comrade in an otherwise irrational family existence. For all those reasons and more, I appreciated his involvement in my life.

Over the next few months following Dad's death, I visited Mom on weekends, but when I did, she was unresponsive. Her fixed stare convinced me she had lost all cognition. With Dad being gone, it seemed like she had given up, though truly her ability to feel anything had long since passed.

That December I thought about a Christmas present for her, which of course was absurd. I considered a nice blanket or an afghan, but discarded the notion once the nursing home staff said she wouldn't be able to recognize such items. Thereafter, I learned that people in her condition could sometimes hear, so I bought her a boom box and some music from her era. The nurses thought it was a good choice, and they played the tunes at her bedside all her waking hours.

In early January, 2000, the nursing home called and informed me that Mom had died of pneumonia. I felt nothing, not because I didn't care, but because I had already grieved her death slowly. A funeral did not make much sense, for all her relatives were dead and her friends had drifted away over the years. Instead I set up a visitation in Stevens Point and another one in Danville. Her coffin was modest, as she had complained bitterly in life about what a rip off a fancy one would be.

I brought Lee up from Plainfield for the visitation in Stevens Point. He stood over Mom's open casket coldly, though nevertheless dutifully. After a minute or two he abruptly asked me to take him back to the group home, in the same manner as he had done whenever he came to dinner at our family home: "Okay, I want to go back now." The only other person who made it to the visitation was my friend Jon, despite it being announced in an obituary in the paper. I felt pretty shitty about the lack of people there, but I knew that Mom had no living contemporaries and had had an isolated existence once her ability to communicate had left her.

In Danville, several people came to Mom's second wake, but Lee was not one of them. I knew better than to ask him to make the trip with me. He barely spent a minute at Mom's visitation in Stevens Point, so I concluded he would not be interested.

There was nothing fancy about Mom's graveside service. A Presbyterian minister agreed to say a few words at it, and all he did was give a prayer incorporating the 23rd Psalm. While Mom had been Methodist growing up, her estrangement from her family made her become Presbyterian, so that's why I asked him to do it. Present were me, a childhood friend of Mom, and a couple of gravediggers, who manned a crane nearby. Extended from the crane was the top of a concrete grave liner that was lowered onto the vault once the coffin was put in it. This seemed altogether too practical to me at the time, but Mom was a practical woman and would have wanted it this way.

Later, I pondered Mom's life just as I had done with Dad's. She had been dealt a bad hand, first with paralysis and then Lee. She certainly did not have privilege, indeed far from it. I thought about her pushing me around in a stroller and the countless things she had done to make things normal with that one good hand. I also considered my brother's belief that she had been out to get him and just how wrong he had been about her. She truly loved him and frankly was his staunchest defender in spite of all he had done to her. Her existence had been marked with no other accomplishment than us two boys, and even that was terribly damaged. Though she faced many challenges, she never gave up. For that example and many others she had set for me, I knew I had been immeasurably blessed.

32

Church and Marriage

My cousin Mark called me after my Dad's death. I hadn't spoken to him since his mother's funeral in Salt Lake City in 1985. Thus, I was quite thrilled to hear from him. I received the call in the family room of my home in Oregon.

"Sorry, I wasn't able to make it to your Dad's funeral," Mark started off.

"That's all right. It's a long ways out here, and besides Norm (Mark's brother) represented your side of the family."

"Did you get the flowers?"

"Yeah, thanks."

"How are you getting along given what has happened lately?"

"Okay, I guess."

"You were always the rock in your family growing up, weren't you?"

"I tried to be, but I am not sure how good I was at it."

"Well, I've been praying for you."

"Thanks. I remember when we were kids, you taught me about the Mormon Church. You were pretty into it back then."

"I still am."

"I want you to know I have always respected your commitment, Mark. After Dad died I even prayed."

"What did you pray for? Do you remember?"

"God's help."

"Since you brought this up, I have a question for you."

"*Uh-oh,*" I told myself. I knew exactly what my cousin was going to ask.

"Would you be willing to talk to the missionaries from the church? I'd teach you myself, but I live too far away."

I got up from my easy chair and began pacing the floor nervously. I had the phone in one hand and ran my fingers through my hair with the other. "I don't know, Mark. Maybe, I guess."

Two sister missionaries from the LDS Church came to my home several days after my conversation with Mark. They were in their early twenties and had angelic faces. I was impressed by their sincerity, and their innocence drew me in. I also listened to them out of respect for my cousin.

I told the missionaries I had always been an empiricist, meaning knowledge for me was gained through the five senses, the processing of that information by one's brain, and the retention of it by a person's memory. One of the missionaries replied that she believed that people possessed a sixth sense. When I asked her what that sense was, she said that it was manifested by a warm feeling in one's heart. She told me that if something were true, he or she would receive confirmation of it through that feeling. She said she believed that this feeling came about as a result of the influence of the Holy Ghost.

I responded that I had always hoped God existed, but I didn't know for sure, and this meant I had no faith. The missionary then eagerly paged through her scriptures and found a passage that said that hope was the seed of faith. If I permitted that seed to grow, faith would be bestowed upon me, she said. But if I failed to water or feed the seed, it would be lost. I was impressed by such words, though I still did not know whether to trust them.

At the end of our conversation, I pledged to come to church the following Sunday. As I went to sleep that night, however,

I wondered if I had made a mistake, perhaps having done so in a moment or period of weakness. I also believed that weakness could sometimes bring clarity to one's thoughts and that adversity could be God's way of making one surrender. So I cast my doubts aside and decided to honor my commitment to come to church.

The local LDS branch conducted services at an elementary school in Stoughton, Wisconsin, a small town near Oregon. The church had rented space there until its new building was completed. The congregation consisted of less than a hundred people, and everyone in it was friendly and sincere. The fact that it was held at a school and involved such a small group gave it a humble air, which in turn gave it a spiritual one.

After church, the missionaries introduced me to a family named the Stevensons, who invited me to their house for dinner that night. Naturally, I obliged. They lived in a half-duplex with their three teenage daughters. One of its walls had a picture of Christ, and an upright piano in the living room had a green Mormon hymnal atop it. Sister Stevenson, a skinny and attractive stay-at-home mom in her mid-thirties, smiled at me when she answered the door, and that smile never left her face the entire time I was there. Her husband was a tall, balding man with muscular arms. He also had a pleasant disposition. At first, I thought the Stevensons' attitude was overdone, but as time wore on I realized it was genuine. They appeared to be the family I always wanted to have, but never did. Maybe it was still possible, I thought.

Brother Stevenson offered an articulate prayer before we ate in which he asked that the food be blessed; he closed the prayer in the name of Jesus Christ. The meal was nothing fancy: chicken breasts, corn, and mashed potatoes. Water was the only drink. Dessert consisted of a cake Sister Stevenson had made. Afterward she cleared the table with her daughters before I had a chance to offer my assistance, and in no time they loaded the dishes in the washer.

In the living room, Brother Stevenson and I talked about the church and my family background. He told me he had a video he wanted me to watch. He slipped it in his VCR as his wife joined us on the sofa. The video was produced by the church and told the story of a young man whose car had stalled on the side of a country road. He looked around and saw miles of empty highway. In time, another man came along and offered him help and gave him a ride to his house, where he introduced him to his family, and they had dinner. The second man then got the first one's car running. The family was LDS, of course, and the video ended with a simple message: no matter how isolated you feel, you are never alone when it comes to God. The message hit home given the circumstances I was facing.

In the months that followed my dinner with the Stevensons, the missionaries taught me the church discussions. The discussions were a lesson-by-lesson explanation of the principles and obligations of the LDS Church. The Stevensons stood by me in this process, and Brother Stevenson ultimately baptized me. Though he and his family later moved away, we maintained contact. I was a very active and strong member, which thrilled Mark and my relatives in Utah. Most importantly, the church gave me a community of people and a sense of belonging I had never had.

As a result of my parents' deaths, I didn't have to deal with my hang-up about a girlfriend or a significant other meeting my family. Lee was still an issue, but there was no urgency in divulging him because people don't necessarily have to mention a brother to a partner right away. I could ease into that. The bottom line was I didn't really have to camp out anymore.

At church one day, I met someone and started dating her. She was an attractive blonde about ten years younger than me and recently divorced. She had four kids ranging from four to fifteen. She was an active member of the church, so we had much in common. Like me, she wanted to have a church life comparable to that of the Stevensons, one in which we would work with the missionaries in acclimating new members. We dated about six months before we got married in September of 2001. We married in Chicago, as that was where the nearest temple stood, and LDS couples typically married in a temple. We did this on the same day of the month that my parents married and in the same city. I had proposed to her in the temple's celestial room several months before. My fiancée broke into tears when I asked her to marry me. I was forty-four years old at the time, about the same age as Dad when he got hitched to Mom.

After our wedding day, we frequently had people over on Sundays for dinner, just like the Stevensons had done with me. We each had callings in the church, and for several years I was scoutmaster of the local LDS scout troop. As for children, the situation worked out well. Since my wife already had kids, I had the family life I had missed growing up. We did not have a baby together, so I did not have to worry about my genes producing a schizophrenic child. We had nice Christmases, with no hiding of knives, or a family member talking to himself or having paranoid or grandiose delusions. And yes, my new wife ultimately met Lee, and miraculously there was no problem.

Unfortunately, while I got along well with my wife's children, she and I drifted apart. The reasons for this have nothing to do with Lee, except for this: because I had missed having a normal family growing up, I felt the need to replace that element of my life too quickly once my parents died. Further, I assumed that my wife would be like the mother in the Stevenson family, but she wasn't. In my haste to compensate, I did not get to know her well enough before I married her. Despite this fact, I really don't feel badly about the failed marriage. At least I gave it a shot and quit camping out.

After my divorce, I moved to a condo in Madison which was closer to work, and my church membership was transferred to a different ward. I didn't know anyone in the new congregation, so I became estranged from the church, and this together with the divorce caused me to reexamine its doctrine and scriptures. Eventually I fell away. I don't regret having joined, however, and I found members of this organization to be sincere and good-hearted. Unfortunately, my involvement in it had occurred at a time in my life when I couldn't be objective about religion.

33

Making Peace with Lee

As time passed following my divorce, Lee seemed to mellow out, as schizophrenics often do. No longer was he violent or dangerous. For the most part he had no paranoid delusions, though he continued to be grandiose. He got along well in his group home placements, for they amounted to an in-between level of structure. He could come and go as he pleased, so long as he told staff where he would be and when he would return. Most significantly, he quit fighting the system. While there had been multiple involuntary commitments and yearly extensions over the years, lately he had only been in treatment on a voluntary basis. He finally came to the conclusion that he needed help.

As a result, my relationship with him improved, and I saw him more often. I remember well an occasion in which my ex-wife and I visited him at the Plainfield Group Home. I found on the bookshelf in the living room a board game that we played as kids—Stratego. I had never beaten him at it in my life, but I asked him to play anyway, and he agreed. I thought that this time I would win, given his years of mental illness and use of anti-psychotic medication. I was wrong. Within a short time, he figured out my strategy and won the game. As we got up from the table, he said, "You had me confused there for a while, Kenny. Nice effort." Some things never change, I guess.

Soon the state shut down the Plainfield Group Home for regulatory violations, and Human Services transferred Lee to another one called the Sullivan House in Wausau, Wisconsin. I probably visited him there a dozen times or so. We went to area malls and shopping centers, and I bought him clothes and took him out to eat.

After Mom's death, a special-needs trust that Dad had set up for Lee's benefit went into effect. The idea of it was to give him limited funds such that his eligibility for Social Security Disability and Medicaid would be maintained. The money in his case was used for bus passes, a library card, clothing, and other necessities. It also paid his way for a group-home-sponsored trip to Nashville, Tennessee. Initially, I was trustee, but after a short time I resigned and turned over responsibility for the trust to a bank.

During the period in which I was in charge of the trust, Lee sent me a letter that read:

> Dear Kenny,
> I would like to buy several houses in Wausau and fix them up. This will require a capital investment of $300,000. Please deposit such funds into my account using Dad's money.
> Sincerely,
> Lee

My brother made a similar request for funds from the bank that took over the trust after me. On that occasion the business scheme had to do with his purported invention of a centrifuge that would supposedly cure AIDS by separating contaminated cells from good ones. Needless to say, the bank did not honor the request.

Initially, I worried that such grandiose ideas were a step backwards. But when I asked Lee about this correspondence, he just laughed. He seemed to be trolling me, in fact. Instead of calling him out on it, however, I laughed too. Henceforth, this was how we dealt with his get-rich-quick schemes. We made a joke of them and any other delusions he still had, and this seemed to make things better between us.

At one of my visits I mentioned to Lee that I had gotten divorced. He told me not to let it bother me, and that things like that just happen in life. He resumed being a mentor to me for one special moment.

In the spring of 2006, I received a phone call from a staff person at an emergency room at Wausau Hospital. The man told me my brother had been admitted for pneumonia. A chest x-ray revealed he had a tumor on his lungs. This was not surprising, since Lee had chain-smoked since he was nineteen. He had smoked every conceivable type of cigarette—menthols, lights, filtered, and non-filtered, whatever he could get his hands on. Thus, I knew what the tumor meant: lung cancer.

In the days that followed, I visited Lee in the hospital and prepared myself for the reality of his death. While I had long ago come to terms with him always being schizophrenic, in my heart I had always hoped he would recover and be productive. I now knew this would never come to pass. My big brother, the one who meant so much to me as a child, was going to die.

A month after I learned Lee was sick, the group home director asked me to accompany a staff person and my brother to an oncologist's office. The doctors had made several attempts to get a good sample of the tumor for biopsy purposes, but had failed. In time, they cut a hole in my brother's neck, went down into his lungs, and obtained the sample they wanted. The appointment had to do with the results of this testing, and I am sure the Sullivan House wanted a family member present when the doctor explained the inevitable bad news to him.

Lee and I and the group home representative went to the clinic in my car and sat in a waiting room for twenty minutes. We could see a dozen easy chairs lined up in a large room next to us. Several had been placed by windows that offered a beautiful view. Adjacent to the chairs were stands for intravenous tubes. I knew the purpose of the chairs immediately, and my gut turned.

In time, a nurse summoned us into a small office with an examination table. After a few minutes, the oncologist arrived. He was in his early forties and had jet-black hair. He wore a white doctor's coat and spoke in a direct, efficient manner. "We now have the results of your testing," he told Lee. "Unfortunately, Mr. Farmer, you have small-cell lung cancer. This particular disease is incurable and its duration typically is a matter of months." He did not expressly tell my brother he would soon die, nor did he give him a specific range of time he had left to live. I had always thought that a physician in such a situation would flat out tell a patient this. Instead, this guy chose an inferential way of explaining things, something more subtle and comforting. What was even stranger was Lee did not react to the news. He just sat there with no expression.

The doctor had him get on the examination table, where he listened to his breathing with a stethoscope. The procedure seemed purposeless, more for show than anything else. After he finished, he told my brother that a port for chemotherapy would be installed near his neck. The goal of such therapy was to reduce the size of the tumor, he said, and to provide a palliative effect during the last months of his life.

Since Lee didn't seem willing to advocate for himself, I asked the doctor if he could operate and remove the tumor once it was small enough from chemotherapy or radiation. He looked at me and said one word, "No." I assumed that the size and location of the tumor made this impossible or impractical, so I did not bother to argue with him. Next, I questioned him about metastasis, and he told me that this form of cancer would move to my brother's bones and brain. He assured me that through radiation therapy that they would try to stay on top of this and make him as comfortable as possible.

I drove Lee back to the group home after the appointment. On the way, he again showed no reaction to what the doctor had told him, not one bit of sorrow, sadness, or anger. Something about schizophrenia or his anti-psychotic medication made it so he didn't worry about death. In fact, he didn't care about anything. He had the same reaction with respect to Mom and Dad's demise, and the news regarding the cause of Mom's paralysis. For a while I considered such an attitude to be useful to the extent it would get a person through life's worst experiences. In the end, I concluded it was better to care, even if it meant I would suffer more.

On Sunday, February 4, 2007, a nurse from Wausau Hospital notified me by phone that Lee would have to stay a few more days before returning to the Sullivan House. He had been there a week while recovering from an infection occasioned by the cancer treatment's compromise of his immune system. He had gone to the hospital several times recently and always made it out within a few days. Since this occasion seemed different, I became concerned and asked to speak to him.

"Hi Lee, are you feeling any better?"

A tired, vacant voice responded in the negative.

"The Super Bowl is on tonight. Are you going to watch it?" I asked in order to cheer him up. In 1967, we had viewed the first one together on our brand new color TV. The Packers played the Chiefs that year, and we audio recorded the game on a cheap reel-to-reel tape recorder we had gotten for Christmas.

"Yeah...the Super Bowl," Lee replied weakly.

Those were his last words.

On Monday, February 5, Lee's oncologist called me just before I left for work. His tone was urgent. "You need to come here right away. Your brother is dying."

After a two-hour-plus drive from Madison to Wausau, I arrived at the hospital. The nurses told me to wear a surgical mask before entering my brother's room and to wash my hands after, due to the severity of his infection and the possibility it could spread. I did as instructed.

The scene was painful to watch. Lee had agreed that heroic efforts such as tube feeding and oxygen should not be administered on his death bed. Thus, he breathed rapidly to gather air, as he lay unconscious. It was the kind of breathing you would expect to hear from a person who had just completed a long foot race. A monitor next to the bed showed his pulse to be very high, though his blood pressure was low. A bag had been attached to him by way of a catheter that hung from the side of the bed. It was partially full of urine, but nothing was dropping into it anymore. The nurse came in and mentioned that the chart did not authorize oxygen, due to Lee's advance directive. She said they would obtain a BiPAP machine to assist his breathing. I left the room and got something to eat at the hospital cafeteria while this was being arranged.

When I returned, the medical staff had the BiPAP mask connected to his face, and it forced air down his throat. His face reddened as the machine pumped over and over into his mouth, causing him to struggle. It seemed as if he were drowning. Finally, the oncologist came in and took the mask off in anger, as if to ask, "Who the hell authorized this?" He then peeled open my brother's right eyelid to determine his level of awareness. He told him that he was going to give him something to make him feel better just like they had discussed. Lee moaned in response. The doctor wrote an order in his chart, and I knew it was for the administration of a heavy dose of morphine. This would alleviate Lee's pain but also hasten his death. I did not try to stop this procedure, though I had medical power of attorney.

I asked the doctor how long it would be before Lee died. "Based on the fact his kidneys are no longer functioning, probably a day or so," he replied. "He's dying from infection, though the cancer has also taken its toll."

"I have to get a few things from my home south of Madison, so I can stay the night in Wausau and be close by when he passes," I told him. "Do I have enough time? It might take five to six hours to drive there and back. If not, I'll stay here and wait."

"He probably won't die for a day or two, so you should be okay," the doctor replied.

I sat with Lee a half hour and left. By the time I got to my house, the phone rang.

"Is this Kenneth Farmer?" a nurse from the hospital asked.

"Yes."

"Your brother just passed away," she said. Lee was fifty-five years old, though for him it must have felt like a hundred.

I indicated to the nurse I wanted to see him when I got there. She tried to tell me it might be better if I waited for the funeral home people to take care of things before I saw him. I insisted, nevertheless. She granted my request and said they would keep Lee in the room until I returned.

I called the group home director and notified him of my brother's demise. I mentioned I would be going to see him, and he asked if it was all right for him to accompany me. I replied it would be nice if he did. In a couple of hours I met him at the entrance to the hospital, and together we made it up to Lee's room. As we rode the elevator, the group home director confided, "You know what? I liked your brother. Hell, he was one of the most assaultive patients ever to come out of Portage County. But I liked him even so."

"He was a good soul," I replied.

We arrived at Lee's room. The door was closed for obvious reasons, but we slipped in quietly. My brother's eyes were open as well as his mouth. We stared silently at him, and I wondered if I should have taken the nurse's advice and waited for the undertaker to improve his appearance. But I felt I had a responsibility to be there, for I had not been with him at the exact moment of his death.

At Lee's bedside, in my head I could hear Mom saying, "He doesn't have any friends, Kenny. Why don't you go down to the den and talk to him?" So I spoke to him just as I had done when he sat on the purple couch. I did so under my breath so the group home director could not hear me. I told Lee I was glad his struggle was over and that things finally would be better for him. There would be no more haunting voices, no more paranoid thoughts, no more urges to do violence, no more loneliness, and most importantly respect from those around him.

Two weeks after Lee's death and after I had already buried him next to my parents in Danville, Kentucky, I got a call from the group director. "Hey, did you have a funeral for your brother or are you planning a memorial service for him?"

"Not really. I didn't think anyone cared."

"Oh, they do all right."

"Come on, who seriously gives a damn about him besides me?"

"The group-home residents."

"That's very kind of them, but—"

"We were wondering if we could conduct our own tribute to him, and we would like for you to attend."

I was dumbfounded. When I had gone to see Lee, the patients at the home never spoke to me or him. They appeared completely oblivious to our presence, and I doubted they had feelings for anyone, much less my brother. Initially, I thought the proposal to be a contrived exercise in sociability, but I agreed to it, if for no other reason than to help the residents in that exercise.

A couple days later Lee's tribute took place at 6 p.m. The group home appeared as always—a two-story house built in the forties with a large front porch. In the driveway a canopy stretched over a picnic table. Seated under it were two residents mindlessly smoking cigarettes and not talking to each other. Inside, I saw some group-home workers cleaning up after dinner. The rest of the residents were barely visible here and there and said nothing to me. In the living room, about ten chairs had been arranged in a circle.

I recognized the group-home director from the hospital and shook his hand. "Thanks for coming," he said. "Was it a long drive?"

"Not too bad."

"Well, I thought we would all sit around and talk about your brother," he suggested, while gesturing toward the chairs.

"Sounds good to me."

The director looked at his watch and announced that it was time to begin. One of the residents went outside and yelled for the two at the picnic table to come in. The rest gathered in the living room. "Here's your chair," the director told me.

I nodded and took a seat.

"I thought we would have everyone say something about Merl," the director told people after they sat down. "Just anything you want, an experience or a conversation you may have had with him. Why don't we start with you, Jeffrey?"

The man next to the director cleared his throat. He was short and pudgy. He appeared to be in his forties and had a balding head with hair that stuck out haphazardly from its sides. His bottom lip had spittle on it. As he talked, his words were slurred, no doubt the result of heavy-duty meds. "Your brother taught me to play chess," he said cautiously.

"He did that for me too," I replied.

The resident smiled for the first time.

"I even beat him," the resident said, then paused for effect. "Once."

Everyone broke out laughing.

"Wow, that's hard to do."

"Just lucky, I guess."

After some silence, the director went to the next resident. "Paul, what do you have to say?"

"Merl taught me the phrase *e pluribus unum*," he replied, barely able to separate the Latin syllables.

"He did?" I asked.

"Yeah, and you know what it means?"

"Why don't you tell us?"

"Out of many, one."

"I think you are right about that."

"It's to do with democracy and voting, Merl said."

"That's true."

"He taught me things like that. He had his books in his room, you know. He called them the Harvard Classics."

"Did he read them?"

"Oh yeah, every night."

"He made me read *Little Men* once," I said. "Was that one of the books he had?"

"I'm not sure."

The next person did not respond to the director's prompt initially. "Don't you want to say something, Eric?"

"I-I." The man gulped back his tears. "I helped him up one time when he fell down upstairs," he said, measured. "He had become really weak, and now and then, we would have to help him."

"I thank you for that."

"No problem. I liked him a lot, and I'm sorry he's gone. He was one of the few people I could talk to."

And so we went around the room. Each person had something nice to say about Lee. I had been fixed on the negative for so long—the violence, the dangerousness, the paranoid ideations, the grandiosity, the commitments, the hospitalizations, and the lack of productivity and self-care. So often the positive had eluded me, but now I was finally hearing it, and I felt proud of my brother for once.

"Ken, do you have something to say?"

A rush of experiences with Lee entered my head: our running in the rain together as children in Erlanger, attacking that wasp nest at Grandmother's, gathering pop bottles when we hiked to the airport, nearly drowning in Iverson Park on ice rafts, playing basketball inside Washington School when we weren't supposed to be in there, running football patterns in the back yard, evading the mosquitoes at the Contents', trying to get their window fixed, and oh so many other things. I could not explain a lifetime, but I had to try.

Finally, the words came out. "My brother taught me everything: to read, swim, skip a rock, throw a spiral, and even give a speech. He encouraged me to become an Eagle Scout and a lawyer. Without him I would be nothing."

I started to cry. There was silence until I recovered, and in a single sentence I boiled it all down: "He touched my life for good."

"As he did for all of us," the group-home director acknowledged.

At this, the tribute ended. A worker called out, "Medication time," at which point Lee's friends and fellow residents, who had been so important in his life as of late, evaporated into the worlds from which they had emerged.

Selected Bibliography for Further Reading

While the goal of this book has been to share the emotional impact schizophrenia had on my brother and my family, I would be remiss if I did not provide some additional sources that might enhance a better understanding of the current mental health system as well as the disease itself. Though improvements have been made since my brother's experience, we have a long ways to go in properly addressing issues associated with this devastating problem. Knowledge is a good thing when it comes to constructive change, and for this reason I definitely encourage readers to educate themselves in this pressing area of public policy.

Learning about commitment laws and procedures in your area would be a good place to start. Two sources that encompass this are: Treatment Advocacy Center, *Know the Laws of Your State,* 2018, www.treatmentadvocacycenter.org; and *Civil Commitment and the Mental Health Continuum: Historical Trends and Principles of Law and Practice,* 2019, www.samhsa.com.

Regarding evaluation of such laws, here are some excellent sources: Brooks, Robert A., "Psychiatrists' Opinion About Involuntary Civil Commitment: Results of National Survey," Journal of the American Academy of Psychiatry and the Law, June, 2007; and Treatment Advocacy Center, *Grading the States: An Analysis of Involuntary Psychiatric Treatment Laws,* Sept. 2020, www.treatmentadvocacycenter.org. The second article provides a grading system that evaluates every state's commitment laws. Thus, if you want to find out how your state rates, this is the perfect source. You may even be surprised which states are the best and which ones are the worst.

Several landmark court decisions are well worth reading since they show the historical origin of our current commitment laws and standards. They include: *Lessard v. Schmidt*, 349 F. Supp 1078 (E.D. Wis.1972) (established major changes in commitment procedures and criteria for commitment in Wisconsin and was a blueprint for nationwide change in this area of law); *O'Connor v. Donaldson*, 472 U.S. 563 (1975)(ruled that a person, who does not pose a danger to self or others and is capable of living without state supervision, can't be involuntarily committed); *Addington v. Texas*, 441 U.S. 418 (1979) (provided that the burden of proof in commitment proceedings is by clear and convincing evidence and not beyond a reasonable doubt).

As to controlling the possession of guns by the mentally ill, an excellent resource on the current state of legislation in this area is: National Convention of State Legislatures, *Possession of Firearms by People with Mental Illness*, Nov. 2021, www.ncsl.org/civil-and-criminal-justice/possession-of-firearms-by-people-with-mental-illness. The federal statute prohibiting committed persons from possessing guns is 18 USC Sec. 922 (g) (4). It should be noted that this prohibition only applies to persons involuntarily committed to a mental institution. Thus, there are many contexts in which dangerously mentally ill individuals can legally possess a firearm, including: patients who have agreed to a voluntary commitment to an institution; persons who, during the course of private counseling, threaten bodily harm to others; people who are merely involuntarily committed to outpatient programs; and various mentally ill individuals who aren't being treated at all. Finally, an interesting article on the actual risk that the mentally ill pose when they come into possession of guns is: Ramchand, Rajeev, and Ayer, Lynsay, *Is Mental Illness a Risk Factor for Gun Violence?*, April, 2021, www.rand.org/research/gun-policy/analysis/essays/mental-illness-risk-factor-for-gun-violence.html.

The two best guides for families of schizophrenics that I have seen are: E. Fuller Torrey's *Surviving Schizophrenia, A Family*

Manual, Seventh Edition, Harper-Perennial, 2019; and Kim Mueser and Susan Gingerich's *The Complete Family Guide to Schizophrenia,* The Guilford Press, 2006. The former book is a detailed explanation of the science behind the disease, its onset, prognosis, causes, and treatment. The latter reference is a very user-friendly source that is particularly good for parents, siblings, spouses, and partners of schizophrenics.

Hopefully these sources will help the reader to become more informed on this subject. Had they been available to me and my family when Lee went through this experience, I believe it would have been more tolerable, though no amount of knowledge or expertise can ever make this problem easy.

Acknowledgments

There are obviously many people I wish to acknowledge for helping me put this work together. They include: Tim Storm of University of Wisconsin Writers and Carol Gaskin of Editorial Alchemy, who professionally edited the book; Don Romundson, attorney and writer, who repeatedly consulted with me on it and helped copy edit it; Dan Goyette, Retired Chief Public Defender in Louisville, Kentucky, who gave me the idea to begin with and was supportive throughout the long and difficult process; Lee's public defender during his first two commitments; my brother's long-standing social worker, Ray Przybylski, who did a lot more for him than the workers involved in his case initially; relatives on both sides of my family; and my significant other, Jo Ellen Bell, who patiently listened to me read the book to her so that it would be a smoother and overall better product.

About the Author

Kenneth Farmer is a retired public defender and prosecutor. His first jury trial took place in 1976 when he was a witness at his brother's civil commitment proceeding at the tender age of 19. Though he has plenty of professional experience dealing with schizophrenia, it is his personal one that qualifies him the most to write this book. He actually went through the tears, disappointment, fear, shame, and blame that thousands of families of schizophrenics endure every day. As a result, he is able to describe with incredible accuracy the heartache as well as the legalities of this horrible disease. In addition to this memoir, he has written two novels involving the criminal justice system: *Chez Betty* and *Real Lawyers*. Thus, he is also a writer, which permits him to tell his story in page-turning detail.